National, International, and Human Security

The Global New Deal, 2nd ed., by William F. Felice

The Ethics of Interdependence by William F. Felice

The Information Revolution and World Politics by Elizabeth C. Hanson

Sword & Salve by Peter J. Hoffman and Thomas G. Weiss

International Law in the 21st Century by Christopher C. Joyner

National, International, and Human Security, 2nd ed., by Laura Neack

The New Foreign Policy, 3rd ed., by Laura Neack

International Negotiation in a Complex World, Updated 4th ed., by Brigid Starkey, Mark A. Boyer, and Jonathan Wilkenfeld

Global Politics as if People Mattered, 2nd ed., by Mary Ann Tétreault and Ronnie D. Lipschutz

Military-Civilian Interactions, 2nd ed., by Thomas G. Weiss

National, International, and Human Security

A Comparative Introduction

SECOND EDITION

Laura Neack

ROWMAN & LITTLEFIELD
Lanham • Boulder • New York • London

Published by Rowman & Littlefield
A wholly owned subsidiary of The Rowman & Littlefield Publishing Group, Inc.
4501 Forbes Boulevard, Suite 200, Lanham, Maryland 20706
www.rowman.com

Unit A, Whitacre Mews, 26-34 Stannary Street, London SE11 4AB, United Kingdom

British Library Cataloguing in Publication Information Available

Library of Congress Cataloging-in-Publication Data Available

ISBN 9781442275256 (cloth : alk. paper)
ISBN 9781442275263 (paper : alk. paper)
ISBN 9781442275270 (electronic)

∞™ The paper used in this publication meets the minimum requirements of
American National Standard for Information Sciences—Permanence of Paper
for Printed Library Materials, ANSI/NISO Z39.48-1992.

Printed in the United States of America

This book is dedicated to the little girl on the front cover, whose name I do not know. May she find safety and better days when she can get back to school with the rest of her Syrian, Iraqi, Afghani, Pakistani, Eritrean, Nigerian, Somali, and Sudanese sisters and brothers, and all of their other sisters and brothers who have been forcibly displaced from their homes. Without education these kids are truly lost, with education they can change our world.

Contents

List of Acronyms   xiii
Preface   xvii

1   The Elusive Nature of Security   1
    Introduction   1
    Defining Security   6
    Whose Security? Or, "What We Seek to Protect
        Reflects What We Value"   8
    Recap   18
    Discussion Questions   18

2   National Security   19
    Introduction   19
    Internal versus External Security   20
    Protecting the State's Core Values   23
    Sovereignty and the Ways of the Sovereign State   28
    Recap   35
    Discussion Questions   35

3   Internal Security   37
    Introduction   37
    The Components of a State: Territory   42

The Components of a State: Effective Government 45

The Components of a State: Legitimacy 48

State Responses to Internal Threats 50

Recap 59

Discussion Questions 59

4 Unilateral Pursuit of External Security 61

Introduction 61

The Security Dilemma 62

Defense 66

Deterrence 68

Defensive Defense 73

Preemptive Self-Defense and Preventive Force 77

Recap 82

Discussion Questions 83

5 Multilateral and Bilateral Responses to External
Security Threats 85

Introduction 85

Military Alliances 86

Why States Join Mutual Defense Arrangements 88

The Costs of Joining Mutual Defense Arrangements 94

Train, Advise, Equip, and Assist Missions 97

Recap 101

Discussion Questions 101

6 International Security: Multilateral Efforts to
Achieve Security 103

Introduction 103

Collective Security and the United Nations 104

The UN Charter on International Peace and Security 109

Multilateral Sanctions Short of Force—Chapter VII,
Article 41 113

Collective Security and All Means Necessary—
Chapter VII, Article 42 123

Recap 129

Discussion Questions 129

7 United Nations Peacekeeping and Peace Enforcement   131
   Introduction   131
   Traditional Peacekeeping   136
   Precedents for a New Era   138
   Peace Enforcement   141
   Multidimensional Peace Operations   146
   Improving Peace Support Operations   151
   Hybrid Peace Operations   154
   Recap   157
   Discussion Questions   158

8 Human Security   159
   Introduction   159
   Defining Human Security   161
   The Geneva Conventions   162
   The Post–Cold War Human Security Agenda   166
   Protecting People from Large-Scale Violence   173
   Civilian Protection Becomes Humanitarian War   179
   The Future of Human Security   182
   Recap   183
   Discussion Questions   184

9 Conclusion: Resilience and Imagination   187

Notes   195

Index   211

About the Author   217

List of Acronyms

ACOTA	Africa Contingency Operations Training and Assistance
AFRICOM	United States Africa Command
AMIS	African Union Mission in Sudan
AMISOM	African Union Mission in Somalia
ANF	Al-Nusra Front
ANZUS	Australia, New Zealand, United States Security Treaty
AQI	Al Qaeda in Iraq
AU	African Union
CEAS	Common European Asylum System
CIS	Commonwealth of Independent States
CRS	Congressional Research Service (United States)
CSTO	Collective Security Treaty Organization
DTO	Drug Trafficking Organization
ECOMOG	Economic Community of West African States Monitoring Group
EU	European Union
GPI	Global Peace Index
GPOI	Global Peace Operations Initiative (United States Department of State)

HDR	Human Development Report
IAEA	International Atomic Energy Agency
ICBL	International Campaign to Ban Landmines
ICC	International Criminal Court
ICISS	International Commission on Intervention and State Sovereignty
IEP	Institute for Economics and Peace
ISIL	Islamic State of Iraq and the Levant
ISIS	Islamic State of Iraq and Syria
MAD	Mutual assured destruction
MENA	Middle East North Africa
NATO	North Atlantic Treaty Organization
NGO	Nongovernmental organization
OPC	Operation Provide Comfort (Iraq)
OSCE	Organization for Security and Cooperation in Europe
P5	Permanent five Security Council members
ROC	Republic of China (Taiwan)
RUF	Revolutionary United Front (Sierra Leone)
SALT I	Strategic Arms Limitations Treaty I
SEATO	Southeast Asia Treaty Organization
SNA	Somali National Alliance (Somalia)
UAV	Unmanned aerial vehicle
UN	United Nations
UNAMID	United Nations-African Union Mission in Darfur (Sudan)
UNAMSIL	United Nations Mission in Sierra Leone
UNDP	United Nations Development Programme
UNEF	United Nations Emergency Force (Sinai Peninsula)
UNFICYP	United Nations Peacekeeping Force in Cyprus
UNHCR	United Nations High Commissioner for Refugees
UNITAF	United Task Force (Somalia)
UNMISS	United Nations Mission in the Republic of South Sudan
UNMOGIP	United Nations Military Observer Group in India and Pakistan
UNOMSIL	United Nations Observer Mission in Sierra Leone

UNOSOM   United Nations Operation in Somalia
UNPROFOR   United Nations Protection Force (Bosnia-Herzegovina)
UNTAC   United Nations Transitional Authority in Cambodia
UNTSO   United Nations Truce Supervision Organization
            (Middle East)

Preface

The first edition of this book was published under the title *Elusive Security: States First, People Last* in 2007. This edition has been retitled, but the basic theme remains. This volume, however, goes beyond the original book because the world has changed substantially since 2007. This new edition needed to accommodate the disintegration of critical countries in the Middle East and Africa, the scope of international networked terrorist groups, and the apparent impotence of the United Nations to do much to help because its member states are still engaged in states-first security-seeking practices. Despite these significant changes, this edition starts where the first edition started—with refugees being denied entry into safe places and terrorism. These phenomena are linked more now than ever, as reflected in these pages.

This edition would not have happened without the professional and personal friendships of Karen Mingst and Eric Selbin, both on the New Millennium Books (NMB) series board. My gratitude goes to them and to the full NMB board for their enthusiastic support for a second edition.

Karen, Eric, and I form a team at *International Studies Perspectives*, as well. The past several years have been easier and more rewarding because of them. Indispensable to this project, too, were Susan McEachern and Rebeccah Shumaker at Rowman & Littlefield— Rebeccah for being the person to bring this to print, and Susan for being a wise, humane, and incisive editor. Finally, my son, Harry Neack, stepped in to help with research as he did on the first edition, and my dog, Lionel, waited patiently to go to the park. Thanks Harry and Lionel, Karen and Eric, and Susan and Rebeccah!

1

The Elusive Nature of Security

In This Chapter

Introduction
Defining Security
Whose Security? Or, "What We Seek to Protect Reflects What We Value"
Recap
Discussion Questions

Introduction

The picture on the cover of this book is of a young girl in a refugee camp. She is a representative of the severe human insecurity that results from the security struggles of states and nonstate actors and the incapacitation of international security organizations.

This little girl was not involved in the spectacular and horrible terrorist attacks in Paris in 2015. In January, terrorists attacked people at the offices of a satirical magazine and a Jewish supermarket, and then in November terrorists attacked people out for an evening of fun at several popular night spots. Nearly 150 people were killed in these combined attacks by terrorists affiliated with a group that calls itself the Islamic State.

This little girl was not involved in the Paris attacks as perpetrator or victim. Instead, she is part of a mass human migration. In 2015, the same year of the Paris attacks, more than a million people entered Europe by "irregular" (undocumented) means. In 2014, fewer than 300,000 irregular migrants had entered Europe. Of the people filing for asylum in Europe in 2015, most had fled civil conflict and lawlessness in three countries: Syria, Afghanistan, and Iraq.[1] The little girl on the cover is a Syrian refugee.

Some of the terrorists who had perpetrated the 2015 attacks in Paris had spent time fighting in the conflict in Syria, although most were French or Belgian citizens or legal residents. Europeans constituted some 21 percent of all foreign fighters in the multisided Syrian conflict.[2] For five years the Turkey-Syria border had been essentially open to people fleeing the conflict in one direction and combatants joining the conflict in the other. Europeans had slipped across that border to fight in Syria, and some had slipped back across to take the fight to Paris. Rumors circulated that one of the terrorists had disguised himself as a Syrian refugee to enter the European Union (EU).

In November 2015, the French prime minister said that Europe should shut its borders to all Middle Eastern refugees. In the beginning of 2016, the Dutch prime minister said the same. In March 2016, terrorists killed thirty-two more people in attacks at the airport and metro station in Brussels. That same month, EU officials announced a deal with Turkey that European countries would return to Turkey all new "irregular migrants" crossing from Turkey to the European Union as a "temporary and extraordinary measure which [was] necessary to end the human suffering and restore public order."[3] Turkey would agree to "take any necessary measures to prevent new sea and land routes for illegal migration opening" and would receive three billion euros, a liberalization of the existing visa policy for Turks seeking to enter and work in the EU, and a renewed commitment from the EU *to talk about* talking about Turkey joining the EU. The EU insisted that it was not engaging in "collective expulsion" or non-refoulement, both of which would be in violation of international law. As politicians talked, the little girl in the picture was trapped in a temporary refugee camp in Serbia close to the Hungary-EU border in May 2016.

We will discuss the national security problems terrorists and other threats pose to states—and to the people living in those states. We will discuss international efforts to secure states—and the people living in those states. This book is about national, international, and human security. The picture on the cover captures, in the face of one little girl, the security failures of states and international organizations. Before we go further into our exploration, we need to pose some obvious questions: What is security? And, whose security? Certainly the people of Paris deserve to be secured against terrorism, and the government of France holds the primary responsibility for this. But what about the more than six million internally displaced Syrians and five million Syrian refugees? Who secures them? And what about the 3,770 migrants of many nationalities who died at sea in 2015 trying to cross the Mediterranean from Northern Africa to Italy. What did security mean for them?

In this book, we explore the threats to and policies and practices of national, international, and human security, with this basic proposition: Security at all levels is elusive. In one sense, security is elusive because it is almost entirely dependent on context and who is speaking and who has power. But more fundamentally, security is elusive because the politics of security remains embedded in a centuries-old ethic that ultimately is self-defeating. That ethic insists that states are the primary and most important international actors, they ultimately can rely only on themselves for protection, and they must keep all options on the table toward the goal of achieving *national* security. The continuation of this states-first ethic ensures that *international* security and, most importantly, *human* security are routinely sacrificed for the preservation of states and their interests.

Security is a concept that can be widened to include almost any facet of state, international, and human existence. Analysts call this "securitization" when politicians attempt to co-opt a policy issue and turn it into a national security issue and a "war on" something in order to further a particular political agenda. Despite the political uses of security, it cannot be denied that the security of life on earth is threatened by global warming. But, in the same way that the states-first ethic impedes the achievement of lasting national, international, and human security, a humans-first ethic impedes the achievement of lasting environmental security. That discussion is vitally important but is too large to take up here. Instead, this book will be limited to a discussion of what it means to attempt to find security from the kind of violence committed by human politics and human-made weapons and violence.

We will begin with an exploration of how states act unilaterally to secure themselves from armed attack whether the source is internal or external. Then our discussion turns to how states have created an international architecture that is meant to provide them international security. Finally, our discussion will be about security in terms of securing human beings in times of conflict and war and beyond. The ordering here is intentional: Historically, states and national security came first, then came the international state system (defined as a system to ensure the external security of states), and then people were brought in. Situating our discussion in this order will demonstrate why states find themselves less secure, not more secure, in an international system that supports and allows conflict, and supports the rights of states (and those who would seek to rule states) to commit violence against human beings. There remain fundamental incompatibilities between state security and international and human security, incompatibilities that can be resolved only through a revolutionary shift in our shared understanding of the "state" and its responsibility to people both within the state and at risk elsewhere. We will discuss how this shift has started, but it still is an uphill struggle—or, if you will, a precarious journey in a rickety, overcrowded boat by desperate and scared people across a turbulent sea. We should add one more element to this metaphor: hope. What puts us in that boat and propels us toward the unknown is the hope that we can and will do better with just one more chance on one more day.

We'll ask this question many times in many ways in this book: What does it mean to be secure? In the first edition of this book, we pondered what it meant to be secure in a world in which a suicide bomber might at any moment walk into a restaurant in Haifa, Israel, and detonate explosives strapped to her waist, murdering nineteen innocent civilians in order to publicize the brutal reoccupation of Palestinian territories by the Israeli army. In response to this attack in 2003, the Israeli government demolished the family home of a suicide bomber and launched a retaliatory air strike against alleged terrorist training camps in Syria, although there was no evidence that the suicide bomber had ever been to Syria. Instead, Hanadi Jaradat, the bomber, was a twenty-eight-year-old woman from Jenin in the West Bank who attended law school and was about to qualify as a lawyer. Her sister believed that Jaradat was motivated by revenge for the killing of her brother and cousin by Israeli forces. What did security mean to Jaradat? What did it mean to her surviving family members who expressed pride in her suicide attack despite the punishment exacted on them by Israeli authorities?

What did security mean to the Jewish and Arab families who jointly owned and operated the restaurant where Jaradat killed herself and nineteen others? What was security to lunch patron Bruriya Zer-Aviv, her son, daughter-in-law, and two grandchildren, none of whom survived Jaradat's act? Were the lives of any Israelis or Palestinians or anyone living in the wider Middle East made more secure when Israel, acting in the name of national security, retaliated for the Haifa bombing by launching air strikes against a location in neighboring Syria and demolishing the Jaradat home in the West Bank?

What is security? This book attempts to sort out the many definitions and referents of security in the first decades of the twenty-first century. The International Commission on Intervention and State Sovereignty has called this a time marked by "a convulsive process of state fragmentation and state formation that is transforming the international order itself."[4] The international order is being transformed by pervasive violence and insecurity as well as unilateral and multilateral efforts to curb this violence and restore security.

This book is offered as a way to understand what governments and security analysts mean when they make claims in defense of national security; what internationalists mean when they seek to protect and strengthen international security; and what international organizations, nongovernmental organizations (NGOs), individuals, and even some governments mean when they assert that the best way to ensure state and international security is first to ensure human security. The international order as we know it privileges states over all others and national security over all else. Issues of international and human security come up in any discussion of national security, to be sure, but current-day notions of and controversies over international and human security can be understood only in terms of their relationship to state security. The failure of the international community to "do something" about terrorism, or humanitarian disasters, or the crimes against humanity being committed by many parties in Syria (and other places) can be understood through an excavation of the foundations of what is meant by national, international, and human security. To understand these related terms, we must begin and remain for a while with the state and its search for elusive security.

Defining Security

Because the international system prioritizes national security, we can start by offering a definition of national security. Over the course of this book (and from country to country), the definition will change slightly. The *Penguin Dictionary of International Relations* says that security is a "term which denotes the absence of threats to scarce values. In principle security can be absolute, that is to say freedom from all threat is the equivalent of complete security."[5] This definition is as good or as bad as any other. "Freedom from *all* threat" sounds like an impossible objective. Can we even begin to name all the threats that might endanger our values? Are there some we might overlook or not understand as threats until too late? If freedom from *all* threat is unimaginable because we cannot imagine all the possible threats that might arise, is there some degree of freedom from threat that will make us feel secure? If we cannot feel 100 percent secure, can we feel 90 percent secure? Is it sufficient to feel 60 percent secure or secure every other day? If we—the people of a country—can agree on the degree to which we want to feel secure, what methods should we take to best achieve that security? Can we or should we attempt to secure all values to the same degree, or are some things more important to us than others? What do we mean by "values" and "threats"? Unfortunately, the dominant understanding of national security has done little to answer these questions in a way that might lead to a more "secure" state or world.

Defining security will remain a persistent problem throughout this book. The definitional problem drives an operational problem: Without a clear understanding of what we are securing and what we are securing against, how do we know when we have found the right policy, doctrine, weapon, or alliance that will in fact secure us? Definitional and operational problems ultimately are political problems. Political problems turn on value judgments, and the ultimate value judgment is determining what must be secured at what expense.

As confusing as this might seem, this book will explore security and its attendant ideas on a practical level. Much of the definitional work has been done for us. Although we might have heated arguments about the proper ways to defend against, say, invasion or terrorism, the starting point for our arguments was established long before any of us were here. The international system of the present day is constructed on very old, very well-entrenched assumptions and definitions.

To say that the starting point for our discussion is long established is not to imply that this starting point is "right" or "correct" or inevitable. Those of us who might wish to construct a less violent and more human-friendly world need to work with what is and has been. This book attempts to set forth what is and has been and to expose the flaws that cause states (and their people and the world) to remain insecure. The current international system has had a long time to develop in the way it has; it cannot easily be dismantled short of a major catastrophic event—and *that* would serve no good purpose! However, this present order could be made more humane and thus more secure at multiple levels. In these pages, we will examine the well-entrenched rules of the security game and how these rules do not help to make the world or the people in it more secure. In doing so, perhaps, we will also see suggestions for how we might revise the rules to obtain real security.

Whose Security? Or, "What We Seek to Protect Reflects What We Value"[6]

Two weeks before the 9/11 terrorist attacks on the United States, a humanitarian crisis was brewing in the South Pacific. Although the crisis would fall off the radar screens of most of the world on 9/11, one country in particular claimed that the attacks had demonstrated why the crisis involved a major national security threat. The story of that crisis in the Pacific can help us begin to delineate national, international, and human security concerns, and take us firmly into the exploration of our first major topic: national security.

On August 26, 2001, an Indonesian ferry packed with people began to sink about halfway between the Indonesian island of Java and Australia's Christmas Island. Acting in reply to the ferry's distress call, the Norwegian-flagged private freighter *Tampa* rescued 438 people. These people were mostly Afghan and mostly men, although there were twenty-six women and forty-three children as well. The rescued people asked to be taken to Christmas Island, but on August 27, Australia refused to grant permission to the *Tampa* to offload the people on its territory. According to the Australian government, all the people were unauthorized migrants—that is, people attempting to enter Australia without visas or other proper documentation.

The Australian government did not want the migrants to set foot on Australian national territory. The government's position was that the Afghans should be taken to the nearest port of call, which would be in Indonesia. Indonesia refused to take the rescued people and warned that it would take blocking action to prevent the *Tampa* from entering its waters. The captain of the *Tampa*, the government of Norway, and the UN High Commissioner for Refugees (UNHCR) insisted that Australia had a moral and legal obligation to assist the rescued people by letting them land on Christmas Island. Although the migrants were no longer on a sinking ship, the *Tampa* did not have adequate facilities or enough food and water for so many people. The living conditions on board deteriorated with each passing day.

Three days into the crisis, the captain of the *Tampa* steered the freighter into Australian waters off Christmas Island. In response,

Australian navy commandos boarded the freighter and took control of it and its crew. The situation remained in this tense stalemate for several more days as regional and international diplomats attempted to find a mutually acceptable solution. Ultimately, New Zealand and Nauru offered to take the Afghans until their claims for asylum were processed. On September 3, the Afghans were transferred to an Australian troopship for transport to New Zealand and Nauru. In a controversial move, Australia agreed to give some US$10 million to Nauru for taking in the migrants.

Why was the Australian government so adamant about not letting the Afghans land on Australian territory? The simplest answer is that the government did not wish to incur responsibility for these people. But a simple answer may not do justice to the security concerns of the Australian government.

The Afghans were not typical, legal migrants to Australia or even tourists, students, or people doing business. They had left behind a country that was mostly under the domination of the repressive Taliban regime; thus, one might safely assume that they were fleeing persecution. If this were the case, the 1951 Convention on the Status of Refugees would apply, and the Afghans could be properly labeled "refugees." By the 1951 Convention, a refugee is

> any person who owing to a well-founded fear of being persecuted for reasons of race, religion, nationality, membership of a particular social group or political opinion, is outside the country of his nation- ality and is unable, or owing to such fear, is unwilling to avail himself of the protection of that country; or who, not having a nationality and being outside the country of his former habitual residence, is unable, or owing to such fear, is unwilling to return to it.

If the Afghans themselves had not been subject to persecution, they may have been fleeing the ongoing violence of Afghanistan's unresolved civil war. By various regional agreements starting with a 1969 policy adopted by the Organization of African Unity and rein- forced by a 1984 declaration by the Organization of American States, the global standard on refugees also includes "persons who have fled their country because their lives, safety or freedom have been

threatened by generalized violence, foreign aggression, internal conflicts, massive violation of human rights or other circumstances which
have seriously disturbed the public order."[7]

By the 1951 Convention and in line with ongoing international customs, refugees have a right to remain in the country of first asylum,
that is, a right to remain in the first country to which they flee. Also by
the 1951 Convention and subsequent practice, host countries agree not
to forcibly return the refugees to their home countries (this is known
as the principle of non-refoulement). Once a refugee enters a country
and claims asylum, the host country is obligated to conduct an inquiry
into whether the person has a proper claim to asylum or safe haven.
The UNHCR was established in the post–World War II period to assist
refugees and states in the logistics of processing asylum claims and
caring for the short-term basic needs of refugees.

Despite international agreements, customs, and expected behaviors, whether and how states grant asylum to claimants is ultimately
left to the prerogative of the state. A state may decide a claimant was
not, in fact, fleeing persecution based on his or her ethnic, religious,
or political affiliation or fleeing to avoid clear threats of violence. As
Laura Barnett explains, "Although [the 1951] Convention guarantees
refugees the right to seek asylum it cannot grant the right to obtain
asylum, as this is strictly a national prerogative. In fact, UNHCR has
no formal supervisory mechanism with a mandate to review state per-
formance."[8] States decide whether and how they will assist refugees
and whether and how they will process and allow asylum claims.
Some states are more generous in this regard, some far less so. The
decision to allow in "unauthorized migrants" is left to states because
the modern international system privileges the rights of states above
all other entities. As Barnett puts it, the concept of refugees has been
entrenched firmly "within the territorial notion of boundaries"—of
state boundaries.[9]

Why would states accept refugees and assist in processing their
claims to asylum? All kinds of humanitarian reasons come to mind.
A basic belief in the dignity and worth of every human being might
lead a country to want to help people fleeing from repressive governments or violent places. Humanitarian concerns might also combine

with political reasons for giving sanctuaries to refugees. During the Cold War, persons fleeing communist countries were given all possible safe haven assistance by the United States. The cause of political prisoners sitting in Soviet jails often preoccupied Western governments and NGOs. Countries might also act on the moral imperative that there is a basic obligation to help people in need.

Why would states refuse to allow in refugees? Many specific and immediate reasons could be given for their refusal. The refugees could put economic strains on the host country, diverting resources from the care and protection of its citizens. The refugees, if admitted and settled into the host country, might create social tensions between different peoples, especially in regard to the availability of jobs and the distribution of finite government resources. The host country may be inundated with refugees, while other just-as-capable countries are left free of the problem. All these reasons were given at various times by Australian government officials, editorial writers, and everyday citizens to justify "pushing off" the Afghan migrants to other countries.

There is an additional reason why Australia might wish to push off these migrants: They might have included "sleepers" or members of terrorist groups who sought to enter Australia in order to live quietly among its citizens while studying how to attack it. This is a problem cast in an especially sharp light by the magnitude of the 9/11 attacks on the United States and the 2002 Bali bombings in Indonesia that specifically targeted Australians. The threat of "sleeper cells" had to be taken seriously by Australian authorities.

When states take in boat people or other kinds of refugees, they make a clear statement in support of the rights and security of the individual person. When states take in refugees, they also signal their participation in and responsibility to international order. When states refuse to take in refugees, they assert a "higher" obligation than the protection of stateless individuals or the protection of international order: That obligation is to defend the state and its interests above all else. This right is firmly supported by the organizing ideas that form the foundation of the international system dating back to the mid-seventeenth century.

The international system since the mid-seventeenth century is what we call *state-centric*; that is, the primary and most important unit in the system is the state. All the "rules" of international behavior as well as the "rules" of domestic politics flow from the primacy of the state. Contemporary discussions of national security, international security, and human security must begin with an understanding of how the state came to be primary. *That* discussion is taken up in the next chapter.

Afghans weren't just fleeing to Australia in 2001; Afghans constituted the second-largest group filing asylum applications in Europe in 2015.[10] The Afghan boat people stuck in the Australian controversy in 2001 were fleeing two decades of conflict in their homeland made worse by the rise to power of the Taliban. They were part of a mass refugee movement at the start of the new millennium, a movement met with stiff state resistance. Speaking to the executive committee of the United Nations High Commissioner for Refugees in 2000, then-secretary-general Kofi Annan assessed that the UNHCR and relevant refugee NGOs had become a tool by which states avoided taking responsibility for refugees. He told the UNHCR:

> You have become part of a "containment strategy" by which this world's more fortunate and powerful countries seek to keep the problems of the poorer at arm's length. . . . And how else can one explain the contrast between the generosity which poor countries are expected to show, when hundreds of thousands of refugees pour across their frontiers, and the precautions taken to ensure that as few asylum seekers as possible ever reach the shores of rich countries?[11]

The Syrian conflict that started in 2011 has resulted in a huge dispersion of human beings, but forced displacement of humans has been a near-constant (but lately growing) feature of international politics. Despite the agitation in the developed world about undocumented migrants over-running national borders, most refugees find refuge in other developing countries. By mid-2016, according to the UNHCR, most Syrians were displaced to Turkey, Lebanon, Jordan, and Iraq. Ethiopia, Iran, and Pakistan also were the hosts of large numbers of refugees—but from other conflicts, not Syria. Even as refugees have been and remain a feature of international politics, Edward Newman noted a decade ago that "one key change in the twentieth century was the move by governments towards regulating migration, in particular, immigration, and toward defining those who were to be granted the special status of refugees."[12] And although it is the fact that the "developing countries shoulder the social and economic strain of the vast majority of asylum seekers and people displaced through conflict and state failure, in both developing and developed countries, governments have for some time been constructing legal and physical barriers against the influx of asylum seekers or those displaced by war."[13]

As we will see in the next chapter, states can do almost anything in the name of national security and national interests, and in the present world order, refugees are the easiest targets with the least ability to protect themselves. The Afghan boat people case study also shows how international collaboration and international agreements get disregarded when national security is said to be at stake—at the ultimate expense of powerless human beings. Even when national leaders may wish to be bold on behalf of humanitarian causes, they may still strike states-first deals, again at the expense of that most powerless group—refugees. Let's consider another case study that makes this point about the states-first security system that leaves states, the system, and the humans in it insecure and at risk.

More than a decade after the Taliban were overthrown in Afghanistan by the combined actions of anti-Taliban forces and the US military, Afghans still were fleeing their country. The International Organization for Migration reported that in 2015 the human beings attempting to enter Europe extralegally came from (in order) Syria, Afghanistan, Iraq, Kosovo, Albania, Pakistan, Eritrea, Nigeria, Iran, and Ukraine. The Global Terrorism Index reports that 78 percent of all terrorist attacks in 2014 were in five of these countries—Iraq, Nigeria, Afghanistan, Pakistan, and Syria. The US military is actively engaged in operations in three of these countries—Iraq, Afghanistan, and Syria.

More than one million migrants were estimated by government officials to have entered Germany in 2015, making Germany the primary destination of migrants. Germany is a committed and some would say dominant member of the European Union. When the Eurozone Crisis began in 2009, German leaders—particularly Chancellor Angela Merkel—resolved to steer the Eurozone ship to safe waters in order to maintain and strengthen the union of Europe. Merkel's views on resolving *that* crisis were often seen as rigid and austere, praised from within Germany but more often than not hated by other Europeans. Merkel's stewardship of Germany and the European Union was characterized by cold-eyed practicality. Her view of a united Europe was based on burden-sharing and responsible, rule-based action by all member states.

In the summer of 2015, the migrant flows turned into a crisis. The sheer number of people overwhelmed local, national, and international entities attempting to register and assist people. In some places, local governments and peoples were welcoming, in other places governments and people felt threatened and were hostile, in all places everyone was overwhelmed. In the middle of August, German officials suspended EU regulations for processing refugees in order to speed up the registration process. For many, this caused the crisis to escalate.

The Common European Asylum System (CEAS) is the result of an ongoing effort by the EU member states (and Norway, Switzerland, Iceland, and Liechtenstein) to establish a system to regularize asylum. In the CEAS, individual asylum seekers can register only one asylum application. Under what is called the Dublin procedures, this application must be made in the first EU country in which the individual arrives. When an individual submits an application, the EU member state is required to determine whether it is the first state of arrival for that person and therefore the responsible state—or not. If the state is responsible, the application must be processed. If not, the person is transferred to the responsible state. As 2015 moved into the summer, Italy and Greece typically did not register migrants and instead let them move on to other EU countries. Both of these countries were still in financial crisis, and it was easier for them to ignore their EU obligations and let people pass through. Both states and their people, though, provided generous assistance to the migrants as they made their way.

In mid-August, German officials issued an internal memo that suspended the Dublin procedures in order to take direct responsibility for the migrants already in Germany rather than taking the time to investigate whether the migrants should be transferred to another EU country. The intention was to speed the processing of claims. Word leaked, and asylum groups spread the news causing more people to attempt to get to Germany, even if they had to walk from Greece. Suddenly, Germany seemed to be opening its arms to refugees, and refugees started moving *en masse* through Serbia (not a EU member), Hungary and Austria, and other countries. Hungarian and Austrian officials were angry, overwhelmed, at times resistant and at other times allowed people to travel through to Germany. At the end of August, Chancellor Merkel both embraced her policy and encouraged other EU member states to share the burden. "If Europe fails on the question of refugees," she said, "then it won't be the Europe we wished for."[14] Merkel was especially proud of Germany's and Germans' responses to helping refugees: "The world sees Germany as a country of hope and opportunity." The task would be hard for Germany but, she said, "we can do it."[15]

The German coalition government was engaged in some public infighting over the suspension of Dublin (a topic for a foreign policy book), while other European states and German media accused Merkel of single-handedly destabilizing Europe. The refugee crisis, of course, had been under way, and the German government had just been reacting to it. By early September, Merkel was doing what she normally did—insisting that all EU members had a responsibility to step up and help the refugees. Germany and Sweden called for a quota system that would distribute the refugee burden among all European states in the spirit of European solidarity. The Eastern European states were particularly opposed to taking in Syrian refugees, with Slovakia saying it would take in only Christian refugees from Syria. France, the scene of a terrorist attack in January, also opposed taking too many Syrian refugees. Recall that the January terrorist attacks in Paris had been committed by second-generation French citizens, some of whom allegedly had spent time fighting or training in Syria.

Despite French opposition to taking in too many Syrians, French and German officials appealed to the members of the EU Parliament for "more Europe" in October. That is, in a familiar refrain for anyone who studies France and Germany in the EU, both countries continued to urge a deepening of EU institutional ties as the answer to the many problems confronting Europe. Merkel even encouraged EU member states to not think in terms of strictly national interests and national security to deal with the refugee crisis: "We must now resist the temptation to fall back into national government action. Right now we need more Europe. Germany and France are ready."[16] This caused the founder of the United Kingdom's Independence Party to quip that "it is an irony that a project designed to contain German power has now given us a totally German-dominated Europe."[17] The UK Independence Party was firmly in favor of the United Kingdom leaving the European Union as a way to assert its own national interests and led the drive for Brexit.

Whether adverse German public opinion changed Merkel's mind, or her hand was forced by her interior minister, or the state-first responses of other EU countries required a different response, German policy took an about-face at the start of November. Rather than taking responsibility for all Syrian asylum claims filed in Germany, the interior ministry said it would only grant Syrians a one-year protected status that would not extend to families. This caused more domestic political arguments and denunciations, and resulted in the deportations of Syrian refugees and the reinstatement of the Dublin procedures. The Austrian interior minister said Germany's new policy was a "return to sense."[18] Within a week, a metaphorical earthquake hit Europe when terrorists affiliated with the Islamic State launched coordinated attacks in Paris, killing 130 people.

On the night of November 13, 2015, the German national football team was in Paris at the Stade de France playing the French national football team in a friendly match. Explosions outside the stadium stopped the game, and the carnage that ensued in the surrounding neighborhood reversed much of the humanitarian impulse to help Syrian refugees. For the first time in more than a decade, EU member states and Turkish officials started negotiating a plan to stop migrants from leaving Turkey for Greece and the rest of Europe. On November 29, a EU-Turkey agreement was announced in which Turkey would stop the migrant outflows and in return would get three billion Euros for refugee assistance, liberalized visas for Turks to enter the EU, and the promised new beginning of talks to bring Turkey into the EU as a member state.

Angela Merkel would go on to be named the 2015 Time Person of the Year by the American media company for extending Germany's welcome to Syrian refugees, but she would also participate in three additional sets of negotiations with Turkey that resulted in a more formalized EU-Turkey Statement in March 2016. The series of agreements with Turkey were criticized by refugee, humanitarian, and human rights groups because of the increasingly authoritarian domestic policies of the Turkish government. Concerns over the treatment of refugees in Turkey multiplied. Nonetheless, the number of migrants leaving Turkey for Europe was cut dramatically from the end of November 2015 through mid-2016.

Thus, one response to the human tragedy resulting from the Syrian war was a multilateral agreement between governments serving their own national interests first. Terrorists in Paris forced those inclined to act humanely toward the Syrian refugees to revert to a states-first default.

We will discuss terrorism in more detail in various chapters, but it is important to note here what was implied earlier in this chapter—most terrorist attacks occur in developing countries, often the same ones experiencing massive forced human displacement. Europe itself had experienced "only" three significant mass casualty terrorist attacks before 2015: the 2004 Madrid train attacks that had killed nearly 200 people, the London tube and bus attacks in 2005 that killed sixty people, and the 2011 killing of 170 Norwegian young people and children by a right-wing, nationalist Norwegian militant. The factual record shows that countries in the Middle East, Africa, and South Asia were much more likely to experience serious terrorist mass casualty attacks than Europe. But how much security will a country want and pursue? How much insecurity will it tolerate? And at what costs? These are issues to keep in mind as we continue our study.

Recap

In this chapter we were introduced to the principle that the international system is state-centric and because of this fact, *national* security comes before international and human security. We began to define "security" while recognizing that it is an elusive concept. We examined various cases in which the national security of states was prioritized over international commitments and the security of refugees.

Discussion Questions

1. What does it mean to say that there is a "states-first" ethic in the international system?
2. Define security. Is it possible to achieve complete security?
3. Discuss the many conflicting security interests involved in the case of the suicide attack on a restaurant in Israel.
4. Discuss the conflicting security interests in the case of the Afghan boat people attempting to reach Australia.
5. What is the internationally recognized definition of "refugee?" Who determines whether a person is entitled to asylum?
6. Describe the dimensions of the refugee crisis in 2015.
7. Discuss the correlation between displaced people and terrorism in reference to the countries of origin of refugees.
8. How did Germany's chancellor attempt to facilitate the settling of Syrian refugees in the European Union? Discuss the consequences of her action.

2

National Security

In This Chapter

Introduction
Internal versus External Security
Protecting the State's Core Values
Sovereignty and the Ways of the Sovereign State
Recap
Discussion Questions

Introduction

National security is prioritized above all other goals in the contemporary global system, and the state itself sets the boundaries for its own security-seeking activities. Consider this quote from a century ago: "The State . . . must create for itself its own imaginary right and necessity for existence, because no other authority can create this on its behalf; and because there does not exist any directive and arbitrative State-authority over all States."[1] The state acts preemptively, marshaling all its power to meet the enemy and answering to no one but itself.

Of course, the *state* does not really act or marshal—in some respects, this is a bit of useful short-hand. The political leaders of the state act. But they act on behalf of the state, and their actions on behalf of the state rise above the acts of private people because the state is prioritized internally and externally. The legal doctrine of sovereign immunity is the principle that the state cannot commit a legal wrong, and so it is above legal obligations and cannot be sued in civil court. This was the stance taken by US president Barack Obama and top administration officials over a piece of legislation allowing US citizens to sue foreign governments for their involvement in terrorist attacks on US soil. The administration's argument was that the bill was dangerous: If Saudi Arabia (the intended target of the legislation) could be sued by the families of 9/11 victims, then the United States could be sued elsewhere. Even liberal political leaders assert the privilege of the state when they or anyone acts in the name of the state. (In chapter 9 of this book we will discuss some relatively new limitations on sovereign immunity in the International Criminal Court.)

There is agreement among states about the essential national security doctrine: States must protect themselves and have a right to protect themselves against threats. States also claim to be the ultimate judge of what is a threat and what must be done about threats. These principles are so foundational to the international system that they are associated with a political philosophy that claims to be about actual reality: Realism. At the same time that there is agreement about these principles, there is considerable disagreement about the national security method. From country to country, and even within countries and particular governments, there is wide disagreement about what steps are necessary to ensure some degree of protection against threats. In subsequent chapters, we will examine the various ways that states seek to secure themselves from internal and external threats.

Internal versus External Security

When the Australian government set up a naval quarantine line to stop boats of unauthorized migrants coming from Indonesia, the government was protecting Australia from what it deemed to be a threat.

The threat posed by unauthorized migrants before 9/11 was not necessarily a national security threat. Instead, the boat people represented more mouths to feed, more jobs to supply, more and different people to accommodate in the societal mix, and so on. The threat posed by boat people after 9/11 was frequently portrayed by Australian political authorities as a matter of national security; political figures worried about the real intention of the undocumented migrants and the possibility that they might form terrorist "sleeper cells" inside Australia. Context matters. One context that sets the stage for how security and threats thereto are defined is whether a matter is internal—and a matter for domestic security actors—or external—and thus a matter for externally oriented security actors.

Keeping would-be terrorists out of Australia is a matter of external security. Identifying and detaining would-be or actual terrorists inside Australia is a matter of internal security. For most countries, security as a function of the government is divided for practical reasons into external and internal concerns. External security in traditional terms—that is, security against a military attack launched from the outside—is handled primarily by defense ministries or departments of defense. Defense ministries are assisted in their duties—or complemented—by other government agencies that have a primarily external face. For example, the US Department of Defense often works with the Department of State and the Central Intelligence Agency (among other government agencies) to provide an external security net for the United States. In the case of Australia, external security is the responsibility of the Department of Defence, the Australian Defence Forces, the Department of Foreign Affairs and Trade, and the Australian Secret Intelligence Service. Uncovering the whereabouts of suspected terrorist sleeper cells among refugees or other immigrant communities inside Australia would be the task of the Australian Security Intelligence Organization, whose actionable information would be tasked to the Australian Federal Police, perhaps with the help of local police.

Internal security is not typically maintained by defense ministries using the national military but tasked instead to internally oriented national security agencies. Often, however, these groups work together. After the November 2015 Paris terrorist attacks, the French government altered policies to facilitate faster and greater cooperation by the Brigade de Recherche et d'Intervention (the special national police) and the military. In Mexico, the Mexican Armed Forces (comprised of the independent Mexican Army and Mexican Navy), under the National Defense Secretariat, operates internally against drug cartels, as do the Policia Federal Preventiva (Federal Preventive Police or more commonly the Federal Police or Federales). In Mexico, these military and civilian security forces are administered by separate—and sometimes competitive—government departments or ministries. The situation is different in the United States where federal law prohibits most uses of the armed forces inside the country. However, national guard units—which often deploy to combat zones outside the country—are sometimes used for internal security purposes.

The distinction between internal and external security drives policy prescriptions for managing security threats. This is the case even in this time of globalized security threats. International, networked terrorism and transnational criminal organizations complicate the policy process because governments are organized to address internal security differently from external security. And, governments hold different views and are bound sometimes by national laws on what kind of force is appropriate within a country versus outside a country, except, of course, in countries in which there are significant internal conflicts. The Assad regime in Syria has used the full military power of Syria and its allies in a total war against many different antigovernment groups—although it claims that the conflict was created and maintained by foreign terrorist groups. The French government is a member of the coalition engaged in an air campaign against the Islamic State in Iraq and the Levant (ISIL, also known as the Islamic State) in Syria and Iraq, yet it uses different tactics against would-be terrorists on French soil. The French government would not order an air strike on a suspected terrorist compound in France—that is, in the predominantly Muslim neighborhoods where so many Muslim young people have become radicalized—but it does use air power against terrorists in many other countries. Depending on the country in question and the historical period, the internal-external divide is of no consequence or is of the utmost consequence for setting the appropriate government response.

We will use this internal-external distinction in our examination of national security since most governments make this distinction. In chapter 3 we examine internal security and in chapter 4 we examine unilateral efforts to defend against external threats. But we will keep in mind that the globalization of security threats has made national security more complicated. Spillover threats are no longer confined to regions and neighborhoods. Weak states, failing states, and states beset by internal conflict become the training camps, home bases, and launching pads for international terrorism and transnational criminal organizations. These phenomena change the security calculation for most states. And, as the security calculation grows in complexity, we can expect states to assert their states-first prerogatives all the more.

Protecting the State's Core Values

With the understanding that national security has both internal and external components and that these are typically addressed using different policies and government agencies, we now will explore what is meant by the term "national security." One of the most widely used definitions of security is credited to Arnold Wolfers. "Security," he writes, "points to some degree of protection of values previously acquired." He continues:

> A nation is secure to the extent to which it is not in danger of having to sacrifice core values, if it wishes to avoid war, and is able, if challenged, to maintain them by victory in such a war. This definition implies that security rises and falls with the ability of a nation to deter an attack, or to defeat it. This is in accord with the common usage of the term.
>
> Security is a value, then, of which a nation can have more or less and which it can aspire to have in greater or lesser measure. . . . Security, in an objective sense, measures the absence of fear that such values will be attacked.[2]

The first part of this definition is about external security, but the second part extends to both external and internal security. Wolfers proposes a definition that allows room for different policies aimed at protecting core values. Even core values are open to variations on theme. As Wolfers says, this variation makes security an "ambiguous symbol."

This is not to say that national security cannot be pinned down or that "national security" is an endlessly expanding term. Wolfers asserts that national security has an established, recognizable discourse:

> We know roughly what people have in mind if they complain that their government is neglecting national security or demanding excessive sacrifices for the sake of enhancing it. Usually those who raise the cry for a policy oriented exclusively toward this interest are afraid that their country underestimates the external dangers facing it or is being diverted into idealistic channels unmindful of these dangers. Moreover, the symbol suggests protection through power and therefore figures more frequently in the speech of those who believe in reliance on national power than of those who place their confidence in model behavior, international cooperation, or the United Nations to carry their country safely through the tempests of international conflict.[3]

Wolfers uses the word "security" interchangeably with "national security." To Wolfers, national security connotes measures taken to protect the "national self" as distinguished from the protection of some narrow group (e.g., the ruling regime) or some more expansive, international interests. The national self is embodied in the state. Protection of the national self—national security—is privileged over protection of the international community or protection of individual human beings in both academic and practitioner accounts of security. R. B. J. Walker explains that this is because

> the meaning of security is tied to historically specific forms of political community. . . . In the modern world, states have managed to more or less monopolize our understanding of what political life is and where it occurs. . . . The security of states dominates our understanding of what security can be, and who it can be for, not because conflict between states is inevitable, but because other forms of political community have been rendered almost unthinkable.[4]

This is not to suggest that national security has no connection at all to international or human security. Remember that we are at the beginning of our exploration and we begin at the beginning. As we will see in chapter 6, international security traditionally is defined in terms of securing the international order for states. When states define their national security in terms of connections to the broader community (as most do in some manner), it is because they perceive that their security cannot be ensured without the assistance and cooperation of others. But the important point remains that in the hierarchy of security referents, national security historically and presently dominates.

What about the national unit that must be secured? States seek to secure their core values. Essentially, all states seek to protect three core values: territorial integrity and protection of citizens, political independence and autonomy, and economic well-being. These three values can be defined quite differently depending on the government and the context, and these three can often come into conflict with one another. For example, to become more economically well-off, a government may choose to deepen interdependence with a common market or economic trade bloc. Entrance into that group, however, might require coordination of some fiscal policies which means that some autonomy in economic decision making is lost. Or a country may choose to be economically less well integrated with others in order to put more emphasis on political autonomy.

States in the Global North tend to put more emphasis on the core value of securing and enhancing economic well-being at the expense of political independence and autonomy. No doubt this is because political independence and autonomy are not as threatened in the Global North as they are in the Global South for historical reasons. There is a recent, glaring exception to this. In June 2016, a referendum was held in Britain on whether it should remain in the European Union or exit. This is what is called "Brexit." Despite the warnings by the private sector and predictions about the overall impact on the British economy, the British public voted for Brexit. After the vote, the British pound fell to a thirty-year low and sat there, while companies and citizens from other EU countries living in Britain worried about what form Brexit would take and when they should plan to leave Britain. The people who voted for Brexit were asserting British independence and autonomy from EU bureaucracy and requirements.

They also wanted to stop allowing the free flow of people from other EU countries into Britain; that is, the vote was also anti-immigrant. It should be noted that the "remain" vote (as in, "remain in the EU") won in Northern Ireland, Scotland, and London. The rest of England outside of London and Wales voted for leaving the EU.

For states in the Global South, the prioritizing of core values is more complicated. Autonomy and economic well-being are not easily separated. For example, since 2008, Brazil's national security policy has emphasized a national strategy of defense and a national strategy of development. Both are engaged simultaneously for the purpose of securing national independence. Imagine a triangle—Brazil puts the core value of independence at the top resting on a base created by the other two core values of defense and development. Independence cannot be secured without defense, and independence cannot be secured without development.[5]

As another example, consider the South African Defence Review of 2014. This is the statement of South Africa's national security priorities. It reads in part that

> national security is centered on the advancement of South Africa's sovereignty, democracy, national values and freedoms, and its political and economic independence. To this end it is clear that there is both a domestic and a regional dimension to national security. Domestically, South African national security focuses on its sovereignty and the related priorities of territorial integrity; constitutional order; the security and continuance of national institutions; the well-being, prosperity and upliftment of the people; the growth of the economy; and demonstrable good governance. As a developmental state, South Africa faces the onerous task of addressing a number of pressing developmental challenges, including poverty, unemployment, inequality and criminality.[6]

Note the description of South Africa as a "developmental state". This characterization signifies that economic values shape all domestic and foreign policies. This has direct implications for *how* national security policy is implemented. The Defence Review explains that the national armed forces play a unique role in South Africa:

Traditionally, Defence Forces have focused purely on the role that they play in the defence of the sovereignty of the nation-state. This Defence Review, however, discusses the broader role of the Defence Force within a developmental state. It does not purely focus on the "what the Defence Force is against" but additionally provides the framework for the "what the Defence Force is for" and consequently "what the Nation expects its Defence Force to do." This includes the positive role it should play in support of nation building, as an adjunct to is traditional role and functions.

The balancing and prioritizing of core values, done well, should sustain the state and make it more secure. But there are times when the unbounded pursuit of a particular core value may result in the *sacrificing* of others, putting countries into something called the "defense dilemma" in which "defense and security are in some sense at odds," according to Barry Buzan. "Defense dilemmas of cost involve straight trade-offs between resources devoted to defense, and resources available to meet other security objectives."[7] For any state, *excessive* resources put into military defense would mean that resources would not be available for pursuing a reduction in poverty, an increase in jobs, a decrease in inequality, and all the other goals a state might want to pursue. But what is excessive? Buzan gives the example of the Soviet Union in 1991:

> The most spectacular example of a cost-defense dilemma is currently unfolding in the Soviet Union. . . . By chronic overspending on military security, combined with the bureaucratic inefficiencies of central planning, the Soviet Union has created an economic and political crisis so massive as to put its entire domestic structure and international position at risk.[8]

By the end of that same year, the Soviet Union collapsed under the weight of its defense dilemma and the Soviet empire was over. Protecting one core value at the expense of another can come at the cost of the state. This is particularly true when the security of that one value is pursued as if to achieve "ultimate security" or the removal of all threats to that value.

Sovereignty and the Ways of the Sovereign State

The essential value that all states seek to protect is their sovereignty. Sovereignty endows the state with rights that no other human grouping is permitted in the international system. Sovereignty, like security, has external and internal components. External sovereignty refers to the situation in which states act as autonomous political units, as "free agents in foreign affairs, negotiating commercial treaties, forming military alliances, and entering into other types of agreements without the supervision of another state."[9] External sovereignty also signifies that states are equal in terms of possessing the "same privileges and responsibilities" as all other states and in claiming the right to use "the same rules of conduct [as all other states] when defending themselves and seeking to exercise influence over others."[10]

The struggle for national security in a world of sovereign and technically equal states may come down to a violent struggle to maintain one's sovereignty against the claims of other sovereign states. For many states today, this might involve a violent struggle against the claims of nonstate actors. Charles Kegley and Gregory Raymond write that the "first right" of sovereignty is "the right to continued national existence, which really [means] the prerogative to use force in self-defense for the acclaimed higher good of self-preservation."[11] Sovereign states retain the absolute right to use violence in the name of preserving their sovereignty. This is true for external sovereignty as well as internal sovereignty.

Internal sovereignty refers to the "supreme decision-making and enforcement authority with regard to a particular territory and population."[12] Just as there is no higher authority than the state in the international system, sovereignty within the state's borders means there is a centralization of power and authority within a single, dominant government.[13] In other words, there are no other competing authorities within the territory of the state. Achieving this centralization of power and authority is no easy process, as will be explained in more detail later in this chapter and in the next. Thus, external sovereignty denotes a fragmentation of authority in the international system, while internal sovereignty denotes a centralization of authority within the political unit of the state.

States and only states are sovereign in the international system. The state is the primary legal entity internationally, and the only entity that has the "right" to use violence. State sovereignty was established in the Treaty of Westphalia signed in 1648 at the conclusion of the Thirty Years' War (1618–1648) in Europe. The treaty divorced the political authority from the religious authority of the Holy Roman Empire in parts of Europe. With Westphalia, sovereignty no longer resided in the emperor and pope but became the prerogative of states and their leaders. That is, sovereignty—absolute decision-making and decision-enforcing authority—moved conceptually and practically from a central political/religious authority to territorial states. Westphalia did not mark the beginning of popular sovereignty, or rule by the people through some form of representative government. Popular sovereignty would not emerge as a political force for another century or so. Instead, Westphalia reified absolutist, maximalist states that could and would claim the right to take whatever measures they deemed necessary to protect national interests and national security.

The world that we live in today was born in the past. The ideas about how we are forced to live in this world today were ideas that made sense to some people in the past. The ideas were not "self-evident truths," but instead were just how people saw the patterns of their own lives, drew some hard conclusions, and learned how to survive in their place and time. As it turns out, those same people codified their conclusions into a treaty whose principles got harnessed to European expansionism and today we all are shackled by the conclusions drawn by some European warlords in 1648. To understand why in the early twenty-first century Bashir Assad, the president of Syria, could routinely drop barrel bombs on his own people, or lay siege to towns and villages to starve Syrians into surrender, or use chemical weapons against Syrian civilians *in the name of the protection of Syria and its people*, we have to understand how the patterns, conclusions, and policies of the Thirty Years' War and the Treaty of Westphalia remain embedded in the politics of the twenty-first century.

Kegley and Raymond have turned a constructivist eye on the Thirty Years' War and the Treaty of Westphalia. To understand Westphalia and its impact on the world today, they suggest, we need to understand the nature of the times that were cemented into the treaty and turned into the "reality" of international politics. The Thirty Years' War was a time of unrelenting brutality originally fought over religious differences. The religious divisions that characterized the early years soon broke down as the war took on its own momentum and became all that was known and knowable by Central Europeans. The war was marked by the decimation of thousands of villages and the deaths of millions.

The factors that kept the war going for so long became foundational elements of the modern—present—international system. Kegley and Raymond conclude that four factors kept the war going: First, the "belligerents became callous in the pursuit of state power." Second, "opportunistic pursuers of personal wealth . . . saw in the role of military entrepreneur a means of achieving social stature and financial gain. Such men had few incentives for a negotiated truce that would end their acquisition of territory and titles as spoils of war."[14] Third, "warfare rationalized the rise of absolute monarchs for desperate people who began to value order over freedom" and saw absolutist states as their only hope for safety. Further, war put back the cause of peace by concentrating "military might in the throne, making state power unassailable for those religious and humanitarian groups that otherwise could make a moral argument for peacemaking."[15] In short order, the rise of the absolutist state meant that democracy and human rights would be put on hold for a hundred or more years. Fourth, Kegley and Raymond conclude that intolerance and mutual disdain locked states into a self-enforcing cycle of mistrust.[16]

In Kegley and Raymond's view, while the Treaty of Westphalia ended the war, it did not construct a better world. The writers of the treaty were warlords, and they locked into place the brutal rules that had developed through much bloodshed and plundering—the very rules that had made them victorious. The victors were surviving warlords, so warlordism was encoded into international politics. The warlords, now in the form of absolutist states, "began to think of warfare as a naturally occurring and appropriate institution."[17] This notion of war as a natural element of international politics remains with us today. The doctrine of raison d'état (by reason of the state or by the need of the state) became the operating principle for states. No sovereign state dwelling in such a brutal world should be *or could be* denied any and all means to protect itself and its interests. We hear this today when political leaders claim that "all options are on the table" for national defense. Further, this recourse to any and all means is not subject to the veto of others because there is no authority above the sovereign state. Leaders began declaring their own wars just and the wars of others unjust, and "the legality of state conduct was now reserved for the state itself to judge."[18] In short, the "reality" asserted by political realists was written onto international and domestic political affairs as a result of a long and terrible European war.

Kegley and Raymond's central thesis is worth repeating at length here, as we see in it the claims made by states today in the name of national security, and in the ways in which these claims undermine the pursuit of a more comprehensive international security that provides for human security. Their thesis is as follows:

> After evaluating the peace treaties . . . that brought the Thirty Years' War to a close, we conclude that the Westphalian settlement was flawed then and that it remains dangerous today. Simply put, in its effort to create a stable international order, Westphalia went too far in liberating states from moral restraints. Expediency overshadowed justice. By legitimating the drive for military power and the use of force, and by placing international stability on the precarious foundation of the successful operation of the balance of power, Westphalia enabled anarchy and amorality to take root in international affairs.[19]

The "reality" of international politics that was constructed on the smoking embers of Europe after the Thirty Years' War did not go unchallenged by those who would assert an international and domestic order based on morality and justice. Hugo Grotius (1583–1645), the so-called father of international law, was a contemporary of the men who constructed the Treaty of Westphalia. As explained by Karen Mingst, "Grotian thinking rejects the idea that states can do whatever they wish and that war is the supreme right of states and the hallmark of their sovereignty."[20] Yet advocates of a law-based international order would take a subordinate place over the centuries to those advocating a "state-first," national interest-first approach. The debate between those who advocated a broader ethic and those who advocated a narrow ethic remains to this day. There are rules now that govern how states interact with other states and nonstate actors in wartime, and rules about how states should treat civilians in wartime, but even these rules are delineated by Westphalian understandings that undermine human security and international security. We will discuss those rules in chapter 8.

One of the legacies of Westphalia is that it is commonly accepted that states operate on a different "code" than do individuals or any other social group. This code distinguishes between appropriate and necessary state action and moral or ethical action, especially regarding the use of violence against threats. Thus, a state can order its own people to die on its behalf in pursuit of national defense through the draft or conscription. Or, a state can kill people as punishment for crimes "against the state" such as murder (although the majority of countries have outlawed the death penalty for any crime). And, of course, a state can determine that *the people of other states* must die so that it may better secure its interests/protect itself. When soldiers die defending their country, the state and its people mourn their loss while declaring their sacrifice to be noble and necessary. Heroes are those who make the ultimate sacrifice to protect the greater good that is embodied in the state. When citizens of other countries die as a result of a state's actions to defend its interests, those lost lives are either "regrettable" and/or "collateral" when they are noncombatants. When the dead are combatants, their deaths are measurable indicators of the successful protection of national security. Lives lost in pursuit of national security are tallied on balance sheets as indications of a state's success or failure.

There is an absence of morality in the ways of the sovereign state. The morality that we come to expect in our normal affairs with other human beings is suspended when considering how states make use of human beings for their own security needs. If a twenty-two-year-old American man were to come upon a twenty-two-year-old Japanese man in 2016 in the Solomon Islands and kill him in hand-to-hand combat, we would be offended and expect some sort of punishment for the killer. But transport these men back in time to World War II and make them soldiers: The American man would be expected to kill the Japanese man and vice versa. Both men would be excused from the normal bounds of what is moral behavior between human beings because they would no longer be individuals but agents of their states. Their cause would be the greater good, and their conscience would be substituted for the national conscience.

The Treaty of Westphalia established the codebook for the realist worldview, but not just for realists. On matters of defending the state, political realists and liberals agree on some essential points: States and only states are sovereign, sovereign states have an absolute right to self-defense, sovereign states have a right to use violence, and sometimes the only option open to sovereign states pursuing their own security is war.

The Treaty of Westphalia also established the principle that states retain a monopoly on the use of violence. Violence is the right of states, and states use violence to confront internal as well as external threats. Some scholars have asserted that violence is "natural" to the state-building process. "State building" means the development over time of effective governing institutions within and institutional control over a defined territory and population. Charles Tilly is widely quoted for his observation that states made war and war made states. Tilly's position, based on the study of the historical development of European states, is that state building is "organized violence."[21] The history of the state system in Europe was a history of political units fighting for survival against other political units. This fight for survival required money and soldiers. Of course, no individuals or groups—internally or externally—gave up resources willingly. Thus, to fight and survive external wars, political authorities used violence to coerce people within their territories to supply much-needed money and soldiers. These resources were necessary for waging the external struggle to conquer the resources of other would-be states. Internally, the successful state was one that expanded its reach into the whole of its territory, defeating peasant uprisings and aristocratic refusals to pay for "national" defense. The successful state was able to institute conscription and taxation systems in the face of considerable and often violent internal resistance. Defeating the internal resistance

was essential to mobilizing the resources for defeating external challenges and further increasing state power and wealth through external
conquest.

Mohammed Ayoob argues that the violence that appears at times to
be ubiquitous in states that were once colonies should be understood
in terms of this "natural" state-building process. Where European
states had the luxury of time and freedom to "complete" this process, former colonies must navigate this process in a truncated time
frame and under constraints imposed by globally accepted international principles. The European states that survived the violent state-
building process are today stable, modern states. Many political units
did not survive to become stable, mature states. Thus, state building is
conceived to be a violent political form of "natural selection."

The state-building process in former colonies was suspended during colonialism or was designed to facilitate the interests of the colonial power. At the conclusion of colonialism, former colonies found
themselves thrust into a modern state system without the benefit
of time and trial that produces stable, modern states (i.e., without
undergoing the same "natural selection" process as the European
states). Additionally, and critically, these new states achieved independence in an international system committed, by virtue of the
United Nations, to the territorial integrity of states.[22] Nonviable political units that were largely colonial artifacts were recognized as juridi-
cally sovereign states even though they would not qualify empirically
as sovereign states.[23] Taken together, the result is what Ayoob calls
"disequilibrium":

> This disequilibrium lies at the root of the chronic political instability
> that we witness in most [Global South] states today. Instability, in
> turn, engenders violence and insecurity, as state-making strategies
> adopted by state elites to broaden and deepen the reach of the state
> clash with the interests of counterelites and segments of the popula-
> tion that perceive the extension of state authority as posing a direct
> danger to their social, economic, or political interests. Given adequate
> time, these conflicts of interest could be overcome peacefully through
> prolonged negotiations . . .
> However, given the short amount of time at the disposal of state
> makers in the Global South and the consequent acceleration in their

state-making efforts, crises erupt simultaneously, become unmanageable as they overload the political and military capabilities of the state, and lead to an accumulation of crises that further erodes the legitimacy of the fragile post-colonial state.[24]

Ayoob offered this analysis thirty years ago, in the first post–Cold War decade. As we will discuss throughout the subsequent chapters, this *was* a decade of ubiquitous violence, as well as a decade of international efforts to stem the violence. But, things have not changed much in some places in the world. Far too many states today are still fragile units in which political violence is pervasive and unrelenting. Fragile states are the source of insecurity for other states because of the globalization of security threats.

Recap

In this chapter, we examined the concept of national security and how all states seek to protect three essential core values. The most essential part of the state is its sovereignty, and so the protection of sovereignty becomes a paramount concern. Sovereignty endows states with rights that no other entity has, such as the right to use violence to pursue national interests. The ways of the sovereign state that are foundational to international politics today reflect a brutal world and brutal worldview developed in Europe centuries ago and transplanted around the world.

Discussion Questions

1. What do we mean by the idea that this is a time of globalized security threats?
2. How do states organize their internal and external security efforts?
3. What is the "national self?"
4. What are the three core values that all states seek to protect?
5. What differences might we find in how core values are prioritized by states in the Global North and states in the Global South?

6. What is Brexit, and how does it alter your previous answer?
7. What is the defense dilemma?
8. What is sovereignty?
9. How was the idea of the sovereign state established?
10. What rights do sovereign states have that no other human groups have?
11. Taking an historical view, what has been the relationship between state-building and violence?

3

Internal Security

In This Chapter

Introduction
The Components of a State: Territory
The Components of a State: Effective Government
The Components of a State: Legitimacy
State Responses to Internal Threats
Recap
Discussion Questions

Introduction

Now we begin to dissect national security. "National" refers to things pertaining to countries or states. "National" in the sense of "national unit" or "national security" or "national interests" does not refer to things pertaining to "nations" in a strict sense. "State" and "nation" are frequently used as interchangeable terms by the popular media, by national governments and political leaders, and even by international organizations—such as the United *Nations*. Strictly speaking, the United Nations is a voluntary grouping of *states* that may or may not be identified as nations. Stateless nations who seek sovereignty, such as those represented by the Hawaiian sovereignty movement, would no doubt be happier if the United *Nations* were actually about nations.

We need to define some terms. A state is what is commonly called a country. A state has an internationally recognized territory, population, and an effective government. States and only states are sovereign; thus, states are the primary units of the contemporary international system and hold primary legal status. Recognition of statehood is conferred on a state by other legally recognized states. Since 1945, membership in the United Nations signifies the recognition of statehood—not because the organization called the United Nations recognizes a new member but because the *member states* of the United Nations recognize the new member. However, membership in the United Nations is not required for recognition; Switzerland has long been recognized by the world's states as a legal state, yet it only formally joined the United Nations in 2002. A final key attribute of states is that states and only states can legally use violence to protect their interests.

A nation is a term that denotes a social/cultural group of people. The group shares history, culture, perhaps a common religion or language or ethnicity, but these latter three attributes are not requirements of nationhood. A nation is not necessarily defined by territory with recognized borders. A nation may claim a particular territory as its homeland and may even reside on that territory, but territory is recognized internationally as belonging to states. The nation is a group of people who have a sense of a common history *as a people* and a sense of a common destiny *for the people*. A nation may seek to become a state in order to better protect the nation against real and potential threats to the group's existence. With statehood comes the legal right to use violence to protect the nation and its interests against all others. The desire to protect the nation is often manifested as nationalism, but states also manifest nationalism, particularly states engaged in wars and foreign crusades. To throw another term into the mix, when we speak about a person's "nationality," we are not referring to the person's connection to a nation, but to a state. Nationality is, in this way, similar to citizenship.

Two examples are useful here. The Jewish people around the world identify as a nation—they are Jewish *people* with a common culture, religion, and history. The Jewish people, like all peoples, envision and work for a future as a people as well. But Jews have many different nationalities depending on where they hold citizenship in the world. Before 1948, there was no Jewish state that could legally use force to protect Jews as people and as *a people*. In 1948, Jewish nationalists declared Israel to be an independent and sovereign *state* whose primary purpose was to defend and protect the Jewish *people*. Since the start of the state of Israel, Jews in Israel are identified by *nationality* as Israelis. Jews in the United States are Americans, Jews in France are French, Jews in Argentina are Argentine, and so on. Some Israelis are not Jewish; some Israelis—again, this is a term that signifies nationality or citizenship—are Arab or Palestinian.

"Arab" is a designation of ethnicity. "Palestinian" is a designation referring to the ethnic Arab people who lived in the area known as Palestine. Arabs live in many countries, primarily but not exclusively in the Middle East and North Africa (collectively called the MENA region). Some of these Arabs are Palestinian, and some are Jordanian or Egyptian, to name a few nationalities. In 1948 when the Jews in Palestine declared the birth of the independent and sovereign state of Israel, they displaced a counterclaim to the area by the Palestinians. Many wars followed, some of which involved other Arab states along with Palestinians, some of which were just between Israel and Palestinian groups. The Palestinians as a nation or people would seek to protect the future of their nation within the legal framework of statehood. So far, Palestine is not a recognized state in the United Nations despite efforts to achieve such recognition. Some Palestinian groups have used violence to promote the cause of the Palestinian nation against Israel. Some Jewish groups used violence to promote the cause of the Jewish nation before the founding of Israel. These examples should suggest the differences between nations and states.

When a political leader or opponent makes a call to the nation, she or he is appealing to the sense of the people *as a people* who have a common destiny to protect. The appeal is more emotional and evokes more commitment than an appeal to defend a legal entity. The reason for this appeal will be explained in more detail shortly. In short,

linking the nation to the state is a move designed to evoke an emotional connection to the group, an emotional connection that would
foster sacrifice for the group, whether the sacrifice is as relatively
small as paying taxes or as large as going to war on behalf of the state.

Although "state" and "nation" are used interchangeably and are
often combined in the phrase "nation-state," the distinctions between
the terms should not be easily dismissed. A "nation-state" signifies
a more or less perfect coincidence between the legal-political state
and the sociocultural nation. Japan is a commonly used example of
a nation-state. By contrast, the overwhelming majority of the world's
states are multinational; that is, they contain within their borders more
than one significant national grouping. Multinational states are not
necessarily problematic; in many states, loyalty to the state coexists
easily with loyalty to one's nation. For example, in the United States,
positive feelings toward the United States as a whole generally do
not interfere with or challenge positive feelings toward one's group
identity and vice versa.

But multinationalism can be the source of troubles within a state.
Separatist nations may wish to break apart from a state and form their
own state with their own government—that is, some nations wish to be
self-determining or self-governing. The desire for self-determination,
or statehood, is especially strong in cases where another group has
dominated the political, cultural, and economic life of the state, using
its position of dominance to threaten the identity and existence of the
minority nation. Such multination states might be called "imperial"
states in which the dominant group exerts control over the nondomi-
nant group.[1] In the imperial multination state, one nation dominates
the other(s) through a variety of means, including at the extreme the
use of genocidal violence, massacre, forced relocations, imprisonment,
forced sterilization and removal of children, to less obviously violent
means such as establishing a national education system dedicated to
promoting a single language and culture, and promoting people in
government—particularly the military and police—who are members
of the dominant group, and so on.

The Soviet Union, despite claims to the contrary, favored ethnic
Russians over all others. In a move taken from classic colonialism,
Russians formed the primary administrative and privileged core

within each of the Soviet republics. This created antagonisms between the majority populations and the dominant Russian minorities. After the collapse of the Soviet empire, Russia intervened in other post-Soviet states on the pretense of giving humanitarian assistance to ethnic Russians. In a case that will be discussed more later, Russia said it was answering the will of the Russian majority in Crimea when Russia annexed Crimea in 2014. The people of Crimea were majority Russian-speaking, and they voted in a controversial election to join Russia two days before the annexation. After the annexation, Crimean Tatars and Ukrainians quickly became targeted by the dominant Russians—and by Russian law. The Tartars were evicted from the offices from which they self-governed under previous Ukrainian law, their television channel was taken off the air, and public leaders and intellectuals were harassed.[2] Crimean Ukrainians had their language removed from school curriculums and newspapers closed.[3] The people of both groups were told to switch to Russian passports or they would be denied rights such as access to health care.

In the case of Iraq, Kurds, Turkmen, and Arab Shi'ia were dominated by Arab Sunnis under British colonial rule and later under the independent Iraqi governments up to and including that of Saddam Hussein. The Arab Sunnis dominated the other groups and, under Saddam Hussein, this domination was often brutal and repressive. Saddam's regime even used chemical weapons against Iraqi Kurdish civilians. After 2003, the Kurds, Turkmen, and Arab Shi'ia feared a return to that status quo, while the Arab Sunnis feared that these other groups would seek revenge on them for the past. The federal system installed in Iraq by the United States, with its "regional" governments and militias for Sunnis, Shi'a, and Kurds, and its shared vice presidencies, was designed, in part, to guard against the further domination by one group over the others. However, during the 2006–2014 Iraqi government of Nouri al-Maliki, Shi'a dominated the government and used the authority of office and law enforcement to harass Sunnis. This created a pool of potential recruits for antigovernment groups such as ISIL.

Multinationalism is not the only source of arguments over "who is the state?" Antigovernment groups of all sorts, including homegrown and internationally inspired terrorists and criminal organizations, create internal security problems for states. Later in this chapter we will discuss the case of Mexico and drug trafficking organizations.

The Components of a State: Territory

Earlier we defined a state as having a defined territory, population, and effective government. It is useful to deconstruct the state and its components in order to understand the difficulties posed by competitive, antagonistic multinationalism, antigovernment sentiment of various forms, and/or terrorism, and to consider solutions to these problems. By understanding the state, we can begin to understand the nature of internally generated threats against the state.

Barry Buzan describes the state as having three components: a physical base, an "institutional expression," and an "idea" of the state.[4] The physical base of a state is the defined territory and population of our definition. Since the beginning of the UN system in 1945, the territorial integrity of most sovereign states has not been threatened by other states. That is, with few exceptions, sovereign states have not attempted to remap other sovereign states by invading and annexing their territory. The Chinese takeover of Tibet in 1950 stands out as one of the few exceptions to this rule. In a few other cases—such as the Indonesian takeover of East Timor in late 1975 and Morocco's efforts since 1976 to alter the demographic makeup of Western Sahara in order to annex it—states have attempted to assert control over territories as they were vacated by the colonial powers (the Netherlands was the vacating colonial power in East Timor and Spain in Western Sahara). And, after Russian gunmen assisted locals in toppling the government of Crimea in 2014, Russia took control of Crimea from Ukraine. Russia claimed to be responding to the Russian majority in Crimea and rectifying a mistake made in 1954 when Soviet leaders administratively moved Crimea out of the Russian Soviet Socialist Republic to the Ukraine Soviet Socialist Republic.

The UN system is founded on the notion of respect for the territorial integrity of all states. States are thus proscribed from invading and conquering other states with the intent to annex the new territory and people. The 1990 invasion of Kuwait by Iraq was met with widespread international disapproval for this reason. Had Iraq attempted to take over Kuwait prior to 1945, it *may* have succeeded because no global organization dedicated to upholding the territorial integrity of its members existed. The precursor to the United Nations, the League of Nations, was dedicated to upholding the sovereignty of its members, but its membership was limited to the small number of independent states. Before 1945, Iraq's success in taking over Kuwait would have been contingent on its sheer military ability to do so and its good relations with the relevant, interested "great power." According to some accounts, in the summer of 1990 the government of Saddam Hussein made strong hints that it intended to take over Kuwait. Having been told by the American ambassador that the US government had no opinion on Iraq's differences with Kuwait but only wanted to see those differences settled quickly, the Iraqi government may have assumed that it was given a green light to proceed by the relevant, interested great power. Unfortunately for Iraq, the US government had not signaled a go-ahead. Facing international punishment as a result of the invasion of Kuwait, the Iraqi government claimed that it had no intention of annexing Kuwait and would leave once a friendly Kuwaiti government was established. This would be more in line with what the US government did the year before when it invaded Panama and replaced the government of Manuel Noreiga with the friendlier Guillermo Endara government.

As the examples of Panama in 1989 and Iraq in the wake of the 2003 invasion demonstrate, the territory of states may be more or less protected by notions embedded in international politics, but particular governments or officeholders may not. Panama did not become part of the United States in 1989, nor did Iraq in 2003. The countries remained intact and more or less independent, with a friendlier government installed in Panama. The post–Saddam governments of Iraq have not been as consistently friendly. There have been cases of states breaking apart (e.g., the Soviet Union and Yugoslavia) and cases of states intervening in other sovereign states, but generally the territorial integrity of states is upheld.

Recently two cases challenge the territorial integrity of states. The first case has already been mentioned in this chapter: the annexation of Crimea by Russia in 2014. In 2010, Viktor Yanukovych was elected president of Ukraine, promising reforms and closer ties with the European Union. Yanukovych, however, was strongly pro-Russian and did not sign a much-anticipated deal with the European Union. Street protests followed at the end of 2013, including some that involved violence committed by state security forces and deaths. In February 2014, Yanukovych fled to Russia and an interim government was installed. The next month, Russian-speaking Crimeans and plain-clothed Russian gunmen/soldiers toppled the administration of the Crimean provincial government. A quick and contentious vote in March for joining Russia was followed two days later by Russia annexing Crimea. The international community condemned the taking of Crimea from Ukraine, placing sanctions on Russia. In the following month, pro-Russian forces—and actual Russian forces—began military operations in Eastern Ukraine to split it off from Ukraine. Russia was punished with more sanctions but as of the start of 2016 the annexation of Crimea stands as the fighting simmers in Eastern Ukraine.

The other case that challenges the idea that territory is protected by the UN and the international system involves the activities of the self-named Islamic State. This group saw its origins in the Sunni group known as al Qaeda in Iraq (AQI), an armed anti-US occupation group that began in 2004. When the leader of AQI was killed by a US airstrike in 2006, the group splintered. One of its pieces renamed itself the Islamic State of Iraq, and then the Islamic State of Iraq and the Levant (ISIL) after conflict began in Syria in 2011. As Zachary Laub and Jonathan Masters write, ISIL "capitalized on Sunni disenfranchisement in both Iraq and Syria."[5] The Syrian regime of Bashar al-Assad favored Alawites, a sect of the Shi'a branch of Islam, just as the Iraqi Maliki government was favoring Shi'a in Iraq. ISIL moved into Syria where it was able to grow in strength, taking and holding territory in Syria and then moving back into Iraq to take and hold more territory. Raqqa, Syria, is claimed as the capital of the new "Islamic State," which its leaders call a caliphate. By the start of 2017, the territorial holdings of this self-declared state had been diminished by a multinational military effort. No state or international organization recognized the "state" of the Islamic State.

The Components of a State: Effective Government

In our definition of state, we included the component "effective government." The government needs to have some administrative authority over all of its territory. Note that the definition says nothing about the relationship between the government and society as in "representative government." Effective government relates to what Buzan calls "institutional expression."[6] The institutional expression of the state is the form and content of the government—the officeholders and the rules by which the officeholders come to power, the national laws, the configuration of legal authorities, and the ways in which the laws are upheld and enforced. As a matter of principle, the shape and form of government within a particular country is not the legitimate business of any other state. But states are often quite involved in the domestic affairs of other states, attempting to shape and influence government type and policies by lobbying, espionage, alliance-building, and so on, and by overt or covert military action, the imposition of sanctions, the offering of rewards, and so forth. The institutional expression of a state may be threatened internally as well. Governments that do not enjoy widespread internal legitimacy may come under political and even military attack from within their own borders. Antigovernment groups of all kinds may take up arms to contend with the legal political authorities. Other groups may take up arms to protect their members when the government fails to protect them in the crossfire.

Mexico's drug war provides an illustration of this last point. The common view of this war is that many different drug trafficking organizations (DTOs) are fighting against the legal authorities and are fighting among themselves. This picture is incomplete because it ignores vigilantism by civilians, some of whom are involved in centuries-old indigenous community policing, some of whom have "taken up arms because the state has systematically failed to protect them," and some of whom have become engaged in criminal activities themselves or absorbed into DTOs.[7] In 2016, vigilante groups operated in about half of the states of the United Mexican States (Estados Unidos Mexicanos, the official name of Mexico indicating that administrative areas are called "states" as in the United States). Two of the worst states for DTO-related violence were also the states with significant vigilantism—Guerrero and Michoacán.[8]

Civilian vigilante groups sprung up because the government was not protecting communities against DTO violence. Drug trafficking in and through Mexico has existed for decades, and violence has been part of it. In places, the police and army were involved in the drug trade or were bought off to allow it. Officially, the Mexican government largely ignored the problem until the mid-2000s. In the early 2000s the number of homicides related to drug trafficking started to increase precipitously. In 2006, President Felipe Calderón started the "drug war" with the dispatch of military personnel and Federales into DTO hotspots, particularly Michoacán. As the drug war heated up, vigilantism increased as well. The International Crisis Group reports that

> though lynching and other vigilante actions have a long history in Mexico, they appear to have increased at the same time as cartel-related violence and crimes have shot up. Between 2005 and 2010, cartel-related homicides quadrupled, according to government figures, while vigilante actions such as lynching rose from four in 2005 to 23 in 2010.[9]

Since the federal and local governments tolerated or allowed drug trafficking and the attendant homicides and violence, civilians—particularly in rural areas—started protecting themselves. Some groups wore uniforms and worked openly as community police, some set up roadblocks and interrogated suspects, others were masked and armed and conducted raids on DTOs. The places where vigilante groups developed were some of the poorest states with few government resources and much less government protection, according to the International Crisis Group.

Meanwhile, Calderón pursued a "kingpin policy" which ended up splintering the DTOs and creating more violence as the lieutenants fought each other for control while rival groups stepped into temporary power vacuums. Vanda Felbab-Brown of the Brookings Institution explains that the situation was grim:

> For years, the Calderón administration callously dismissed the violence, arguing that it was an indicator of government effectiveness

in disrupting the drug trafficking groups. Indeed, the arrests and killing of top *capos* did splinter the DTOs and set off internal succession battles among ever-younger *capos*. The decapitation policy also sparked external power competition—frequently violent—among the drug trafficking groups in a complex multipolar criminal market where the DTOs have struggled to establish stable balances of power and territorial control.[10]

Calderón's successor, Enrique Peña Nieto, claimed to be altering the kingpin policy but ultimately followed suit. The kingpin policy for both administrations failed to plan for the predictable splintering of the DTO. Felbab-Brown recommends that when the government hunts for kingpins, it should also conduct "a systematic strategic analysis of how and where a capture would trigger violent contestation among local criminal groups, what groups might be tempted to enter a territory from outside and how to preposition law enforcement forces to deter and immediately counteract such outbreaks." Simply, "without the state becoming stronger in the territory of the weakened group, some criminal entity will regenerate or recapture that space."[11]

Government inaction, then misdirected action, created more violence and more violent actors by splintering DTOs, thereby causing greater need for vigilantism. But the violence in Mexico was not just committed by DTOs or armed vigilantes, and government actors were not always the enemies of the DTOs. During Calderón's administration, the US military worked closely with the Mexican marines against the cartels, an institution the United States found to be more professional and less corrupt. Peña Nieto changed this policy by using the army more than the navy and marines. This was a nod to Mexican nationalism, because the army was more nationalistic and opposed to US involvement—but the army was reportedly more corrupt.

Additionally, Mexican military forces were known for killing opponents rather than taking prisoners. As reported in the *New York Times* in May 2016, the International Committee of the Red Cross calculates that in armed combat there are on average four to seven injuries sustained for every one death. In Mexico, "the opposite is true." The army killed eight people for every one injured, and the marines killed thirty people for every one injured. From 2007 to 2012, 158 military personnel died, while the military killed 3,000 people. This toll has been attributed to the military's own assessment of the institutions of the government: "In Mexico, where fewer than 2 percent of murder cases are successfully prosecuted, the armed forces kill their enemies because they cannot rely on the shaky legal system."[12] Further, the military used torture and forced confessions when prisoners were taken, acting largely unaccountable. "Of the 4,000 complaints of torture that the attorney general's office has reviewed since 2006, only fifteen have resulted in convictions."[13]

Violence by Mexican government authorities against civilians engaged in nondrug-related activities was common as well. In one particularly notorious case, forty-three student teachers were "disappeared" in September 2014. The student teachers had stolen some buses for transportation to a demonstration. The temporary stealing of buses was an act so common that "bus companies generally instruct the drivers that in the event of a student hijacking, they should remain with the buses to ensure their safe return."[14] That students could engage in the temporary theft of buses speaks to the lack of appropriate law and order and the lack of civilian respect for what law and order there is. The police and gunmen hunted down the students, attacking the buses with gunfire and tear gas. Students, bystanders, and passengers in other buses and vehicles were injured in the chaos. The forty-three disappeared students have never been found.

In some deeply troubled places in Mexico, when the state is not involved in the violence it seems unable to unwilling to stop it, providing an extreme illustration of what happens when the institutional expression of the state fails.

The Components of a State: Legitimacy

This leads us to Buzan's third component of the state—the "idea" of the state:

> The idea of the state is the most abstract component of the model, but also the most central. The notion of purpose is what distinguishes the idea of the state from its physical base and its institutions. The physical base simply exists. The institutions govern . . . but their functional

logic falls a long way short of defining the totality of a state. . . . In a properly constituted state, one should expect to find a distinctive idea of some sort which lies at the heart of the state's political identity. What does the state exist to do? Why is it there? What is its relation to the society it contains?[15]

The idea of the state speaks to a positive linkage between society and state. Essentially, it is a measure of how legitimate the state (and here this would mean the institutions, laws, and office holders) is in the eyes of its population or how much and how well the state is supported by the people. It is important to note that this may or may not relate to *individual* officeholders. In states with regular, routinized changes in officeholders through regular elections, popular support for the idea of the state may not reflect popular support for a particular set of officeholders. The system *itself* may be viewed as legitimate even when the policies and personalities of officeholders are rejected. The "idea" of the state should not be imperiled by unpopular government officials who can be turned out of office in a no-confidence vote or new election. However, there may be people or groups within the country who do not see the system—the institutions, laws, and officeholders—as legitimate. Not all of these turn to violence to demonstrate their antigovernment views, but those that do pose clear law and order problems (when the scale is small) or security threats (when the scale is larger).

What is legitimacy? "Legitimacy" can mean "legality," but a legal government may not necessarily be acceptable, correct, or just in the eyes of the people—or in the eyes of some of the people. Legitimacy requires legality, but legality is not enough. In March 2011 (and for some, well before March 2011), significant numbers of Syrians did not recognize the Assad government as acceptable, correct, or just, although the Assad government was the legally recognized government of Syria. At the same time, some Syrians *did* recognize the Assad government as legitimate. The situation in Syria is an illustration of what Buzan means with this oxymoron: "The state is a major source of both threats to and security for individuals. Individuals provide much of the reason for, and some of the limits to, the security-seeking activities of the state."[16]

If individuals are the "reason for" the state, then how can the state also be a source of insecurity to them? Recall in the previous chapter that the state-building process historically involved coercion and extraction to eliminate internal competing authorities and to harness the people and resources in the territory to the external struggle against other states. The people were made to bend to the will of the state so that the state could survive externally. If the external threat is sufficiently ominous, the leader of the state can justify coercive and extractive practices as necessary for the common survival. But governments make this claim just as easily against internal threats; if the internal threat is sufficiently dire, the people must bend to the will of the state for the common survival. And, governments will also blend the two threats to justify security-seeking activities against people who normally might be considered citizens of the country. When antigovernment demonstrations started in Syria in March 2011 (as part of the Arab Spring), the demonstrators demanded government reform and greater political freedom. In response, the Assad regime sent military troops to forcibly stop the demonstrations, which transformed the demonstrations into armed insurrection. Once the antigovernment forces were armed, Assad claimed that foreign terrorists and agents were acting through local malcontents to harm the security and stability of Syria and its people. This merging of threats allowed the government to use its full machinery of violence internally, causing what was estimated at the end of 2016 to be nearly 500,000 deaths, six million internally displaced Syrians, and five million Syrian refugees.

State Responses to Internal Threats

Buzan asks a question that makes sense here: "If the state becomes a major source of threat to its citizens, does it not thereby undermine the prime justification for its existence?"[17] John Locke, the social contract theorist of the seventeenth century, gave an answer to this question that should resonate with people in democracies: If the state or the monarchy makes war on the people, then it has lost its justification for existence. The social contract is the agreement among people about how they will live together in a political society and what authority can be legitimately exercised over them by a government. Locke might agree with some of Assad's armed opponents that Assad had broken the social contract and thus their cause was righteous.

The Arab Spring of 2011 was an uprising by the peoples of many Middle Eastern and North African countries attempting to overthrow illegitimate authority in order to strike a new social contract between themselves as citizens and between citizens and their states. In representative democracies, the social contract is based on the notion that the state has only that authority that is given to it by the people. Sovereignty does not reside in the entity of the state, but in the people—popular sovereignty—who agree to limit their own absolute sovereign rights in order to live peacefully and productively with each other. Because the grant of authority to the state is limited, the state has no right nor need to be intrusive in the lives of the citizens. This idealized state is called a minimalist state. Democracies are based on this ideal.

The minimalist state is one end of a continuum. The other end is the maximalist state. States facing existential threats operate as maximalist states in which all the people and resources are dedicated to the preservation of the state. The state becomes more than the grant of authority given to it by the sovereign people, and the people become less than sovereigns and more like parts of the machine of the state.

Democracies may operate at times like a maximalist machine state when engaged in total war, but the extraordinary power exercised by the state is still considered to be granted to the state for the limited purposes of meeting the immediate threat. The US government's use of internment camps for American citizens and permanent residents of Japanese ancestry during World War II is one stark example. This policy forced more than 110,000 people into camps away from the West Coast because the US government feared that these people would sympathize with and help the government of Japan. This was the case even though more than 60 percent of the interned people were US citizens. (And, there were no internment camps for Americans of German ancestry.) This extraordinary, maximalist measure was taken two months after the Japanese bombing of Pearl Harbor and lasted until the last internment camp was closed in 1946.

After the November 2015 terrorist attacks in Paris, the French parliament approved a state of emergency granting the government extraordinary powers, including the right to carry out raids and put people under house arrest. The parliament extended the state of emergency and some of the extraordinary powers twice to cover potential threats that might arise during two international sporting events happening in the summer of 2016. The extended emergency powers allowed the government to ban demonstrations and limit the movement of people and vehicles. The sporting events were not attacked. Instead, the city of Nice was the scene of a terrorist act that killed eighty-four people on Bastille Day, July 14, 2016. The government announced that it would continue the state of emergency. The threat to France and its people came in part from alienated and radicalized French young people supported, trained, and assisted by external jihadist groups, particularly ISIL. An appropriate French response—beyond extending immediate extraordinary law enforcement powers—would need an external component aimed at ISIL and an internal component aimed at creating a positive linkage between "France" and the alienated Muslim youth. These two components would take very different forms.

It is the case that sometimes governmental actions taken by minimalist, democratic states in times of heightened threat tend to become institutionalized rather than being removed after the threat abates. This institutionalization of extraordinary government powers can change the very society that the measures were meant to protect. In December 2004, the highest court in Great Britain, the Law Lords, overturned parts of the Anti-Terrorism, Crime and Security Act of 2001, which had been enacted after the 9/11 terrorist attacks on the United States. The law had permitted the British Home Office to detain indefinitely and without charge foreigners suspected of terrorist activities. The Law Lords found the law to be a violation of European human rights laws, but the ruling went even further. One of the judges wrote, "The real threat to the life of the nation, in the sense of a people living in accordance with its traditional laws and political values, comes not from terrorism but from laws such as these."[18] To put it another way, the law, designed to defend Britain, posed more of a threat to the British nation and its core values than that which it was designed to counter. The particular response to the terrorist threat embodied in the legislation ran counter to the critical values of the nation.

Democratic states with open societies tend to be more reactive than proactive to potential internal threats. In one sense, the reactionary nature of a democracy's response to terrorism is related to the fundamental social contract struck between the people and the government. Democracies are intentionally open societies, and the role of government in open societies is to promote and maintain the openness. The openness means that governments typically do not engage in acts of prevention, waiting instead until an attack provokes the need for a "cure." Unfortunately, the cure that is chosen may be as momentous as the terrorist attack. As Laura Donohue warns, "When an open society has been taken advantage of [by terrorism] the immediate response is to close it."[19]

Democratic governments are responsive governments by design, and a terrorist attack prompts a government *not just to respond*, Donohue warns,

> but it must be *seen* to respond. And not just to terrorism in general, but to each significant attack. Following the 1974 Birmingham bombings [in the United Kingdom], for example, Westminster introduced the Prevention of Terrorism (Temporary Provisions) Act. After the August 15, 1998 Real IRA bombing in Omagh, Northern Ireland, the United Kingdom adopted the Criminal Justice (Terrorism and Conspiracy) Act and the Republic of Ireland introduced the 1999 Criminal Justice Act. . . . Following the 1995 attack by Timothy McVeigh on the Murrah Federal Building in Oklahoma City, the United States' Congress adopted the 1996 Antiterrorism and Effective Death Penalty Act. And within weeks of September 11th, America witnessed, amongst other provisions, the adoption of PL 107–56, the "[Uniting] and Strengthening America by Providing Appropriate Tools Required to Intercept and Obstruct Terrorism (USA PATRIOT) Act of 2001."[20]

As is true for any security issue, government responses to terrorism tend to take two forms: those dealing with internal vulnerabilities and those dealing with external vulnerabilities. Because of the difficulties involved in trying to close down all the possible external sources of terrorism, governments may conclude that they can be more effective turning inward. Donohue details the extent of such activity in the United States in the wake of the 9/11 attacks:

> Between September 11, 2001, and January 11, 2002. . . Congress proposed more than 450 counterterrorist resolutions, bill, and amendments. (This compared with approximately 1,300 total in the course of US history.) Within four months of the attacks, more than two dozen new measures became law. President Bush issued 12 Executive Orders and 10 Presidential Proclamations related to the attacks. Only a handful addressed the war in Afghanistan. Most dealt with the domestic realm, the consequences of September 11, and the United States' preparedness for future terrorist attack.[21]

These emergency laws, which have the impact of abridging civil liberties, become regularized over time as temporary emergency measures become permanent. Since terrorism remains a distinct possibility and since governments are supposed to protect their citizens from terrorism, "security forces become reluctant to relinquish" powers. Meanwhile, calls to restore a pre-attack political order (i.e., restore curtailed civil liberties and limit government intrusiveness) are met with derision and questions about whether the source of the calls is appropriately patriotic.[22] Civil liberties get curtailed, noncitizens get legally scapegoated, presumptions about innocence and free speech rights get eroded, and power becomes concentrated in the hands of the executive in order to deal more effectively with terrorists. Counterterrorist measures in liberal states move these states away from the liberal ideal of minimalist government toward the illiberal ideal of a maximalist government, all in the name of preserving and protecting "the people."

Additionally, there is a built-in institutional dynamic that encourages this movement away from minimalism and toward maximalism. Attempts to reorganize government bureaucracies to conduct better counterterrorism get frustrated by entrenched interests who do not want power and money shifted away from their agencies. Individual rights, conversely, are more easily curtailed because individuals (citizens but especially noncitizens residing within the country) have less immediate political clout than do government agencies. Thus, for political reasons, we might expect a government confronting a terrorist threat to increase police investigatory and detainment powers at the expense of individual civil liberties rather than reorganize itself to make counterterrorism efforts more efficient and effective.

National leaders prone to maximalist tendencies—in nondemocratic states—are inclined to perceive the existence of a "national security" threat in order to strengthen their powers. Indeed, they might even facilitate the rise of a threat in order to justify steps against political opponents as they seek to strengthen "regime security." In the first four years of the Syrian conflict, the Assad regime insisted that there was no true Syrian opposition to it—instead, the regime was fighting foreign terrorists. There *were* foreign fighters and terrorists in Syria, primarily (but not exclusively) in the form of ISIL and al-Nusra. Despite the presence of foreign terrorists and the claims made by the Assad regime that it was defending the nation against terrorists, government and pro-government forces rarely attacked ISIL locations.[23] Reuters reported in 2015 that the Assad regime was the top buyer of petroleum from ISIL. US officials estimated that ISIL had made $500 million in trading oil with Assad and, to a lesser extent, Turkey.[24] When Russian forces joined the conflict on behalf of Assad in 2015, they, too, refrained from attacking ISIL and instead attacked other opposition forces including those supported by the West. The presence of ISIL and its barbarism were convenient scapegoats and boogeymen for a regime claiming that there was no political uprising against it but only a foreign terrorist threat. The fear of ISIL was intended to drive Syrians and most of the outside world into the arms of the Assad regime as the lesser of two evils.

The Assad regime did not just stumble upon ISIL as a convenient "enemy." William McCants explains that the regime facilitated the rise of terrorist groups starting in 2011 in order to give it a blank check for dealing with political protests:

> When Syrians began peacefully protesting against their government in 2011, the Assad regime released an unknown number of jihadists from prison. The release was calculated to foster violence among the protestors and give Assad a pretext for a brutal crackdown. It worked. As a Syrian intelligence officer would later reveal, "The regime did not just open the door to the prisons and let these extremists out, it facilitated them in their work, in their creation of armed brigades."[25]

Assad wanted the Syrian Spring to be armed so he could use brutality to silence protestors. To accomplish this, he helped terrorists arm
themselves. When ISIL set up shop in Syria, Assad "turned a blind
eye, happy to let the Islamic State threaten his domestic and foreign
enemies as long as it didn't threaten him."[26]

The Assad regime's violent response to the peaceful protests against
it quickly drove many Syrians into taking up arms. The maximalist
tendencies of a regime engaged in security-seeking behaviors against
its own people will encourage people to take up arms against the
unjust state authorities. There is a tipping point to all violence, or
diminished returns to use a crass economics idea. The more violence is
used against a people, the more likely they will be to take up violence,
justifying more state violence against the people. This explains the
early days of the Syrian conflict.

Syria is a case study in how the maximalist state operates. Well
before the Arab Spring came to Syria in March 2011, Syria was a mul-
tiethnic, multireligious country run as a police state under the control
of a ruling family. Hafez al-Assad was an air force officer who came
to power in a succession of coups. He ruled from 1971 until his death
in 2000, at which point his son, Bashar, was "elected" president. In the
late 1970s, the Muslim Brotherhood organized and protested Hafez
al-Assad's government. The government, particularly the security and
intelligence organs, was dominated by Alawite, a Muslim sect that
is affiliated with Shi'a Islam. The Muslim Brotherhood is Sunni. By
1980, the Brotherhood was engaging in urban guerilla warfare against
the regime. Assad responded with overwhelming force, crushing the
uprising in what is called the Hama massacre of 1982. The military
destroyed Hama, killing somewhere between 1,000 (the official state
toll) and 40,000 people. After Hama, the regime grew more restrictive
and oppressive of the people. A cult of personality was supported
by the regime and the institutions of state and civil society. Human
rights deteriorated. The regime was supported by a small number of
people who benefited from it, to the exclusion of the rights of all others. Syria under the Assad family was a police state—what in the Latin
American context of the 1970s and 1980s would be called a "national
security state." We can borrow a term from Buzan and say that under

the Assads Syria was ruled by "pure coercion"[27] rather than rule authorized and guided by a social contract based on a shared commitment to the idea of the state. There were reasons Syrians took to the streets in March 2011.

Maximalist states may not be legitimate in the eyes of the people, but rule by pure coercion can sustain itself for some time with dire consequences for human beings. Because maximalist police states rely on the use of coercion and violence at every level of society, the blowback is bound to take similar form. Violence begets violence, as the old and true saying goes. Locked-down societies are not fully locked down; antigovernment sentiment might be on slow simmer for years.

As discussed, Hafez Assad confronted the Muslim Brotherhood with force, including a month-long government siege and destruction of Hama in February 1982. The Brotherhood members who survived were imprisoned or fled Syria. One who fled was a Syrian jihadist named Abu Khalid al-Suri who later became close to Osama bin Laden's second in command, Ayman al-Zawahiri. Suri was subsequently captured and returned to Syria to a prison that "held many of Syria's political prisoners, including the jihadists [Bashir] Assad would later release [at the start of the Arab Spring]. When the Assad regime freed Abu Khalid, Zawahiri quickly reestablished contact."[28] Suri went on to become an intellectual guide of jihadists, including those running another anti-Assad jihadist force in Syria, the Nusra Front or Jabhat al-Nusra.

The slow simmer of antigovernment sentiment in Syria was turned into a boil by the Assad regime when it released prisoners at the start of the Arab Spring. But Assad had done far more to create the conditions that exploded into multiside war in Syria. Again, as recounted by McCants,

> When ISIL decided to set up shop in Syria, it already had a network in place. Syrian president Bashar al-Assad had funneled hundreds of jihadists into Iraq to fight against the United States. According to the U.S. government, in 2007, 85 to 90 percent of the foreign fighters in Iraq had come through Syria. ISIL had received many of those fighters and had maintained its facilitation network in Syria after the end of the [US] Iraq war.[29]

Assad had a hand in the growth and training of ISIL, and despite the West's opposition to Assad, the Western war against ISIL will probably keep Assad in power in Syria.

Extensive civil disorder and a "disproportionate security apparatus"[30] are characteristics of maximalist states. The human beings living in such a state may be subject to state-conducted or opposition-conducted violence for generations. And, depending on where such a state may be and what it may have that is of interest to others, the outside world may or may not have much concern for the humanitarian disaster that becomes normal everyday politics.

Until, that is, people start fleeing. The flight of refugees prompts neighbors, at the very least, to take notice of a conflict. We are in an era of massive human flight. The United Nations High Commissioner for Refugees (UNHCR) reports in *Global Trends 2015* that 65.3 million people were forcibly displaced from their homes worldwide. Of these, 21.3 million were refugees, and half of them were under the age of eighteen. Additionally, ten million people were classified as stateless in 2015, that is, there were ten million people denied a nationality or a formal relationship with a government and so denied the rights that citizens enjoy. In 2015, 33,972 people a day were forced to flee their homes.[31]

This massive human flight results from extensive civil disorder and violence in places where governments are either participants in the violence or are powerless in the face of factional violence. The UNHCR reports that in 2015, three countries accounted for 54 percent of the refugees: Somalia, Afghanistan, and Syria. The top nine refugee-producing countries were (in mid-year): Syria, Afghanistan, Somalia, South Sudan, Sudan, the Democratic Republic of Congo, Myanmar, Eritrea, and Iraq.[32] Even general knowledge of these countries confirms that these are sites of massive humanitarian disasters. When we match these against the Global Terrorism Database list of countries with the highest number of terrorism-related deaths, the pattern becomes clearer. The countries with the highest number of terrorist-related deaths (in 2014) were, in order, Iraq, Nigeria, Afghanistan, Pakistan, Syria, Somalia, Ukraine, Yemen, Central African Republic, and South Sudan. Half of the countries on the refugee-producing list are on the list of countries with the highest number of deaths by terrorism for roughly the same time period: Afghanistan, Central African

Republic, Iraq, Somalia, South Sudan, and Syria. Five of these states—Afghanistan, Central African Republic, Somalia, South Sudan, and Syria—are on the list of the ten most fragile states on the Fragile States Index for 2015.[33] This index used to be called the Failed States Index, and these cross-comparisons suggest why. Any one of these countries could be a poster child for the lack of good fit between the institutional expression and the idea of the state.

The Global Terrorism Index 2015 reports that just five countries—Iraq, Nigeria, Afghanistan, Pakistan, and Syria—accounted for 78 percent of the lives lost because of terrorist attacks in 2014.[34] The same index reports that 92 percent "of all terrorist attacks between 1989 and 2014 occurred in countries where political violence by the government was widespread." And, more evidence that violence begets violence, "in the last 25 years, 88 percent of all terrorist attacks occurred in countries that were experiencing or involved in violent conflicts. Less than 0.6 percent of all terrorist attacks occurred in countries without any ongoing conflict and any form of political terror."[35]

Recap

In this chapter, we examined the important differences between "state" and "nation," and the complex relationships between the components of a state. We paid particular attention to the issue of legitimacy, and noted how legitimacy is eroded when states fail to provide security or when states become a source of insecurity for their own citizens. We charted how government failure in Mexico led to the rise of alternative authorities in the form of drug trafficking organizations and vigilante groups. And we observed how maximalist states like Syria create antigovernment forces and terrorist groups as a result of their efforts to rule by pure coercion.

Discussion Questions

1. Explain the differences between a "state" and a "nation."
2. Define "nationality" and explain its meaning in relationship to the state.

3. How might multiple nations within a state lead to instability and violence?
4. Discuss the few cases in which the territories of states have been threatened since the founding of the United Nations.
5. Explain the origins of ISIL.
6. What would an "effective" and "legitimate" government look like?
7. Discuss why vigilantism is on the rise in Mexico.
8. Discuss the difference between a minimalist state and a maximalist state and how security threats move one type toward the other.
9. Discuss the conflict in Syria within the framework of maximalist states and their use of political violence.
10. Describe the correlations between high numbers of displaced persons and refugees and extensive civil disorder involving state-directed violence.

4

Unilateral Pursuit of External Security

In This Chapter

Introduction
The Security Dilemma
Defense
Deterrence
Defensive Defense
Preemptive Self-Defense and Preventive Force
Recap
Discussion Questions

Introduction

The pursuit of external security, like the pursuit of internal security, is an absolute right of the state. Article 51 (Chapter VII) of the United Nations Charter upholds this right even as it seeks to establish the means by which external security can be guaranteed collectively:

> Nothing in the present Charter shall impair the inherent right of individual or collective self-defense if an armed attack occurs against a

Member of the United Nations, until the Security Council has taken
measures necessary to maintain international peace and security.

The UN Charter envisions a world in which states are secured against
external threats by the mutual respect shown by all states for the territorial integrity of all other states. External security is also promised by
the threat of collective security or the collective punishment of aggressors. These topics are discussed later in this book, but no discussion
of national security post-1945 is complete without acknowledging the
important context of the UN system.

The United Nations is a system based on reciprocal exchanges. In
exchange for the promise of protection through collective security,
states agree "that armed force shall not be used, save in the common
interest." This relinquishing of the use of armed force in the pursuit
of a state's foreign policy goals does not, as noted earlier, impair the
state's "inherent right" of self-defense. As this chapter will explore,
states can and some do take this "inherent right" to extremes. Further-
more, the UN system is a *voluntary* system of reciprocal exchanges,
and states are *more or less* bound by membership obligations (some
states seem more bound than others, some far less bound). Thus, the
use of armed force in statecraft remains a present reality in international politics, as much as the use of state violence remains present
in state-building and state-maintenance activities within states. States
threaten and use armed force—and they erect stockpiles of armaments
for these purposes. Even in the UN system, collective security cannot
be maintained without a credible threat of military punishment for
aggressors, and a credible threat depends both on significant military
capabilities and on the willingness of states to use those capabilities.

The Security Dilemma

As discussed in chapter 2, what we have come to accept as the reality of international politics was born on the bloodied fields of Central
Europe during the Thirty Years' War. "The war bred a pessimistic
mood: evil was seen as ubiquitous and *realpolitik* seemed to offer the
only viable tactics for advancing one's interests in a callous world."[1]

The long legacy of Westphalian principles demonstrates "that when a practice (such as war making) becomes widespread, these customs tend to become obligatory."[2]

What we call the Westphalian peace treaty initiated a system between states that did not attempt to guarantee international peace but instead "created a war called 'peace.'"[3] The first element of this system that came to be taken as a given was that the international system is characterized by anarchy, which is to say that "there is no international political authority invested with a legitimate monopoly of force capable of enforcing peace, protecting states against aggression, and guaranteeing that their rights will not be violated."[4] Given the predominant value placed on state sovereignty in international politics, no overarching international political authority *could* be created. International treaties could be struck and accords arranged, but these would be premised on the understanding that national security interests might at any time require a state's departure from such treaties and accords.

Anarchy does not imply chaos, nor does it imply a lack of rules and order. Instead, the order that was struck after Westphalia was founded on the realist notion of the balance of power. Balance of power refers to the distribution of power across the international system, particularly among the greater or major powers although this can also be used to discuss regional systems and regional powers. This balance is more than a distribution of power because it is also a system by which great powers attempt to prevent any one of their ranks from becoming more powerful and perhaps hegemonic. War is not necessarily the first resort in such a system, as war is not always the most efficient way to maintain the balance. Thus, great powers calibrate and recalibrate the balance through arms acquisitions, negotiations, short-term alliance formation, and then, if necessary, war.

The balance-of-power system established in European affairs did not ensure peace but regularized war as a means by which some states consolidated their power over other Europeans and ultimately over much of the world. The world wars of the first half of the twentieth century can be understood in some sense as balance-of-power wars, but by this time the European great powers had been joined by the United States, China, and Japan.

The balance-of-power system, as realists think about it, also does not preserve a stable status quo or equilibrium. John Mearsheimer maintains this is "because the international system creates powerful incentives for states to look for opportunities to gain power at the expense of rivals, and to take advantage of those situations when the benefits outweigh the costs. A [major] state's ultimate goal is to be the hegemon in the system."[5] Writing in the midst of a great power war—World War II—Nicholas J. Spykman made this same observation:

> The truth of the matter is that states are interested only in a balance (imbalance) which is in their favor. Not an equilibrium, but a generous margin is their objective. There is no real security in being just as strong as a potential enemy; there is security only in being a little stronger. There is no possibility of action if one's strength is fully checked; there is a chance for a positive foreign policy only if there is a margin of force which can be freely used.[6]

Similar sentiments are voiced in the domestic politics of many countries whose leaders call for "peace through strength." As will be discussed in chapter 6, elements of the balance-of-power system get incorporated into the UN collective security framework, although the free use of war to regulate the distribution of power across the great powers is prohibited.

Of course, if all states—or all ambitious states—seek more power at the expense of others, then this creates a dilemma for all states. Analysts call this the security dilemma. As explained by Glenn Snyder,

> The term is generally used to denote the self-defeating aspect of the quest for security in an anarchic system. The theory says that even when no state has any desire to attack others, none can be sure that others' intentions are peaceful, or will remain so; hence each must accumulate power for defense. Since no state can know that the power accumulation of others is defensively motivated only, each must assume that it might be intended for attack. Consequently, each party's power increments are matched by the others, and all wind up with no more security than when the vicious cycle began, along

with the costs incurred in having acquired and having to maintain their power.[7]

In chapter 1, we saw the case of Australia's refusal to allow the landing of some Afghan boat people in August 2001. Australia's ongoing efforts to manage the security threat posed by boat people (as potential terrorists) resulted in a 2004 policy announcement aimed at defending Australia from boat people. The Australian prime minister declared that Australia would begin to enforce a 1,000-nautical-mile maritime security zone to protect against shipborne terrorists who would threaten Australian territory and offshore oil interests in the Timor Sea. Any ship entering the zone would be required to produce detailed information on its cargo, crew, and destination(s) when challenged by the Australian navy. By the declared size of the zone, the territorial waters and even the sovereign territory of Indonesia, Timor-Leste, Papua New Guinea, and New Zealand would be violated by Australia.

Officials in Indonesia and New Zealand, as well as those in Malaysia whose waters and territory would not be directly affected, quickly warned Australia not to violate other states' sovereignty or international maritime law. Although Australian officials tried to reassure the neighbors, some were not so easily placated. Indonesia had had prickly relations with Australia since the 1970s and Indonesia's annexing of East Timor. When ethnic conflict erupted around East Timor's independence referendum in September 1999, the Australian prime minister declared Australia to be the "deputy" of the United States in Asia as Australia led a multinational military intervention force into East Timor. These bad relations were intensified over the August 2001 Afghan boat people episode when Australian officials implied that Indonesia had encouraged the people smuggling that sent illegal migrants toward Australia. Adding more fuel to the fire since 2002 were repeated pronouncements by the Australian prime minister that Australia reserved the right to launch preemptive strikes in neighboring countries to prevent terrorist attacks. If any specific country were to feel threatened by the new Australian maritime security zone, it would be Indonesia. By realist logic, Indonesia would be foolhardy *not* to respond with some heightened military posture to Australia's latest affront.

Not all states appear to be seized by the dynamics of the security dilemma, to be sure. But whenever central authorities are faced with what they perceive to be serious threats to their existence, sovereignty, status, or prestige, we are sure to see elements of this self-defeating cycle.

A critical problem for national leaders is how to gauge threats in a system that is by definition abundant with threats. Further, national leaders must somehow convince other states that their actions are simply defensive and are not intended to be threatening (unless the game of threats is on, and in a realist world this is the operative assumption). In sorting out threats, Klaus Knorr makes the distinction between *actual* threats (which he says can be precise as well as vague), *potential* threats, and *systemic* threats. The determination of whether a threat is actual or potential is always made more dangerous by systemic threats:

> Today's friendly neighbor may become dangerous tomorrow, because, for example, he has acquired additional territory or superior technology or a strong ally or a different government. The observation that interstate changes in intentions and capabilities can unpredictably lead to dangerous threats follows from the very structure of the international system in which each unit is militarily sovereign. We call this, therefore the *systemic* threat. It means that, over the longer run, no state-actor can ever be certain of its security.[8]

What do states *do* when perceiving actual or potential threats in the face of the "reality" of the security dilemma and the ongoing systemic threat? States need to be prepared at all times to defend themselves.

Defense

All states' national security policies are aimed at protecting their territory and population, political independence and autonomy, and economic well-being. Countries define each of these—and the perceived threats to each of these—in different ways, sometimes directing their efforts inward and sometimes outward. Even within particular countries, different national decision makers may define and perceive values and threats differently. Another important idea to keep in mind is that the protection of any one value or set of values often comes at the expense of one or more others.

Defense in its most essential form involves the ability to withstand a physical attack on one's territory. This understanding "rests on an essentially autarkic notion of the state as a unit self-contained and self-reliant in all the major political, economic and cultural elements of life. Its principal military need is to defend its domestic universe from disruption by external military attack or internal disorder."[9] One obvious shortcoming of this notion of national defense is that it is a remnant of "the largely bygone days when most important state interests could be protected by military force."[10] In a broader sense—for some but not all countries—national defense has come to involve the use of military force to protect core values or interests, whether those values are located within the state's borders or not. But for now, we will stay with the idea of defending one's own territory from attack in order to expand on the concept of defense.

Another obvious shortcoming of the term "defense" conceived as the ability to withstand an invasion attempt is that invasion itself is increasingly unlikely given the sheer magnitude of the military power necessary to invade and conquer another country successfully. Historical examples of more powerful states invading and attempting to occupy less powerful states such as the Soviet Union in Afghanistan in the 1980s and the United States in Iraq from 2003 to 2009 demonstrate how much overwhelming force and power are required to carry this out. Most countries do not face potential enemies who possess this kind of overwhelming military power.

Instead of the threat of an invasion attempt, most states must protect against the possibility of an enemy using force or violence to cause unacceptable *damage* to territory, population, or critical infrastructure. Such an attack might be carried out through the use of aircraft, ballistic or short range missiles, covert special operations, drones, suicide attacks, and so on. The attacker could be a state as easily as a nonstate actor (and here the identity of the attacker would in part determine the form and method of the attack), and the attacker need not possess power capabilities on par with the target's. This last statement is especially true in an age of defending against transnational terrorism committed by nonstate actors.

Defending against such an attack—an attack not intended to invade and conquer but simply to cause harm—requires the use of more than military force. Or, it requires military force that is used not to stop the harm when it is about to happen but to stop the harm *before* it begins.

Deterrence

To deter is to stop something from happening that has not yet started to happen. A deterrence strategy involves stopping an attack by would-be attackers by threatening dire retaliatory consequences. Just as an attacker may not possess the military power to attempt to invade and conquer a country and thus resorts to the use of force to hurt the opponent for its political goals, a targeted country may not possess the military power to be able to thwart an invasion attempt but may well have the military power to hurt a would-be attacker. The ability to threaten damage to one's opponent is more attainable than the ability to defend against or threaten invasion.

Let's consider an example. India and Pakistan became independent from the United Kingdom in 1947 and proceeded to enter into their first war with each other. Another war between the two came in 1965, and a war in 1971 ended with Pakistan loosing territory that became the independent country of Bangladesh. In 1999, the two countries fought what is called the Kargil War. India and Pakistan remain at odds with each other presently. India has a military advantage over Pakistan in terms of ground forces and hardware. In 2015, India's armed forces numbered 1,150,000, while Pakistan's numbered less than half of that at 550,000.[11] India also had two aircraft carriers, attack submarines, and superior airpower. "It's distinctly possible," writes Kyle Mizokami, "that any future war between India and Pakistan would involve limited action on the ground and full-scale fighting at sea and in the air. India has the upper hand in both, particularly at sea where it would have the ability to blockade Pakistani ports."[12] Since Pakistan cannot sustain or win a conventional war with India, how can it defend itself? Pakistan has developed nuclear weapons, and the United States has supplied it with sophisticated aircraft that could deliver those weapons. That is, Pakistan has a nuclear deterrent against Indian military attacks. This is not the end of this story, however, because deterrence is a tricky thing.

India also has nuclear weapons. It has more nuclear weapons than Pakistan and superior aircraft and land-based missiles, and was scheduled to deploy a nuclear-armed submarine in 2016. By the logic of deterrence, though, because both sides have nuclear weapons, both sides are deterred from attacking because of the fear of nuclear retaliation. Let's explore the idea of nuclear deterrence a bit and then we will return to India and Pakistan. Nuclear weapons put the security dilemma and the ambiguous role of military weapons as both protectors and destroyers of life into the starkest relief.

Most of our understandings of and expectations about nuclear deterrence arise out of the development of the American-Soviet nuclear relationship. The American-Soviet nuclear relationship in its first years was asymmetrical, with the United States in possession first of a monopoly on and then a predominance of nuclear destructive capability. In the time that the Soviets lacked sufficient weapons and delivery systems to threaten substantial damage to US territory, the United States possessed what is called first-strike capability. This is the capability to substantially eliminate the enemy's ability to retaliate to any degree. One result of this first-strike capability was the US threat of massive retaliation in response to any Soviet efforts to increase Soviet territory or influence. This asymmetry characterized the relationship until around the start of the 1970s.

By 1972 and the signing of the Strategic Arms Limitations Treaty (SALT I), the Soviet nuclear weapons program and arsenal had achieved essential equivalence to the US arsenal in terms of nuclear destructive capacity (which includes both warhead stocks and reliable delivery vehicles). The Soviet Union had achieved second-strike capability, or the ability to absorb a nuclear attack by the United States and still have sufficient nuclear weapons remaining to retaliate and inflict comparable and unacceptable damage. The United States, too, possessed second-strike capability; thus, a superpower war theoretically would ensure mutual assured destruction (MAD). The *mutual* recognition of MAD meant that the idea of direct war of any sort between the superpowers was supposed to be "unthinkable." By virtue of both sides acquiring second-strike capability, the superpower relationship reached the "maturity" of stable nuclear deterrence.

Understood this way, MAD freed the superpowers from the inevitable self-defeating drive of the security dilemma. Both sides in such a relationship should and would understand the consequences of their mutual actions and thus would be mutually deterred, restrained, and *reassured*. Further, neither side would be provoked by uncertainty and the lack of trust to continue arming and taking other more provocative moves.

Of course, despite the "achievement" of MAD and many arms control and disarmament treaties signed between the two superpowers, neither seemed so reassured by their "mature" relationship that they stopped arming. And, proxy war conducted by one or the other was ubiquitous during the Cold War as each made use of local conflicts in their meta-level conflict. Even after the Cold War ended and the Soviet Union collapsed, Russia and the United States continued to develop or planned to develop new nuclear weapons systems.

Deterrence—and particularly nuclear deterrence—admits to the basic inability of a state to protect its people and territory. A deterrent strategy admits this inability and asserts that a country will harm others in order to provide something like defense. A nuclear deterrent strategy threatens massive and potentially irremediable harm to others as a way to protect people and territory. Does it work? And does it work for all threats in the same way?

France is a nuclear power; it was the fourth country to attain operational nuclear weapons. After the 9/11 terrorist attacks on the United States, France revised its nuclear policy to make it explicitly and overtly designed for defense and deterrence in a world in which major power conflict was far less likely than an attack on one's vital interests by a smaller opponent. The French government let it be known that in case of a threat against its people, territory, or interests, France would issue a final warning, or ultime avertissement. This final warning would be a "single, limited strike on military targets. If an adversary persisted, the final warning would be followed by a massive strike."[13] This final strike without a doubt would employ nuclear weapons, as France had long rejected a "no-first-use" policy.

The French nuclear arsenal and deterrence strategy has not been able to protect France from jihadist terrorist attacks. The nature of the opponent—radicalized French citizens and legal residents assisted and/or inspired by ISIL—makes the use of nuclear weapons unthinkable. Even if France were to make the unthinkable decision to attack ISIL positions in Iraq and Syria with nuclear weapons in retaliation for the terrorist attacks in Paris and Nice, it is highly doubtful that the problem of radicalized Muslim youth living in France and in Europe would disappear.

At its most basic, deterrence has a lot of moving parts that must all happen together to make it a workable strategy. First, the state threatening deterrence (nuclear or not) must have the means to make good on the threat and must be perceived as being fully committed to carrying through with the threat. The opponent must understand that the threat is real. If the opponent does not believe the threat is real, the opponent will not be deterred. What is the best way to convince an opponent that the threat is real—that the threat can be done and *will be done*? Thomas Schelling contends that

> unhappily, the power to hurt is often communicated by some performance of it. Whether it is sheer terroristic violence to induce an irrational response, or cool premeditated violence to persuade somebody that that you mean it and may do it again, it is not the pain and damage itself but its influence on somebody's behavior that matters. It is the expectation of *more* violence that gets the wanted behavior, if the power to hurt can get it at all.[14]

France has demonstrated its willingness to use force in Syria, Libya, Mali, and other countries and conflicts, but as a democratic country with a strong commitment to human rights, it will not use the same kind of force against internal armed opponents, or at least not at the level of violence that governments use against external threats.

Moreover, French military policies alone cannot eliminate the internal terrorist threat, although military attacks against ISIL positions in Iraq and Syria might weaken the external support for internal terrorism.

Returning now to India and Pakistan, since both states possess nuclear weapons their relationship *might* approach one of stable nuclear deterrence. Using ideas from the American-Soviet nuclear relationship, we might assume that because both India and Pakistan have nuclear weapons they would be mutually deterred from fighting a direct war with each other, because any confrontation could escalate into a nuclear confrontation. Recall also that Pakistan has less military capability—conventional and nuclear—than India. This might mean that Pakistan might be *more* restrained in its interactions with India to avoid war. However, in the spring of 1999, Pakistani regular troops and irregular forces invaded Indian territory in Kashmir causing a war with India. The Kargil War ended only because the US Bill Clinton administration engaged in high-level crisis diplomacy to get each side to back down. It remains uncertain who started the Kargil War on the Pakistani side, but whoever they were they were not deterred by India's conventional or nuclear superiority and the threat of unacceptable damage.

Two more problems of deterrence should be mentioned here. First, analysts usually discuss deterrence in terms of a bilateral relationship, or a two-player game to use game terminology (favored by people who think about these things). Very little in world politics is bilateral. The "game" of nuclear deterrence played by India and Pakistan needs to take into account other "players." The United States alters the balance of power (or balance of terror) between India and Pakistan in its weapons sales to both sides and with the US-Indian nuclear agreement of 2005. China, too, is an unnamed but significant player with nuclear weapons pointed in India's direction. Additionally, China militarily occupies parts of Kashmir as well as territory in another Indian state as a result of the Indo-Chinese border war of 1962. India suffered a major military defeat in that war and since then has perceived China to be a primary security threat. India's nuclear arsenal thus is partly directed against the Pakistani threat and partly directed against the Chinese. Moreover, China "has been the principal provider of nuclear and missile technologies to Pakistan" as a counterweight to India.[15] A two-state situation of stable nuclear deterrence might be destabilized by all the other self-interested actors in the game.

This brings us to the final problem of deterrence which foreshadows a discussion yet to come on the use of preventive force. Preventive force involves a military operation aimed at eliminating a future threat that has yet to materialize. In 1981, Israel launched an airstrike on a nuclear plant under construction at Osirak in Iraq. The attack was both to stop a threat emerging from Iraq *and* to deter Iran from developing its own nuclear weapons capabilities in the future. Jennifer Taw cautions that,

> a show of force could have a deterrent effect on potential enemies, but it could also serve to strengthen their resolve. The Iranian government, having seen the effects of Israel's attack on the Osirak reactor, did not decide against nuclearization, but instead ensured that its own nuclear development facilities would be far less vulnerable than Iraq's had been.[16]

Just as one cannot control whether one's opponents may understand the message conveyed by a deterrence policy, one also cannot control how the opponent may react. Hardening one's resolve to continue is the opposite of heeding the threat and stopping. As a strategy to defend one's people and territory, deterrence is the name of the game, but not one that is fail-safe.

Defensive Defense

There is an alternative notion of defense that would reject any kind of deterrent precisely because deterrence is embedded in realism and is too dangerous. This alternative view is that a state should deploy a military force that is "manifestly defensive" or, as Geoffrey Wiseman explains, a military force that "is defensive, and is seen by one and all to be so, not just in stated overall purpose, but also in its inherent characteristics."[17] Such a defensive posture would be intended to serve as a "shield" rather than a "sword" and ideally would not be a shield that could serve as cover for the wielding of a sword. It is worth noting at this point that very few countries have ever adopted a defensive defense policy, but if the goal is human security and a less violent world, then it is an idea that should be discussed.

"Defensive defense," "nonprovocative defense," and "nonoffensive defense" are related terms suggesting "a conventional approach to [defense] aimed at creating an environment that [favors] defensive strategies and operations rather than offensive options. According to this view, offensiveness can be derived from the structure of a military and [defense] forces should therefore have defensive structures and capabilities that are not threatening to other countries."[18] Johan Galtung proposes that we

> locate the definition of the offensive/defensive distinction in geographical space: *can the weapon system be effectively used abroad, or can it only be used at home*? If it can be used abroad then it is offensive, particularly if that "abroad" includes countries with which one is in conflict. If it can only be used at home then the system is defensive, being operational only when an attack has taken place.[19]

Wiseman tells us that "a central assumption of non-provocative defense concepts is that manifestly defensive capabilities provide reassurance to others about intentions."[20] Reassuring others is hardly the stuff of realism and the security dilemma. Instead, Wiseman contends that advocates of nonprovocative defense attempt to "reverse the deterioration process" associated with the realist security dilemma.[21]

In post–World War II global politics, defensive defense arose in response to the absurdities of the Cold War and nuclear deterrence. Alternative defense notions arose with the development of peace research studies (rather than security studies), especially in Scandinavian countries.[22] These alternative defense notions were incorporated into Swedish prime minister Olof Palme's advocacy of common security—or security *with* other states rather than against other states.[23] In some ways, the European Union is based on the notion that European states must be secure with one another, since war anywhere in Europe was war everywhere in Europe.

Alternative defense concepts that are "manifestly defensive" encourage national leaders to be self-aware and self-reflective about how one's own actions are perceived internationally.[24] Because it is so difficult for others to assess motivations and because it is possible to use ostensibly defensive weapons for offensive purposes, national leaders need to configure their resources in defensive modes that would make reconfiguration impossible or so time consuming that would-be targets would be alerted long in advance of any attack. Transparency in the deployment of actual, material defensive forces would be the key to reassuring others. To Galtung, the ideal defensive defense strategy would involve immobile defensive systems having only a local impact area or, less ideally, short-range systems with a limited impact area. Long-range systems with extensive potential impact areas would qualify only as offensive systems.[25] Additionally, defensive defense puts heavy emphasis on nonprofessional, generally conscript armies and militias that would go to war only reluctantly and then only to defend national territory.[26]

In a practical sense, after World War II, Japan and Germany were required to assume defensive defense postures as part of the terms of surrender and occupation. Nonprovocative defense postures may be particularly well suited for the postwar reintegration of losing states, especially from the standpoint of former targeted/victimized states. In some sense, the sanctions regime imposed on Iraq after the 1991 Gulf War can be understood as imposing a defensive defense posture on Iraq.

By way of a more elaborate example and one that does not involve a defeated enemy, Wiseman describes Switzerland's "deterrence by denial," through which it would "deter attack by setting a high price for invasion":

> In theory, the Swiss concept of "general defence" involves the entire population. There is no professional army; arms, ammunition, and uniforms are kept in homes; and a well-trained militia force capable of mobilizing some 680,000 troops (comprising men 20 to 50 years of age) is trained to fight within the country's borders.
>   In the event of an external armed attack, the armed forces would assume the major role in defending the country. . . . Should large parts of Switzerland become occupied, citizens would carry out activities ranging from guerrilla warfare to sabotage and civil disobedience.

No form of retaliation or punitive action against the adversary's population is planned. Switzerland would rely heavily on passive defences, such as obstacles against tanks, anti-aircraft missiles, and early-warning radar systems.

Undoubtedly, these military preparations are manifestly defensive. Switzerland seeks only to defend its territory, it does not threaten others, and will not fight unless attacked.[27]

There are some problems with the notions of nonprovocative defense. One might question whether a state in a dangerous neighborhood—such as the Middle East or South Asia—ought to risk a defensive defense posture. Perhaps only states that are especially important to all parties to a potential dispute—such as Switzerland during World War II—or, conversely, countries that tend to be peripheral to the central issues of world politics might be successful in adopting defensive defense strategies. Additionally, in this age in which nonstate actors pose critical security threats (more so than states in most cases), it may be nearly impossible to invoke civil defense strategies; the goal of nonstate actors is not to invade and occupy but to do significant harm to a target state.

Another tough issue arises in that we live in an age marked by intrastate rather than interstate conflict. A defensive strategy that depends on arming and mobilizing a population for homeland defense may well be suicidal for any given government under conditions of probable and impending civil ruptures, conflict, and war. Galtung warns as well that,

A policy of defensive defense is not offensive against an outside adversary, but could be highly offensive against an inside adversary. The types of weapons that are described . . . as being defensive are defensive because they cannot reach outside national borders in any significant manner. But they can certainly hit inside those borders, otherwise they would not have any capability at all. And they would not necessarily distinguish between external and internal foes of the regime. As a matter of fact, they are exactly the type of weapons that a repressive government might use against insurgent forces, whether their claims are justifiable or not.[28]

Finally, as Galtung admits, *"defensive defense presupposes a high level of national self-reliance in defense matters.* If weapon systems are not supposed to be quick, long range, and mobile, then they cannot be transported from one country to another in order to help that other country (rather than attacking it) either."[29] This has implications for military alliances as well as for international security arrangements like the United Nations that depend on member states' offensive military capabilities. Galtung proposes that the undermining of military alliances is a long-term good: "Clearly, a country which is used to relying on allies, and particularly on a superpower ally, will not mobilize all its defense resources." But "if one really means what one says, that freedom is worth a fight, then that fight has to be done by nobody else than oneself."[30] But what happens in those cases when groups such as ISIL or Boko Haram or governments such as Syria's Assad regime or Libya's Qaddafi regime turn defensive resources against their internal foes? Who comes to the aid of civilians caught in the cross fire or civilians caught in the genocidal plans of a monstrous government? Even in an idealized world in which states harbor no aggressive intentions toward one another, human security still may be imperiled by deadly internal arguments over who composes the state and nation.

Preemptive Self-Defense and Preventive Force

This chapter started with the statement that states enjoy an inherent right to self-defense. This right is upheld in Chapter VII, Article 51 of the UN Charter: "Nothing in the present Charter shall impair the inherent right of individual or collective self-defense if an armed attack occurs against a Member of the United Nations, until the Security Council has taken measures necessary to maintain international peace and security."

In most, if not all, cases, when a state uses force outside its borders, the justification for the violence will typically be self-defense or the defense of vital national interests. Historically, the claim of self-defense was the only acceptable justification for states intervening in other states even when humanitarian disasters were under way in the targeted states. *How* and *for what* and *when* a state may act in self-defense brings us to the topics of preemptive self-defense and preventive force.

Note that Article 51 says that there is a right to self-defense "if an armed attack occurs" and "until the Security Council has taken measures." Self-defense exists in that space. And, the armed attack must "attain a certain scope and magnitude."[31] And further, when the attack of "a certain scope and magnitude" is committed by a nonstate actor, the attack "can count as armed attacks only if the terrorist group is under the 'effective control' of a state."[32]

Does a state have to wait and be a victim of a serious attack before it can act, or can a state preempt an attack? Preemption is considered to be acceptable under certain circumstances. Richard Betts explains that preemption or preemptive war is "unobjectionable in principle, since it is only an act of anticipatory selfdefense in a war effectively initiated by the enemy."[33] Preemption, Betts tells us, is "legitimate in principle and sometimes advisable in practice."

In the context of international jurisprudence and accepted state practices, Neta Crawford delineates four necessary conditions that must be met in order to conduct a legitimate preemptive strike or war:

> First, the party contemplating preemption would have a narrow conception of the "self" to be defended in circumstances of self-defense. Preemption is not justified to protect imperial interests or assets taken in a war of aggression. Second, there would have to be strong evidence that war was inevitable and likely in the immediate future. Immediate threats are those which can be made manifest within days or weeks unless action is taken to thwart them. This requires clear intelligence showing that a potential aggressor has both the capability and the intention to do harm in the near future. Capability alone is not a justification. Third, preemption should be likely to succeed in reducing the threat. Specifically, there should be a high likelihood that the source of the military threat can be found and the damage that it was about to do can be greatly reduced or eliminated by a preemptive attack. If preemption is likely to fail, it should not be undertaken. Fourth, military force must be necessary; no other measures can have time to work or be likely to work.[34]

Chris Brown agrees that preemption is justifiable in terms of self-defense. "States, it is presumed, do not have an unqualified right to use force in international relations, but they do have the right to defend themselves—a right established in customary international law and reaffirmed in the UN Charter—and, crucially, are under no obligation to allow an aggressor to strike first." Yet this right is indisputable only when "there is an imminent threat of an unprovoked aggression."[35]

Before the 2003 invasion of Iraq, the Bush administration claimed that it urgently needed to act before a mushroom cloud appeared over cities in the United States. It contended that the United States was faced with such "an imminent threat of unprovoked aggression." Iraq would not directly attack the United States, but rather it would transfer weapons of mass destruction to terrorists who would use the weapons in the United States. Despite the lag between the Iraqi government's transfer and the actual (potential) attack, the claim was that time was of the essence. But, this time lag is important in whether an action can be preemptive self-defense, despite Bush administration claims. Additionally, the International Court of Justice ruled in the case of *Nicaragua v. United States of America* that providing weapons and support to terrorists or other nonstate actors does not constitute an "armed attack" as envisioned in Article 51.[36]

What would constitute a legitimate preemptive use of force if the 2003 invasion of Iraq was not? Richard Betts argues that the case of the Israeli attack on Egypt and Syria in 1967 is the "most promising" of real-world cases to fit the category.[37] In the month before the 1967 Six Days' War between Israel and the Arab states, Egypt took a number of actions that became increasingly threatening to Israel. First, the Egyptian government of Gamal Abdel Nasser moved the Egyptian army into the Sinai Peninsula. Second, Egypt ordered United Nations peacekeepers out of Sinai where they had maintained a cease-fire line since the 1956 Arab-Israeli war. Third, Egypt blocked the Straits of Tiran, cutting Israel off from the Red Sea. Finally, Egypt signed a defense pact with Jordan.[38] These four acts committed in a single month constituted an imminent threat of an armed attack, to which Israel responded with a preemptive attack on Egypt.

If the US war on Iraq that began in March 2003 was not a preemptive war for self-defense, what was it? Domestic critics of the Bush administration have called the war an "elective" war much like elective surgery that is chosen not because one's life and health are in jeopardy but because of the benefits that might accrue from such a procedure. The elective use of force would be for some perceived political, military, or economic gain and not to prevent immediate substantial harm to vital national interests.

In international relations scholarship, there is a concept of preventive war which we will distinguish slightly from preventive force (although this may be splitting hairs). Randall Schweller defines preventive war as "those wars that are motivated by the fear that one's military power and potential are declining relative to that of a rising adversary. . . . States wage preventive wars for either offensive or defensive reasons: to take advantage of a closing window of opportunity or to prevent the opening of a window of vulnerability."[39] Betts would add that "the rationale for preventive war is that conflict with the adversary is so deep and unremitting that war is ultimately inevitable, on worse terms than on present, as the enemy grows stronger over time."[40] These explanations of preventive war mesh with reports that Bush administration officials had long sought to "finish" the "unfinished business" of the 1991 Gulf War by removing Saddam Hussein from power.

The Russian annexation of Crimea in 2014 was proceeded by the appearance of Russian gunmen in Crimea who assisted in the toppling of the Crimea government. After Crimea, the Russians encouraged and assisted armed separatists in Eastern Ukraine in a war that simmers into 2017. Russia's relations with Ukraine could be characterized as a conflict that is "so deep and unremitting" that something worse was inevitable. And, Russia's actions can clearly be characterized as actions "motivated by the fear that one's military power and potential are declining." Many analysts argue that the expansion of NATO into Russia's sphere of influence pushed Russia into acting in Crimea and Eastern Ukraine, as well as elsewhere.[41]

Having said all this, the war in Eastern Ukraine is more typical of the contemporary use of preventive force. This "preventive use of force entails the discretionary, anticipatory use of armed force to foil the emergence or development of a prospective threat," according to Jennifer Taw.[42] Preventive force "is inherently contradictory—an offensive action intended to have a defensive effect against a threat that has not yet developed." An example of this is the 1981 Israeli destruction of Iraq's nuclear plant at Osirak. The Osirak plant nuclear reactor was being built by a French public-private initiative. Although France and Iraq said the plant was for civilian purposes, Israel saw the plant as an existential threat. However, the threat was not imminent since there was no nuclear fuel at the plant when it was destroyed. The attack was an elective action about what might occur in the future.

Taw offers a rational choice perspective on when a state might elect to engage in preventive force. States must weigh "the costs of the use of force, retaliation, and criticism," and stronger states can bear the costs more so than other states.[43] She offers what she calls "pragmatic criteria" for evaluating whether a threat is ripe for the use of preventive force. The threat must be "observable prior to maturity" and thus not a surprise attack. The threat must be "predictable in [its] intent or consequences." The threat must come "from identifiable political entities," and these entities must be "targetable."[44] Since there is a wide array of nonmilitary options available to states that might be more cost-effective for deferring or defusing the threat, since military options can always be used after exhausting some mix of nonmilitary options should the threat continue to mature, and since the threat has not yet reached maturity and may still as yet fizzle out, we can logically conclude that preventive force is not a useful first option for most states.

Yet, the lived reality of people in Afghanistan, Pakistan, Iraq, Syria, Yemen, Somalia, Nigeria, and elsewhere can attest that some states feel quite free in their use of preventive force. All of these countries are beset by conflict in which local and/or external actors have used air strikes and attacks by unmanned aerial vehicles (UAVs), also known as drones. Robert Farley explains that drones have been used in combat "since at least World War II, and they've made up an important part of the aerial arsenal ever since. In the last two decades, however, the massive expansion of communications bandwidth has combined with the ongoing miniaturization of electronic components to produce a Golden Age of UAV technology."[45] According to the New America Foundation, seven countries have used drones in combat: the United States, Israel, United Kingdom, Pakistan, Iraq, Nigeria, and Iran, and nineteen countries possess armed drones.[46] Although Farley contends that armed drones are being used only by countries that are already engaged in airstrikes against opponents—and so drones are just another tool in their metaphorical toolbox—armed drones make the calculation about whether to use preventive force less costly and therefore easier.

Pakistan has used armed drones against Pakistani terrorist groups within Pakistan. The United Kingdom used armed drones in 2015 to kill two British citizens in Syria for their terrorist-related activities. The United States used armed drones in 2011 to kill two US citizens in Yemen in 2011. One of these, Anwar al-Awlaki, was killed in a so-called personality strike against a named terrorist leader; the other (his teenage son) was killed in a "signature strike" which is a strike against a suspected but unidentified militant whose "pattern of life" makes it likely that the person is engaged in terrorism.[47]

When the United States used a drone to kill Anwar al-Awlaki in 2011 in Yemen, it was in response to his incitement of terrorist acts in the United States. He was believed to have incited the terrorist shooting of thirteen people at Fort Hood, Texas, in 2009, among other acts. This targeted killing fits what Plaw and Reis call an "emerging" ethic of acceptable preventive force[48] because it was clear that al-Awlaki intended to continue to encourage terrorist attacks and the Yemeni government was "not willing or able to suppress the threat." The other US strikes in Yemen using conventional air strikes as well as UAVs have not all been about the prevention of future terrorist acts. Instead, American military forces were deployed to Yemen to give support to the government against al Qaeda in the Arabian Peninsula (AQAP). Multilateral and bilateral military operations that take the form of "train and assist" missions like those in Yemen will be discussed in the next chapter.

Recap

In this chapter, we examined how the realist drive to acquire power in an anarchic system results in the security dilemma. We also discussed the changing nature of "defense" and how deterrence is substituted for defense. This, however, does pose a challenge for states because deterrence is somewhat unprovable as a working strategy; India's nuclear deterrent did not prevent Pakistan from launching an attack on India in the Kargil War. Nor did France's nuclear deterrent and demonstrated willingness to use air power against terrorist groups abroad stop terrorist groups from attacking France at home. Finally, we examined the differences between preemptive self-defense and the use of preventive war and preventive force, and how technological advances—like armed drones—increase the probability that states will use preventive force more often in the future.

Discussion Questions

1. What are the implications of anarchy for national security?
2. Discuss how realists would agree with the call for "peace through strength."
3. Explain how the security dilemma works to undermine national security.
4. Discuss how the traditional notion of defense has been altered, particularly in an age when invasions are less likely than terrorist attacks.
5. What is stable nuclear deterrence and mutual assured destruction?
6. Can the military relationship between India and Pakistan be described in terms of stable nuclear deterrence?
7. Explain why France's nuclear deterrent is unable to defend against terrorist attacks within France.
8. What is defensive defense? How would a world of states dedicated to defensive defense undermine international efforts to protect people from mass killing?
9. Discuss the differences between the use of preemptive force and the use of preventive force. Which is considered acceptable self-defense?
10. Discuss how drone technology makes it more likely that states will choose to use preventive force, particularly against nonstate actors.

5

Multilateral and Bilateral Responses to External Security Threats

In This Chapter

Introduction
Military Alliances
Why States Join Mutual Defense Arrangements
The Costs of Joining Mutual Defense Arrangements
Train, Advise, Equip, and Assist Missions
Recap
Discussion Questions

Introduction

In the fifth year of the war in Syria, sixty-six countries participated in various ways in a coalition to defeat ISIL, according to a US Congressional Research Service (CRS) report.[1] That is, a broad coalition was engaged in various acts, some of them violent, in Iraq and Syria. The United Nations Security Council had passed a number of resolutions calling on member states to work together to defeat terrorism and extremist ideology. Resolution 2249 (November 20, 2015) called upon

> Member States that have the capacity to do so to take all necessary measures, in compliance with international law, in particular with the United Nations Charter, as well as international human rights, refugee and humanitarian law, on the territory under the control of ISIL also known as Da'esh, in Syria and Iraq, to redouble and coordinate their efforts to prevent and suppress terrorist acts committed specifically by ISIL also known as Da'esh as well as ANF [Al-Nusrah Front], and all other individuals, groups, undertakings, and entities associated with Al Qaeda, and other terrorist groups, as designated by the United Nations Security Council . . . to eradicate the safe haven they have established over significant parts of Iraq and Syria.

This broad, nonbinding authorization covered some of the warring parties in Syria and Iraq, but not all of them. And, the military coalitions present in Syria were often working directly against each other—although they all could claim to be fighting under the authority of 2249. In this chapter, we will discuss responses to security threats that take the form of multilateral or bilateral military agreements.

Military Alliances

Alliances are "formal associations of states for the use (or non-use) of military force, intended for either the security or the aggrandizement of their members, against specific other states, whether or not these others are explicitly recognized."[2] Glenn Snyder explains that alliances are a "formal subset" of alignment. "Alignment amounts to a set of mutual *expectations* between two or more states that they will have each other's support in disputes or wars with particular other states."[3] Stephen Walt says alliances and alignment are essentially the same thing and loosens them up in terms of formality. Walt defines an alliance as a "formal or informal arrangement for security cooperation between two or more sovereign states."[4] Basically, in a military alliance two or more states pledge to come to the assistance of the other when faced with a military threat or attacked. An alliance is a mutual defense pact against an external threat. States may also refer to these as collective defense arrangements.

Whether a military alliance must be formalized is of no consequence to some analysts, but important to others. For instance, Walt contends that "there has never been a formal treaty of alliance between the United States and Israel, but no one would question the level of commitment between these two states."[5] Writing some years later, James Stavridis argues that the United States needed to sign a formal military treaty with Israel in order to assuage Israel's insecurities, particularly after the nuclear agreement with Iran.[6] Stavridis acknowledges that there are dozens of military and nonmilitary agreements with Israel that should reassure it. What Stavridis suggests, though, is that formal alliances can act to reassure allies when they may sometimes have very different views and political goals. What Walt points to is the expectation of mutual assistance that comes with close alignment regardless of whether the relationship is framed by a treaty, and, importantly, how others—particularly potential and real foes—perceive the commitment between the allies. Perceptions of commitments are important in gauging the strength of a mutual defense arrangement.

In the next chapter, we examine the United Nations as a collective security organization. Members of a collective security organization pledge not to use force to settle disputes among them. Peace is the goal of the organization, and any actor who breaks the peace is punished by the collective membership. The threat of collective punishment and the benefits of peace keep most actors in check. The Inter-American Treaty of Reciprocal Assistance (the Rio Treaty) of the Organization of American States is also designed to keep peace within the group. A collective defense arrangement, on the other hand, starts with an acknowledgment that there is an external threat to one or more of the members of the arrangement. The members pledge their mutual defense against the external threat (real or not-yet-materialized), which hopefully deters any attack but defends against it if the threat materializes. Both kinds of arrangements—collective security and collective defense—work because of the perceived strength of the commitment made by the members to the group. If the commitments are perceived to be strong, foes should be deterred. If the commitments are perceived to be weak, then foes may not be deterred. Of course, *whether* a foe will act on that perception of weakness is an entirely different subject.

Why States Join Mutual Defense Arrangements

There are many reasons why states would join a formal military alliance. One reason is to create peaceful ties between old adversaries. The alliance moves the old adversaries into the future together. Another, more immediate reason to form an alliance is to balance against an external threat. States also may join a military alliance in order to be associated with the winning side after a war or for the benefits that accrue to members, such as military hardware, technology, and intelligence. We will discuss each of these reasons to ally with some examples.

First, it is important to note that before the end of World War II, states generally did not choose to formally align with each other in peacetime. Alliances were engaged to balance against a rising threat in anticipation of an imminent war. Some states may have been closer diplomatically to other states because of shared cultures, religions, political systems, or even ruling families, but states tended not to lock themselves into alliances absent a tangible reason.

At the conclusion of World War II, some states began to formalize their military relations with key allies. This period was marked by multilateralism, or what Miles Kalher calls the "international governance of the 'many.'"[7] John Gerard Ruggie explains that "multilateralism is an institutional form that coordinates relations among three or more states on the basis of generalized principles of conduct; that is, principles which specify appropriate conduct for a class of actions, without regard to the particularistic interests of the parties or the strategic exigencies that may exist in any specific occurrence."[8] The United Nations is the most prominent manifestation of multilateralism in this period. Two multilateral mutual defense arrangements from this same period were also designed to create formal mechanisms for maintaining peace between members, particularly members who were once adversaries. The Rio Treaty, created in 1947 and mentioned earlier, is both a collective security and collective defense arrangement. In 1949, the North Atlantic Treaty Organization (NATO) was signed to pledge mutual defense among the countries of Western Europe and North America. NATO was designed, in part, to maintain peace between old adversaries as well as balance the threat posed by the Soviet Union. As the first secretary-general of NATO once said, NATO was designed "to keep the Russians out, the Americans in, and the Germans down."

"Keeping the Russians out" points to another reason for joining a military alliance—to balance against threats. In one of the classic studies on alliances, Walt concludes that the primary reason states join alliances is to balance against threats, and, even among allies, a common ideology is "less powerful than balancing as a motive for alignment."[9] NATO was not just designed to keep the United States tied to the peace of Europe, but it was also about balancing against the threat of the Soviet Union. The world had entered the Cold War period in which the major powers would not fight each other directly for fear of total—and in time nuclear—war. Yet, the sides were arming themselves as if to go to war at any time. NATO was a way to deter the Soviet Union from attacking Western Europe, and a way to defend Western Europe should the Soviets not be deterred. Initially, NATO had twelve members—Belgium, Canada, Denmark, France, Iceland, Italy, Luxembourg, Netherlands, Norway, Portugal, United Kingdom, and the United States. In 1952, Greece and Turkey—two old foes—joined, followed by the Federal Republic of Germany (West Germany) in 1955, and Spain in 1982. Other countries would join later.

The threat posed by the Soviet Union provoked a multilateral response binding Western Europe and North America. However, that same threat—and the one presented by Communist China during the Cold War—did not inspire a "NATO in Asia." Christopher Hemmer and Peter Katzenstein argue that "multilateralism is a particularly demanding form of international cooperation. It requires a strong sense of collective identity in addition to shared interests."[10] They add,

Shaped by racial, historical, political, and cultural factors, U.S. policymakers saw their potential European allies as relatively equal members of a shared community. America's potential Asian Allies, in contrast, were seen as a part of an alien and, in important ways, inferior community.[11]

This notion of "shared community" might speak to another reason why states choose to join multilateral defense arrangements—or perhaps why the United States would initiate such arrangements in some places but not others. The United States formed a multilateral defense treaty with Australia and New Zealand, and the multilateral Southeast Asia Treaty, but the latter was with Australia, New Zealand, France, the United Kingdom, the Philippines, and Thailand. Only two Asian countries were members, and one, the Philippines, was a former US colony. The administration of Barack Obama made efforts to refocus US military attention to Asia, but the demands of counterterrorism campaigns in the Middle East, South Asia, and Africa made this pivot difficult. Additionally, the Obama administration's main priorities in this pivot were first about trade and the creation of the Trans-Pacific Trade Pact (and so not security related) and then focused on re-energizing *bilateral* treaty commitments. The United States has existing bilateral defense treaties with the Philippines, Japan, and South Korea.

These multilateral treaties—NATO, ANZUS, SEATO—and the three bilateral treaties—with the Philippines, Japan, and South Korea—are the combined *treaty-based* collective defense arrangements of the United States. Yet the United States has extensive military commitments. In a study of all US defense pacts from 1948 through 2010, Michael Beckley presents the astounding finding that "the United States is legally obligated to defend a patchwork of nations that spans five continents, contains 25 percent of the world's population, and accounts for nearly 75 percent of global economic output."[12] We will return to Beckley's study when we discuss the disadvantages of mutual defense arrangements.

Of course, nothing in the world is done in a vacuum, as the realist security dilemma illustrates. The launch of NATO created a threat against which the Soviet Union needed to act, especially after a rearmed West Germany joined NATO in 1955. The Soviets responded with their own mutual defense arrangement, the Warsaw Treaty

Organization or Warsaw Pact. NATO and the Warsaw Pact countries became entangled in a security dilemma that ultimately resulted in putting the world on the edge of nuclear mutual assured destruction. The Warsaw Pact consisted of the Soviet Union, East Germany, Bulgaria, Hungary, Poland, Czechoslovakia, and Romania. Like NATO, the Warsaw Pact was also designed to keep harmony between its members, but "harmony" was defined by the Soviet Union and enforced by Soviet military incursions in Hungary and Czechoslovakia. Indeed, the Warsaw Treaty was the culmination of a series of Soviet-imposed, asymmetrical bilateral agreements between the Soviet Union and the countries of Eastern and Central Europe designed to promote Soviet interests and security first and foremost.[13]

The Warsaw Pact did not survive the end of the Cold War and the dissolution of the Soviet Union. NATO not only survived but expanded. The NATO website says that NATO has an "open door policy" for admitting new members, and that its "enlargement process poses no threat to any country" but is instead "aimed at promoting stability and cooperation, at building a Europe whole and free, united in peace, democracy and common values."[14] In 1999, NATO admitted the Czech Republic, Hungary, and Poland to its ranks. In 2004, Bulgaria, Estonia, Latvia, Lithuania, Romania, Slovakia, and Slovenia were admitted. Then, in 2009, Albania and Croatia were admitted. Additionally, NATO has a Partnership for Peace program for military-to-military cooperation with other former republics of the Soviet Union and Yugoslavia and five non-NATO European Union members.

Why would states join NATO after the Soviet threat? Some realists might call this bandwagoning behavior aimed not at self-preservation from a threat but for "self-extension" and "for profit."[15] Randall Schweller says that bandwagoning behavior can take many forms: (1) "jackal" bandwagoning for profit or the spoils of war; (2) "piling on" near the end of a war when the outcome is clear and the goal is to avoid being punished for not taking sides during the war; (3) "wave of the future" bandwagoning to take part in the next order; and (4) "contagion" bandwagoning.[16] Near the end of World War II, the United States and the United Kingdom encouraged a form of piling on and wave of the future bandwagoning. States wishing to be original members of the soon-to-be-formed United Nations needed to sign onto the 1942 "United Nations Declaration." This was a treaty that obligated states to engage in maximum war effort and to not form a separate peace with Germany and Japan. That is, to be founding members of the United Nations, states would need to pile on the winning allied side of World War II. Piling on would ensure states a place at the table to determine the wave of the future, to use Schweller's terminology.

It may be the case that some states who joined NATO or the Partnership for Peace program after the Cold War were piling on the winning side with the aim of benefiting from the new world order. However, for many states from the former Soviet Union or Eastern or Central Europe, joining NATO also was an act of balancing a threat: Russia. Following the collapse of the Soviet Union, Russia quickly created a regional post-Soviet organization called the Commonwealth of Independent States (CIS) in late 1991. Some former Soviet republics refused to join, notably Azerbaijan and Georgia. The Russian response was to force these states into the CIS. As Neil MacFarlane explains:

> Elements of the Russian military assiduously manipulated the civil conflicts in the [Transcaucus] region (notably the Nagorno-Karabakh conflict between Azerbaijan and Armenia and the conflicts between Ossets and Abkhaz on the one hand and Georgians on the other in the Republic of Georgia) in order to return the governments of the region to a position of subservience.[17]

When Georgia declared its independence from the Soviet Union in 1991, separatist movements developed within Georgia's borders in South Ossetia and Abkhazia. Georgia refused to join the CIS at which point the separatists received aid and arms from Russia. Fighting between Georgian forces and the separatists resulted in a cease-fire in 1992 and the deployment of Russian, Osset, and Georgian "peacekeepers" in South Ossetia. Georgia then joined the Russian-led CIS after all. (Both Georgia and Russia joined the NATO Partnership for Peace program in 1994.) The situation in the separatist regions was not resolved but rather continued to simmer until Putin became president of Russia in 2000, and the "Rose Revolution" of 2003 brought to the

Georgian presidency Western-leaning Eduard Shevardnadze. Russian policy then turned to undermining Georgia. According to Michael Emerson, Russia

> not only protected the secessionist entities, Abkhazia and South Ossetia, but [Russia has] been consistently devious in evading any serious peace and reconciliation negotiations, either under UN or OSCE auspices. It has engaged in policies of creeping annexation, notably through issuing Russian passports to these populations, and installing Russian officials in key security positions. It has tolerated or encouraged provocative actions by the separatists, as typified by the artillery shelling of Georgian villages of South Ossetia in the days and months leading up to the invasion.[18]

Further, Emerson notes, "Russia tried but failed to crush Georgia politically with economic sanctions in 2006."

When Georgian forces retaliated against Ossetian attacks in August 2008, Russian forces invaded with land, sea, and air, as well as cyber forces, creating "Europe's first war of the 21st century."[19] The war lasted a few weeks and concluded with a cease-fire arranged by the French president. Russia withdrew its forces from other parts of Georgia, but remained in South Ossetia and Abkhazia. That same month, Russia recognized these republics as independent states, a move widely condemned internationally. Georgia considers South Ossetia and Abkhazia to be Russian-occupied territories. In 2015, Russia maintained 7,000 troops in South Ossetia and Abkhazia.[20] Georgia quit the CIS in 2008 and began what it hoped would be steps toward accession to full NATO membership.

In 2008, Ukraine also began what it hoped would be accession to NATO membership. Writing in 2008, Emerson quipped that Russia engaged in actions aimed at destabilizing Ukraine as if to send this clear message: "If you persist in your NATO aspirations, Russia will create difficulties to the point of destruction of your statehood."[21] Then, in March 2014, on the heels of a popular uprising that unseated the Russian-leaning Ukrainian president, Russia annexed Crimea and the next month started a war helping pro-Russian separatists in Eastern Ukraine. These actions got Russia kicked out of the G-8

(Group of 8 industrialized countries) and targeted with significant economic sanctions, but the frozen war continued. Some 20,000 Russian troops were stationed in Crimea as of 2015. At the 2016 NATO summit, the US ambassador to NATO suggested that NATO expansion was on hold for the next few years, particularly because members would not be able to reach consensus on the memberships of Georgia or Ukraine.[22] For both countries, membership in NATO could not be characterized as bandwagoning behavior given the real security threats they faced from an aggressive Russia. Unfortunately for them, the NATO countries were not prepared to take on formal allies who were so threatened.

Finally, to conclude this discussion of why states join military alliances, it is the case that countries gain in tangible ways from alliances. Beyond the pledge of mutual defense, states gain access to military hardware, training, and intelligence. Consider Australia: At the end of the Cold War, Australian leaders toyed with the idea of making a more prominent foreign policy shift toward China or Indonesia in anticipation of the rising profile of these states. This talk ended with the Australian-led enforcement action in East Timor in 1999 and the government's pledge to be the deputy to the United States in Asia. The military alliance with the United States gives Australia "privileged access to U.S. military hardware and training," training that gives Australia access to "the most technologically sophisticated and proficient" forces in the world.[23] More, being a close ally to the United States allows Australia to purchase sophisticated military technology from American companies that are strictly limited by the US government in terms of to whom they sell. And, along with these benefits comes access to US intelligence networks and technology.

The Costs of Joining Mutual Defense Arrangements

As with anything, if there are benefits, there are probably costs. When countries join military alliances, they face actual financial costs or dues. Countries also face less tangible but more serious costs in terms of greater exposure to threat, the possibility of entrapment, and the fear of abandonment. Additionally, alliances may be asymmetrical, serving the interests of the most powerful member before the others.

Alliances present variations on the security dilemma. States join alliances to deal, in part, with their insecurities, but they may become the targets of threats because of the exposure caused by declaring their alliance with particular states. Australia has been singled out for special attacks by jihadist terrorist groups because of Australia's partnership with the United States. Australian citizens were the target of deadly bombings in Bali, Indonesia, in 2002. The bombings left 202 people dead, 84 of whom were Australian. Osama bin Laden later claimed that these bombings (conducted by Jemaah Islamiyah) were payback for Australia's support of the United States in the war on terror and for Australia's intervention in East Timor in 1999. The threat to Australia continued into 2016, when ISIL called on its supporters to commit lone-wolf attacks against Australian landmarks.

The classic fear of realists is that a peacetime alliance can lead to entrapment by a risk-taking ally. Entrapment involves one ally dragging another into an unnecessary and undesired war of choice that does not serve the interests of both allies. For realists, the fear of entrapment must be weighed against the fear of abandonment. Abandonment is self-defining: being left to face an adversary alone. To manage the fear of abandonment, a state may try to make itself indispensable to its ally, but in doing this, the state may be increasing its own risk of being entrapped by the risky foreign policy of the ally. After the Cold War ended, the fear of abandonment held by the Western European allies of the United States diminished because the Soviet threat had receded.

In the absence of a strong adversary, the cement of the alliance dissolves, and strong policy differences that erode faith in the commitment of allies may emerge. After the end of the Cold War, the disintegration of the Soviet Union, the end of the Warsaw Pact, and the admittance of many former Warsaw Pact members to NATO, real and persistent questions were raised about the purpose and durability of NATO. The organization began to reinvent itself as a peacekeeping and/or peace enforcement arrangement and a way to expand the European zone of peace. The 9/11 terrorist attacks on the United States seemed to give NATO a new purpose. On September 12, 2001, the NATO governing council invoked the Article 5 mutual defense clause for the first time in NATO's history. Despite this, the early US war in Afghanistan was marked by American efforts to avoid a kind of entrapment by its allies. The Bush administration preferred to fight the new war on terror with "floating coalitions" when needed, but mostly preferred the freedom of unilateralism. The NATO allies were sidelined to remote locations in the early years of the military operations in Afghanistan. In doing this, the United States avoided the need for joint decision making that might have limited its range of actions. This had an unintended consequence when the Bush administration sought to take its allies into war against Saddam Hussein in Iraq. By 2002, allies France and Germany were refusing to be entrapped in Bush's war of choice and actively opposed the coming war.

In a recent study, Beckley tests two competing perspectives on alliances: "entanglement theory"—which is loosely entrapment—and "freedom of action theory" which "maintains that great powers can avoid entanglement by inserting loopholes into alliance agreements, sidestepping costly commitments, maintaining a diversified alliance portfolio that generates offsetting demands from different allies, and using explicit alliance commitments to deter adversaries and dissuade allies from initiating or escalating conflicts."[24] Beckley asks whether the vast web of US military alliances "entangles the United States in wars that it would otherwise avoid."[25]

To test the two theories, Beckley examined every militarized international dispute involving the United States from 1948 to 2010. His conclusion is that despite the many military alliances in which the United States is entangled, the "freedom of action theory" is most supported by the data. In the few times that the United States got entangled in a militarized international dispute, "U.S. actions were driven by an alignment of interests between the United States and its allies, not by alliance obligations. In fact, in many cases, U.S. policymakers were the main advocates of military action and cajoled reluctant allies to join the fight."[26] Beckley concludes that "the U.S. experience . . . suggests that great powers can dictate the terms of their security commitments."[27]

This finding, of course, means that lesser powers should have more entrapment or abandonment fears than greater powers. Maybe recognition of this—and the history of the Warsaw Treaty—made former Soviet republics and allies less willing to enter into security arrangements with Russia. Recall that Russia started the Commonwealth of Independent States (CIS) in 1992. Russia added a Treaty of Collective Security to the CIS, but not all of the CIS members signed onto that treaty. Russia renamed the treaty the Collective Security Treaty Organization (CSTO) in 2002, but the rebranding did not make more states join it. As of 2016, the CSTO was composed of Russia, Armenia, Kazakhstan, Kyrgyzstan, Tajikistan, and Belarus. Uzbekistan was a member of the original treaty from 1992 through 1999, but it sat out from 1999 to 2006. Then, in 2012, Uzbekistan withdrew again from the CSTO to form a closer military relationship with the United States.[28] An assessment by GlobalSecurity.org is that "Moscow's nominal allies in the Collective Security Treaty Organization (CSTO) are either too weak (Kyrgyzstan), too self-centered (Armenia), or not loyal enough (Tajiskistan)."[29]

Given the weak commitments within the CSTO, Russia seemed to acknowledge that it could not rely on its military alliances. GlobalSecurity.org concludes, "The Russian Armed Forces aim for full strategic and operational self-sufficiency, even as they exercise with [the] CSTO and Shanghai Cooperation Organization."[30] This puts Russia in a bind because of NATO's plans to open new outpost command centers in Bulgaria, Estonia, Latvia, Lithuania, Poland, and Romania in 2016.

Train, Advise, Equip, and Assist Missions

The Congressional Research Service (CRS) report referenced at the start of this chapter about the global campaign against ISIL explains that "in Brussels in December 2014, 60 of these partners agreed to organize themselves along five 'lines of effort.'" These were:

- "supporting military operations, capacity building, and training (led by the United States and Iraq);
- "stopping the flow of foreign terrorist fighters (led by The Netherlands and Turkey);
- "cutting off IS access to financing and funding (led by Italy, the Kingdom of Saudi Arabia and the United States);

- "addressing associated humanitarian relief and crises (led by Germany and the United Arab Emirates); and
- "exposing IS' true nature (led by the United Arab Emirates, the United Kingdom, and the United States).[31]

This list demonstrates the many ways that states can assist other states, whether in war, or fighting terrorists or criminal organizations, or just in peacetime for capacity building.

The coalition, named Operation Inherent Resolve, also involved an explicit military component being carried out by twenty-seven states. There were "three primary military components: coordinated air strikes, training and equipping local security forces, and targeted special operations, some based out of Northern Iraq while others . . . [were] in Syria."[32] Because Operation Inherent Resolve is ongoing as of this writing and because of the fact that parties to this conflict have different goals, are often at cross-purposes, and have different levels of risk tolerance,[33] this operation is only being used here to illustrate the types of train, assist, equip, and advise activities states undertake with partner states.

Many countries in the anti-ISIL coalition were NATO countries, but NATO as an organization was not involved. Most of the coalition partner countries engaged in training and capacity building with Iraqi forces. Participants included Australia, Belgium, Canada, Denmark, Estonia, Finland, France, Germany, Hungary, Italy, Latvia, the Netherlands, New Zealand, Norway, Poland, Portugal, Spain, Sweden, United Arab Emirates, United Kingdom, and the United States. The largest training forces came from the United States, Italy, and France. Train and assist missions were also undertaken by these countries in order to increase the Iraqi forces' ability to retake areas from ISIL. More direct combat activities such as air strikes and air-combat support operations were undertaken by many of these same states along with some Arab states.

The coalition's train and advise mission puts extra emphasis on supporting Kurdish Peshmerga (troops) in Northern Iraq. American special forces were embedded with the Kurdish Peshmerga; the US military had been partners with the Kurds since Operation Provide Comfort in April 1991. The Obama administration had pledged that there would be no American "boots on the ground" fighting in Iraq, but the *Guardian* (London) quoted a Peshmerga volunteer contradicting this pledge: "The joke going around here is there are no boots on the ground because they're all wearing sneakers."[34] The US mission also involved equipping the Peshmerga, a partner that the United States seemed to prefer over others in the area. The United States also wanted local Arab fighters to merge with the Peshmerga. As one Syrian Arab fighter told the *New York Times*, "The U.S. doesn't trust anyone except the Kurds."[35] In August 2016, the Obama administration announced it was sending 4,000 more troops and additional hardware and money to Iraq to fight ISIL, including more than $400 million targeted specifically for the Kurdish Regional Government. Similarly, US special operations forces assisted Syrian Kurds, and a group the United States liked to call the Syrian Democratic Forces fighting against ISIL in Syria.

The United States special operations forces were on other train, advise, and assist missions outside of the Iraq-Syria theater. As of mid-2016, the United States had approximately 9,000 special operations and other forces involved in the NATO-led Operation Resolute Support in Afghanistan and in separate unilateral US counterterrorism actions there. The goal was to build the Afghans' capacity to defend Afghanistan through training on the use of heavy weaponry and aircraft, among other tasks. But these missions clearly went beyond training since the US military still was sustaining regular casualties in Afghanistan.

Beyond Iraq, Syria, and Afghanistan, US special operations were involved in Mali in support of French military operations; Niger to build the capacity of Niger, Nigeria, and Chad in the fight against Boko Haram; Mauritania to counter al Qaeda in the Islamic Maghreb; Uganda to counter the Lord's Resistance Army; and in Somalia and Kenya to help fight against al Shabaab.[36] The US special forces in Somalia and Kenya engaged in raids and air strikes in support of the hybrid African Union/United Nations peace operations there (discussed in detail in chapter 7). These kinetic operations were undertaken with local governments in order to build their capacity and focus their training on countering terrorism and criminal organizations. Kinetic operations in Africa fell primarily under the US Africa

Command (AFRICOM). AFRICOM is the newest of six American global geographic combat commands.

The European Union also had kinetic operations under way to build local capacity in border security and the interdiction of human traffickers and people smugglers in Libya, the Mediterranean, Ukraine, and Moldova. The EU also conducted successful antipiracy operations off the coast of Somalia. Meanwhile, the EU assisted in security sector reform and human rights training in Bosnia-Herzegovina, Kosovo, Ukraine, Moldova, the Palestinian territories (along with border security training), and Afghanistan. Military monitors and trainers were also assigned to assist in United Nations operations in Mali and the Central African Republic.

Beyond kinetic missions, the United States was "the largest bilateral donor for peace operations in Africa. The United States has deployed few of its uniformed personnel as peacekeepers in Africa, instead focusing on supporting other actors through various train-and-equip and assistance programs."[37] These programs were conducted by both the departments of defense and state. Paul Williams reports that the US train and assist programs were conducted bilaterally with twenty-five African countries out of fifty-four total on the continent. Two programs—the Global Peace Operations Training (GPOI) and the Africa Contingency Operations Training and Assistance (ACOTA)—cycle troops from thirty African countries through ten-week pre-peacekeeping deployment classes.[38] The United States also began an African Peacekeeping Rapid Response Partnership and Security Governance Initiative to enable individual African countries and the African Union field peace support operations. Williams reports that in the Security Council, both the Bush and Obama administrations prioritized United Nations peace operations in Africa, giving "strong political support to UN operations, which is particularly important when host countries threaten those missions."[39] United Nations peace operations will be discussed in chapter 7.

Finally, the United States dramatically increased its military and policy aid to Africa, according to the Center for International Policy. Department of Defense security assistance increased 775 percent from 2014 to 2016, surpassing aid to Africa from the Department of State.[40] And the motivation for this largess—and the special operations and train and assist missions—is clear, as almost all of the Defense aid was for counterterrorism. This is demonstrated in AFRICOM's five-year plan begun in 2016 that prioritizes in order: (1) neutralizing al Shabaab in Somalia, (2) eliminating the ISIL threat in Libya and shoring up that fragile state, (3) containing Boko Haram in West Africa, (4) "disrupting illicit activity in the Gulf of Guinea and in Central Africa," and finally (5) building "African partners' peacekeeping and disaster assistance capabilities."[41]

Recap

In this chapter, we explored military alliances or mutual defense arrangements asking why states join such organizations and the drawbacks to such membership. Beyond formal military treaties, states also participate in a range of bilateral military activities that are designed to build the capacity of partners against terrorism, criminal organizations, and other threats. In the next chapter, we examine global multilateral efforts to achieve national security and international security as manifested in the United Nations. The UN system is a collective security system which differs from the collective defense arrangements discussed in this chapter.

Discussion Questions

1. Discuss how a military alliance creates expectations for allies and foes alike.
2. Describe the differences between a collective security arrangement and a collective defense arrangement.
3. Discuss the effect of military alliances on old foes.
4. What are the benefits that accrue to states when they join military alliances?
5. What is NATO, and what was its historical purpose?
6. Describe how NATO has enlarged to include some former Soviet republics and former Warsaw Treaty states.
7. What role did NATO enlargement play in the Russian military intervention in Ukraine?

8. Discuss the nature of the relationship between Russia and its partners in the CIS and the CSTO.
9. Describe how military allies try to balance the fear of entrapment against the fear of abandonment.
10. Discuss the many ways that states provide bilateral military assistance to other states, whether by treaty or by simple agreement.
11. Where are the places in which the US military is engaged in train, advise, equip, and assist missions?
12. Discuss the reasons that the United States and the European Union provide military assistance to states in Africa.

6

International Security
Multilateral Efforts to Achieve Security

In This Chapter

Introduction
Collective Security and the United Nations
The UN Charter on International Peace and Security
Multilateral Sanctions Short of Force—Chapter VII, Article 41
Collective Security and All Means Necessary—Chapter VII, Article 42
Recap
Discussion Questions

Introduction

More than a decade ago, in December 2004, the United Nations Secretary-General's High-level Panel on Threats, Challenges and Change issued a report titled *A More Secure World: Our Shared Responsibility*. In one passage, the panel gave this explanation for why states should work together to maintain a system that ensures international security:

> No State, no matter how powerful, can by its own efforts alone make itself invulnerable to today's threats. Every State requires the cooperation of other States to make itself secure. It is in every State's interest, accordingly, to cooperate with other States to address their most pressing threats, because doing so will maximize the chances of reciprocal cooperation to address its own threat priorities.[1]

The panel may have been thinking about the 9/11 attacks on the United States. Even the United States was not secure against a plot hatched in faraway Afghanistan. And, even when states try to act responsibly toward others, policies—no matter how good—have an impact on other states' security. As we discussed in chapter 1, German efforts to speed up the settlement of Syrian refugees created chaos for other European states. In this chapter, we will discuss how states seek to secure themselves by creating an international security system that is built on an acknowledgment of deep interdependence. International security refers to a system of arrangements and activities constructed by states to protect states.

Collective Security and the United Nations

The twentieth century was noteworthy for many things, good and bad, arguably the greatest of which (in terms of overall impact) was and remains globalization. The century began and ended in periods of globalization with the interim years witnessing global wars and global institution building designed to protect and ensure globalization's impact. Globalization—"the process of increasing integration of the world in terms of economics, politics, communications, social relations, and culture"[2]—created the necessity for a new way to manage the international order.

After World War I, and again after World War II, global leaders agreed that what the world needed was a new international system that worked better at managing international power relations, in order to preserve and facilitate global economic relations. This new system would be based on the theory of collective security. "Collective security" refers to a universal system in which members consider international peace to be primary and indivisible. An act of aggression anywhere in the world is considered an action against the whole or against the peace. Aggressors would be confronted with an overwhelming preponderance of power in the form of collective punishment. This collective punishment would be implemented automatically and by obligation. The threat of this collective punishment would deter would-be aggressors and protect the peace. Both collective security and balance-of-power theories were based on what Inis Claude called the "paradox of 'war for peace,'" in which "the fulfillment of the urge for peace is to be achieved by the possession of capacity to fight and the assertion of the will to fight."[3] Importantly, the preponderance of power in a collective security system would be available "to everyone for defensive purposes, but to nobody for aggressive purposes."[4] Thus, non–great powers would be "emancipated" from great power rivalries, and no state would be permitted to become "so preponderantly powerful that it can trespass with impunity upon the basic interests of other states."[5]

Advocates of collective security did not propose to ignore or downgrade state power in international relations. In Claude's words,

> Balance of power and collective security have the merit of maintaining a steady focus on the *state* as the object of central concern. They reflect awareness of the fact that the problem of international order can be accurately defined only in terms of the necessity of developing methods for controlling the exercise of power by these constituent entities of the world system. They are addressed, in short, to the reality of the multistate system.[6]

After World War I, the League of Nations was formed to manage international power relations in a globalized world. The League was not universal in its membership, and it was not committed to honoring the sovereign rights of all nations—colonized peoples were denied their right to self-government and were not represented in the League. Further, the League did not bind in all the great powers; the United States remained removed and distant. Finally, the League did not ensure the sovereign rights and integrity of even its members, and soon its failure was apparent with the start of World War II. After World War II, another effort was made by the great powers to construct an institutionalized international security system called the United Nations (UN).

The origins of the United Nations are found in several procla-mations issued during World War II. These proclamations, taken together, declared a desire for peace, the right of states to exist free from the threat of aggression, the need to respect the sovereign rights of all states, and the need to create a *system* that would discourage states' use of armed force. These proclamations also signaled that as early as 1941 certain great powers were already planning the postwar order.

The UN system would have six principal organs, each of which had a role to play in preserving the new international security system. These organs were the Security Council, the General Assembly, the Secretariat, the Economic and Social Council, the Trusteeship Council, and the International Court of Justice. The International Court of Jus-tice would help establish a body of international law that would bring regularity and predictability to interstate legal affairs. The Trusteeship Council (now essentially defunct) would oversee the end of colonial rule and the potentially violent transition from dependent territory or colony to sovereign state. The Economic and Social Council would pro-vide a variety of programs and agencies tasked with eliminating the socio-welfare causes of violent conflict and war. The Secretariat would provide an international civil service dedicated to the execution of the UN's agenda, blind to national preferences. The General Assembly would provide a democratic one-country, one-vote forum in which the many issues confronting the world's peoples would be openly discussed and in which the member states would exercise democratic oversight over the other organs. Finally, the Security Council would be the primary organ of the United Nations, tasked with maintaining and restoring international peace and security. The Council's design demonstrated both the UN founders' affection for collective security and their conservative embrace of great power politics.

As might be expected after a war, the most powerful members of the winning side of World War II gave themselves a privileged posi-tion in the new UN system and ensured by the UN Charter that their status would not be challenged by rising great powers. Although the UN Charter obliges states to abstain from the use of military force except in the common good, and Chapter VII obliges states to assist in the preservation of international peace and security, the Charter effectively does not restrict the great powers from using armed force themselves. Article 23 of the Charter establishes that the Security Council is composed of fifteen members: ten nonpermanent members holding two-year nonconsecutive terms and the permanent members, or P5—the United States, Great Britain, France, the Soviet Union/Russia, and China. The permanent members were given the responsibility to maintain the new order militarily, as well as the privilege of the veto to control the order's shape. The veto power is the ability of any one of the permanent members to stop an action of substance on war and peace even if that action is supported by the majority of the other members of the Security Council. The veto power makes it unimaginable that the Council would approve any resolution condemning the use of force by any of the P5. In the history of adopted Council resolutions, it is rare to find even a suggestion that any of the five ever used force against another state. For example, the US war in Vietnam was not the subject of a single Security Council resolution. The Security Council also never formally discussed the Soviet war in Afghanistan.

In late 2002 and early 2003, as the United States and ally Great Britain began to make a case for forced regime change in Iraq, the Americans and British tried to obtain Security Council support for their proposed action. Although the issue was debated in the Council, no formal vote on the war was ever taken because of the certainty that Russia, France, and/or China would veto the resolution and because of the uncertainty of even a "moral" majority in favor of the proposed military action. More to the present point, the Security Council did not vote to *condemn* the intervention as an act of aggression and/or the unlawful use of force since such a vote would be subject to a US and/or British veto. Given the nature of the great power arrangement codified into the Charter, no one reasonably could expect the Security Council to try to stop the United States and Great Britain. In 2016, four of the P5 (the United States, United Kingdom, France, and Russia) were engaged in military actions supporting different sides of the Syrian war, and China was involved in military actions to secure its interests in the South China Seas, yet these uses of force have not once been condemned by a Security Council resolution.

Writing forty years before the 2003 invasion of Iraq, Claude noted how the United Nations failed to restrain the great powers *and* how it was never designed to restrain them. The real value in the United Nations was its ability to cause the great powers to be self-limiting:

> The best hope for the United Nations is not that it may be able to develop a military establishment which will enable it to exercise coercive control over great powers, but that it may be able to continue the development of its capability to serve the interests of the great powers—and of the rest of the world—by helping them to contain their conflicts, to limit their competition, and to stabilize their relationships.[7]

How much the great powers have exercised self-control is arguable. However, it is the case that none of the P5 have walked entirely away from the United Nations even when they objected to particular actions or inactions.

The P5 veto power extends to the General Assembly as well. By Article 108, Charter amendments must be adopted by a two-thirds vote of the General Assembly with the concurrence of the permanent members of the Security Council. As of 2016, the United Nations had 193 members. A resolution to amend the Charter would *fail* if 192 members voted *for* the resolution and *one* of the P5 voted against it. One of the most contentious of possible UN Charter amendments has involved the recomposition of the Security Council permanent membership. Many UN member states have called for the democratization of the Security Council and/or the end of the P5 veto. In 2005, upon the sixtieth anniversary of the founding of the United Nations, a many-fronted initiative was engaged to increase the permanent membership of the Council. This movement was supported by many and sabotaged by many; it was sabotaged by countries large and small reacting to the possibility that someone else might gain permanent membership. For example, although Japan had for many years made the second-highest financial contributions to the United Nations, its possible inclusion in the permanent membership was opposed vehemently by veto-wielding China *and* by the China-conscious United States.

The veto casts into stone the power distribution of 1945 (or even earlier). Both this institutionalizing of great power status and the fact that the veto would give the P5 the ability to act in ways inconsistent with the Charter were seen as the costs of forming the United Nations.

The UN Charter on International Peace and Security

The UN Charter contains two chapters devoted to dispute settlement: Chapter VI covers the Pacific Settlement of Disputes, and Chapter VII details what actions the Security Council may take in response to threats to international peace and security up to and including the use of armed force. Chapter VI, Article 33, starts with what seems to be an imperative that

> parties to any dispute, the continuance of which is likely to endanger the maintenance of international peace and security, shall, first of all, seek a solution by negotiation, enquiry, mediation, conciliation, arbitration, judicial settlement, resort to regional agencies or arrangements, or other peaceful means of their own choice.

Despite the use of the imperative "shall" there is no penalty for failure to seek peaceful resolution. Although the secretary-general is not mentioned in Chapter VI, it is usually the secretariat that is tasked by the Security Council with Chapter VI duties. Peacekeeping that does not involve Chapter VII authority to use "all means necessary" generally is said to fall conceptually between Chapters VI and VII, as will be elaborated on in chapter 7.

Chapter VII contains the muscle of the UN system and offers limits on national and collective self-defense. The first provision of Chapter VII, Article 39, states that it is the Security Council that determines whether "any threat to the peace, breach of the peace, or act of aggression" has occurred. Should such an act be identified, Article 41 allows the Security Council to restore the international status quo through authorizing measures short of the use of force, such as economic sanctions or the disruption of communications and diplomatic relations. In a later section of this chapter, we will discuss sanctions placed under the authority of Article 41. Article 42 states that "should the Security Council consider that measures provided for in Article 41 would be inadequate or have proved to be inadequate, it may take such action by air, sea, or land forces as may be necessary to maintain or restore international peace and security." Examples of Article 42 actions will also be discussed in this chapter.

Article 43 instructs states to undertake to assist the Security Council's measures by providing assistance including maintaining ready armed forces. Air forces also should be kept on the ready, as per Article 45. By Articles 45, 46, and 47, a Military Staff Committee composed of the chiefs of staff of the militaries of the permanent members should coordinate with and otherwise assist the Security Council in enforcing mandates. Article 50 allows third-party states to consult the Security Council when Chapter VII authorizations create special economic problems for them.

Finally, Article 51 specifies both when states may take actions in self-defense and when states should turn over their defense to the Security Council. This article was discussed in some detail in chapter 4, but with reference to the beginning section on self-defense. The entire Article 51 reads,

> Nothing in the present Charter shall impair the inherent right of individual or collective self-defense if an armed attack occurs against a Member of the United Nations, until the Security Council has taken measures necessary to maintain international peace and security. Measures taken by Members in the exercise of this right of self-defense shall be immediately reported to the Security Council and shall not in any way affect the authority and responsibility of the Security Council under the present Charter to take at any time such action as it deems necessary in order to maintain or restore international peace and security.

In this chapter, we will focus on the second part of the article. Note that a state has the "inherent right" of self-defense but only "until the Security Council has taken measures necessary to maintain international peace and security." If a state could depend on the Security Council to authorize assistance, it would not have to face aggression or the threat of aggression alone. A state would be relieved of the burden of defending itself by itself. This, in turn, would mean that states would be relieved of the burden of heavy defense spending. Jonathan Soffer writes that most of the early members of the United Nations looked forward to cutting their defense budgets once the United Nations became fully functional.[8]

By the second sentence in Article 51, a state acting in self-defense must immediately report the measures it takes and, by standard interpretation of this phrase but not by its explicit language, limit its measures to those considered proportional. Also in the second sentence, any measures taken in self-defense do not affect the authority of the Council to take "such action as it deems necessary." Beyond the previously mentioned issue concerning *whether* the Council would act, this raises the hypothetical situation of a state taking actions in immediate self-defense that are deemed to be disproportionate to the original attack and thus those very acts might be interpreted as threats to international peace and security. The Council might then order measures against the state that was originally attacked.

To make Chapter VII work—which is to say, to preserve international peace and security—the preponderant military power of the community would need to be harnessed and commanded by the United Nations. By Articles 43 and 45, members are instructed to conclude agreements with the Security Council regarding armed and air forces ready and on call for Chapter VII operations. Early negotiations over the UN system suggested that member states understood Articles 43 and 45 to require the creation of standing UN forces. According to Soffer, the United States was at the lead in this interpretation, pushing hard for a large UN force: "The Americans wanted a huge force of twenty land divisions, thirty-eight hundred aircraft, three battleships, fifteen cruisers, six carriers, and eighty-four destroyers, and they were prepared to make the bulk of the naval and air contributions."[9] The permanent members were in disagreement over what size forces were necessary; none of the others embraced the US vision for such a large force. There was also disagreement over what kind of contributions would be made by the P5—would they contribute equally to the UN forces, or would they make comparable contributions? Equal contributions would result in a much smaller force than the United States proposed; comparable contributions would draw on each country's relative strengths but also would have the practical effect of making some states contribute ground forces while others would just contribute air forces.[10]

Without accord among the permanent members, the issue of whether there should be a standing UN force was resolved by default—there is none, there has been none, there likely will never be one. Instead, drawing on Articles 43 and 45, the Security Council instructs the secretary-general to negotiate separate agreements with members about what forces they could make available to the United Nations when asked to do so. Countries still maintain the right to say no to particular requests, reading no obligation into these standby agreements. The resulting problems with this arrangement have been demonstrated in numerous UN peacekeeping operations—operations that ought to require (in theory) far less of a military force than would a collective security action.

A related problem involves the training and preparedness of troops available on a standby basis. Force commanders could safely assume that a *standing* force would be trained for the many specialized tasks that might be entailed in UN operations—from rapid reaction forces to civilian policing. Further, a standing force presumably would be equipped with the weapons, vehicles, communications devices, food, water, shelter, and all the other necessities of an effective military force. However, experience from UN peacekeeping operations has shown that the level of training and discipline of standby contingents varies greatly by country. Countries send their troops into UN peacekeeping operations with vastly different material possessions and needs. The lack of a standing UN force that is already trained and equipped contributes to situations in which peacekeeping force commanders must divert their attention and resources from the mission and turn instead to the training and equipping work that should have been performed in advance of the mission. Some states, acting bilaterally, have been assisting in the training of other states' forces for the purposes of participating in UN peacekeeping. And, governmental and nongovernmental groups share peacekeeping training ideas and best practices through organizations such as the International Association of Peacekeeping Training Centres.

By not finding common ground on the matter of standing UN forces, the P5 set the stage for an ineffective, inefficient system of standby arrangements for UN military operations. The founding members of the United Nations understood how critical a standing force would be to the new international security system, yet they failed to agree on the most basic details of such a force, leaving to the secretariat the almost impossible task of cobbling together standby forces.

Failure also marked discussions about how a UN force would be commanded. Chapter VII provides for the creation of a Military Staff Committee (MSC) composed of the chiefs of staff of the permanent members or their representatives (Article 47). Working together and using consensus decision making, the MSC would be responsible for the "strategic direction of any armed forces placed at the disposal of the Security Council." Strong disagreements among the permanent members about how the MSC would execute its duties doomed it from the start. In the two cases in which the United Nations embarked upon a collective security action, the lead country pushing for Chapter VII action *opposed* the use of the MSC. The United States preferred in both cases to put its own military in command of the multinational forces, intentionally sidestepping the MSC in order to avoid multilateral decision making. In Korea, the US position was that the MSC had to be sidelined in order to avoid the Soviet veto.[11] In the 1991 Gulf War, the Soviets strongly endorsed activating the MSC,[12] but the US administration was not inclined to share command and control with any other country. Eventually, in 2005, a World Summit of UN member states recommended the elimination of the MSC.

Multilateral Sanctions Short of Force—Chapter VII, Article 41

The United Nations embodies realist ideas—as realized in the veto-wielding P5—and idealist ideas—as in collective security. Another idealist notion embodied in the UN system is that force should be used only after the exhaustion of all other means. If there are measures short of force that can make a bad actor cease and desist, then those measures are used first. Article 41 of Chapter VII authorizes such actions:

> The Security Council may decide what measures not involving the use of armed force are to be employed to give effect to its decisions, and it may call upon the Members of the United Nations to apply such measures. These may include complete or partial interruption of economic relations and of rail, sea, air, postal, telegraphic, radio, and other means of communication, and the severance of diplomatic relations.

A collective security system is the ultimate deterrent. If functional, no actor would break the international peace because of the threat of unacceptable punishment at the hands of the collective community of states. The intention of collective security is to deter breaches of the peace. But when a breach has occurred, action must be taken to make the bad actor stop the bad behavior. This requires something called compellence.

Compellence is in many ways the opposite of deterrence. Compellence is an act intended to make an actor stop doing something that it is already doing. The targeted actor must stop its use of force against someone else, or end its occupation of another state, or the targeted actor must stop building weapons of mass destruction, and so on. In the first case of sanctions discussed here, compellence was used to stop a bad actor from building weapons that could be used in any future attacks on its neighbors. Additionally, compellence was used to stop that actor from harming its own civilians. Where deterrence is in some ways hypothetical only because it cannot be proven to have caused the intended good behavior, compellence can be demonstrated to have worked—because the targeted actor stops doing the bad action—but it requires an enormous show of solidarity and sometimes force to be successful. The UN sanctions discussed next were designed to compel behavior.

When the international community agrees to a set of sanctions and some enforcement mechanisms, we say that a sanctions *regime* has been instituted. International regimes have an accepted meaning, as the "principles, norms, rules, and decision-making procedures around which actor expectations converge in a given issue-area."[13] A sanctions regime establishes the principles and norms that set out why the sanctions are necessary, the rules that show how the sanctions will be performed, what the target must do, and what will be done if the target does not comply. The sanctions regime also sets out what the target must do to be relieved of the sanctions. A UN sanctions regime is embedded in the decision-making procedures of the United Nations and so is controlled by the Security Council.

To be effective, a sanctions regime needs to be multilateral—and ideally global. The goal of the sanctions is to cut a bad actor off from financial and other material resources that can be used to pursue the illicit and proscribed actions. With the funds or resources cut off and the costs of bad behavior mounting, a rational bad actor will decide to modify its actions and comply with international demands. When a significant number of states—or a single significant state—remain outside the sanctions regime and do not respect the terms of the regime, the target may be able to replace old trading partners with new ones and thereby evade the sanctions. Keeping states engaged in the collective action required of a successful regime can be tricky since states may have national interests that dictate continued interaction with the targeted state. That is, the temptation to defect from the regime may be more attractive than the benefits of staying firmly inside the regime.

Contemporary UN sanctions regimes have been designed to target high-ranking officials and state and state-related entities engaging in the bad behavior. For example, in the lead-in to the UN Security Council civilian protection mandate in Libya (discussed in chapter 8), the Council imposed sanctions on members of the Libyan government involved in the procurement of mercenaries. The Qaddafi government did not maintain a large military force but instead relied on the protection of mercenaries. Qaddafi himself came to power through a series of military coups, and thus he appreciated the danger of a standing army to a totalitarian government. The mercenaries in Qaddafi's military came from the broader neighborhood—primarily Chad, Mali, Niger, Sudan, and Somalia. When the Arab Spring demonstrations turned violent in Libya, the government sought to increase the size of the mercenary forces it could deploy against the armed opposition.

That is, officials went on recruiting trips to bring in more mercenaries. Some of the UN sanctions, therefore, imposed a travel ban on members of the government so that they would stop flying to other countries to hire and bring back more armed fighters.

Sanctions regimes are targeted in order to minimize their impact. Blanket sanctions are those imposed against an entire country and its economy. Such sanctions have a direct impact on civilians who often have no power to influence government policies, particularly the policies that have caused the imposition of sanctions. Contemporary sanctions regimes acknowledge the need to protect civilians from harm and so are targeted against the powerful. However, those in power may try to limit the impact of sanctions on themselves by extracting more resources and sacrifices from civilians. Ultimately, then, even targeted sanctions can hurt civilians.

The three cases discussed next demonstrate the use of UN sanctions for compellence purposes. These cases don't include the sanctions imposed on Russia for its annexation of Crimea and involvement in fighting in Eastern Ukraine. The sanctions on Russia were imposed by Western states and not through the UN Security Council. Since Russia is a veto-wielding member of the Security Council, the Council was unable to compel Russia to return Crimea to Ukraine and remove its forces and support from the antigovernment forces in Eastern Ukraine.

Iraq

The UN sanctions against Iraq after the 1991 Gulf War were designed to limit threatening international behavior by Iraq and to compensate Kuwaiti victims for Iraq's invasion of their country. In short order, the sanctions were expanded to limit Saddam Hussein's government from harming people within Iraq.

At the conclusion of the 1991 Gulf War, UN Security Council Resolution 687 (April 3, 1991) welcomed "the restoration to Kuwait of its sovereignty, independence and territorial integrity and the return of its legitimate Government." Resolution 687 also noted that during the crisis and war, Iraq had threatened to use weapons of mass destruction on and conducted unprovoked attacks against third-party countries, and threatened to use terrorism and take hostages outside of Iraq. All these activities were noted as being against various international conventions signed by Iraq, and were threats to international peace and security. In light of all this, the Security Council imposed certain conditions on Iraq in order to limit its ability to threaten its neighbors and the international peace. Specifically, Iraq was compelled to "unconditionally accept the destruction, removal, or rendering harmless, under international supervision," of chemical and biological weapons and stocks of related agents and all ballistic missiles with a range over one hundred and fifty kilometers. Further, Iraq was to "unconditionally agree not to acquire or develop nuclear weapons or nuclear-weapon-usable material or any subsystems or components" or to develop and maintain any facilities designed for nuclear weapons–related purposes. These restrictions effectively formed the bulk of the sanctions regime designed to contain the threat Iraq posed to other states.

In order to ensure Iraq's compliance with the prohibitions, Iraq was required to provide full reports on the whereabouts of restricted materials and facilitate on-site international inspections, destruction, removal, or rendering harmless of all such materials. Later Security Council resolutions established how Iraq would pay compensation to Kuwait and others for all damages incurred in Iraq's occupation of Kuwait. These resolutions also established the "oil for food" fund that would allow the sale of petroleum products for the importation of food and other essential civilian needs, such as medicines. This aspect of the sanctions regime was designed to limit the impact of the sanctions on civilians. The sanctions regime imposed on Iraq amounted to an imposition of a defensive defense posture as discussed in chapter 4.

Within days of Resolution 687, the Security Council also passed a resolution that was aimed at the domestic behavior of the Iraqi government. This unprecedented intrusion into the domestic affairs of a sovereign member of the United Nations set the stage for the idea that states and the United Nations have a responsibility to protect civilians (discussed in the next two chapters). But that idea would not present itself for another decade. The sanctions regime on Iraq did not end when Iraq came into compliance; instead, the sanctions regime ended when the United States spearheaded an invasion in 2003.

North Korea

The sanctions regime against North Korea began in 2006 after North Korea conducted its first nuclear weapon test in early October. Previous international negotiations with North Korea had fallen apart. In Resolution 1718 (October 14, 2006), the Security Council condemned the tests, demanded that North Korea no longer conduct tests nor launch ballistic missiles, demanded that North Korea return to its commitments under the Non-Proliferation Treaty (NPT) and allow the International Atomic Energy Agency (IAEA) access to all nuclear sites. In the words of the resolution, the Security Council declared:

> that the DPRK [North Korea] shall abandon all nuclear weapons and existing nuclear programmes in a complete, verifiable and irreversible manner, shall act strictly in accordance with the obligations applicable to parties under the Treaty on the Non-Proliferation of Nuclear Weapons and the terms and conditions of its International Atomic Energy Agency (IAEA) Safeguards Agreement (IAEA INFCIRC/403) and shall provide the IAEA transparency measures extending beyond these requirements, including such access to individuals, documentation, equipments and facilities as may be required and deemed necessary by the IAEA.

The sanctions were designed to compel North Korea to end its nuclear weapons and ballistic missiles programs. It is useful to recall some of the history that led to this moment. A decade earlier, in 1994, the United States signed a bilateral agreement with North Korea called the Agreed Framework. The Agreed Framework was intended to use incentives rather than sanctions to accomplish the goal of keeping North Korea from developing nuclear weapons and ballistic missiles. In the first phase of the agreement, North Korea would freeze all nuclear weapons–related activity. In the second phase, the United States and its allies would construct two light-water nuclear energy reactors and supply heavy fuel oil. By the third phase, North Korea would dismantle all weapons-related activities. The IAEA (affiliated with the United Nations) would conduct inspections and install permanent surveillance cameras at sensitive sites in North Korea. The first phase of the agreement commenced—that is, North Korea did its part—but the promised construction of the nuclear reactors never occurred, nor did the normalization talks begin. Despite the one-sided nature of the interactions, North Korea's nuclear weapons program was in deep freeze when the more aggressive Bush administration replaced the Clinton administration in 2001.

The George W. Bush administration's antipathy to the North Korean regime was displayed with flair in the famous "axis of evil" proclamation in January 2002. This proclamation was accompanied by the Bush doctrine of threatening preemptive strikes against rogue states. During the course of 2002, as the Bush administration was moving toward war in Iraq, it refused to engage in discussions with North Korea. In early December 2002, North Korea responded by kicking out the IAEA inspectors and dismantling the inspection cameras. North Korea indicated that it would move ahead with its nuclear weapons program unless the Bush administration would sign a nonaggression pact with it. Declaring that the North Korean threat lacked credibility, the Bush administration downplayed any worries that North Korea would restart its weapons program. By January 2003, North Korea announced that it was withdrawing from the Nuclear Nonproliferation Treaty and had reopened the long-shuttered nuclear facility at Yong-byon. Caught by some surprise, the Bush administration declared that the situation warranted multilateral diplomatic efforts, and at the same time the administration launched the Proliferation Security Initiative, a multilateral initiative in which 105 countries agreed to the idea of interdicting shipments to stop the spread of weapons of mass destruction and related materials.

Six-Party Talks between North Korea, the United States, South Korea, China, Japan, and Russia began in 2003. Little progress was made on the talks, and North Korea moved forward in converting a formerly sealed stockpile of 8,000 spent nuclear fuel rods into weapons-grade plutonium. By the reckoning of the head of the IAEA, North Korea had produced five or six nuclear weapons by the end of 2004. While the Six-Party Talks seemed to pick up intensity in 2005, North Korea continued its activities. In the beginning of October 2006, North Korea tested a nuclear warhead. The United Nations sanctions regime against North Korea began less than a week later.

The full United Nations sanctions regime against North Korea through 2016 was created by six Council resolutions. Each resolution was authorized under Article 41 of the Charter. Each resolution came after a provocative act by North Korea. The Council resolutions demanded that North Korea dismantle its nuclear weapons program, refrain from missile tests, and rejoin the Nuclear Nonproliferation Treaty and the Six-Party Talks. That is, each resolution demanded some kind of active compliance by North Korea.

The sanctions against North Korea involved export restrictions on North Korean sales of weapons to other countries, an import ban on goods and materials used in all nuclear weapons–related and missile-related activities, a ban on luxury goods aimed at the elite, an asset freeze and travel bans on top officials, and a ban on exporting coal. Countries were asked to honor the ban and help with the interdiction of suspected sanctions-breaking goods.

As of the start of 2017, the sanctions regime had not compelled a change in North Korea's behavior. In June 2009, North Korea conducted an underground nuclear weapons test. In late 2012, it successfully launched a satellite which was a violation of the ban on the development of technology related to a nuclear weapons program. In 2013, North Korea tested another nuclear weapon. In 2016, North Korea conducted another nuclear test and launched another satellite. Each provocation resulted in a new Security Council resolution in a tit-for-tat cycle.

Why did the sanctions regime fail? One reason is that the North Korean government was willing to shift the costs of the sanctions onto its people, allowing funds to continue to flow into weapons and missile development. Another reason was that China was not inclined to fully honor the sanctions regime, although it voted for each part of the regime. Similarly, other countries were not committed to upholding the sanctions regime. North Korean missiles continued to be sold to Iran, Syria, Pakistan, and even to Yemeni Houthi rebels who used the missiles in their fight against the government of Yemen and its supporter Saudi Arabia.[14] And, the North Korean government seemed adept at off-shoring its money-making activities. Writing in 2016 in the *International New York Times*, Jim Walsh and John Park opined that the sanctions would continue to fail as long as North Korea's out-of-country money-making activities continued.[15] Walsh and Park contended that much of this off-shoring was taking place in China where Chinese business partners were especially willing to break the sanctions and make money off North Korea's ambitions.

Iran

The sanctions regime imposed on Iran started in July 2006, a few months before sanctions were first imposed on North Korea. For a few years prior to 2006, Iran and the IAEA had been going back and forth about whether Iran was enriching uranium beyond a level needed for civilian purposes. Eventually the IAEA declared that Iran was noncompliant on previous agreements and referred the matter to the Security Council. The first round of sanctions was aimed at stopping the production and enrichment of uranium and the development of ballistic missiles. Several more rounds of resolutions resulted in the blocking of financial assistance and loans to the Iranian government and allowed for the interdiction and inspection of cargo. The last Security Council resolution targeted oil profits and banking.

From 2006 through 2010, the Security Council imposed four rounds of sanctions on Iran. During this time, the Iranian government was an ambivalent negotiating partner, yet despite the fact that the government was controlled by hardliners Iran never broke off talks completely. The costs of the sanctions did begin to fray the control of the hardliners, and the internal power started shifting in favor of those who wanted to talk to the West on nuclear matters in order to find some relief from the sanctions. Then the sanctions got ratcheted up, but not by the United Nations.

The United Nations sanctions were complemented by sanctions imposed by the United States and the European Union. These sanctions took a sharp upward turn in 2012. In particular, the European Union banned all oil and petrochemical imports from Iran and restricted indemnity for oil tankers. The European Union was the largest importer of Iranian oil, and the insurance restrictions on tankers meant few companies would risk shipping Iranian oil. The US treasury secretary estimated that the combined international sanctions in 2012 reduced Iran's economy by 15 to 20 percent.[16] The next year, a more moderate president, Hassan Rouhani, was elected in Iran and, with the support of the Supreme Leader Ali Khamenei, authorized a fuller engagement with the negotiations. Rouhani was elected, in part, to bring about an end to the sanctions and get Iran back into the international community.

At this point, it is instructive to think about the North Korean and Iranian sanctions regime cases side-by-side. In the North Korean case, a key state—China—was a constant defector from the sanctions regime, giving North Korea a steady funding source, while other states continued to buy military hardware from North Korea. In the case of Iran, key states—particularly the European Union—were willing to lean into the sanctions regime by initiating their own more intense sanctions. North Korea has never been integrated into the world economy, and so it could get by on the earnings allowed by China and weapons-seeking states. Iran was highly interdependent with the world economy prior to the sanctions regime and so was badly injured by the sanctions. And, finally, the North Korean leaders could shift the costs of the sanctions onto their people, while the Iranian leaders—working in a hybrid political system that does have regular elections—responded to the economic distress of the Iranian people by deciding to find a way to end the sanctions.

Despite opposition in corners of the international community, a nuclear agreement was concluded between Iran and the so-called P5+1 (the United States, United Kingdom, France, Russia, China, and Germany) in July 2015. The agreement "put stringent limitations on Iran's uranium-enrichment program," eliminated Iran's "plutonium pathway to nuclear weapons," and "put in place enhanced international monitoring and accountancy to promptly detect and deter Iranian noncompliance."[17] Further, before the sanctions could be lifted, Iran had to take concrete actions to stop enrichment and related activities and have its actions verified by the IAEA. Thus, the agreement would not be one that required the international community to trust Iran since Iran would actively complete some steps in order to get the sanctions lifted. And, the agreement had a ten-year "snap back" clause that the sanctions would be instantly reimposed if Iran were found to be cheating, and some restrictions on Iran's behavior would continue for twenty-five years after the agreement. In January 2016, the IAEA verified that Iran had met the concrete requirements of the deal and the sanctions began to be lifted.

Collective Security and All Means Necessary—Chapter VII, Article 42

The United Nations can authorize the deployment of military force in different ways. We will discuss peacekeeping and peace enforcement in chapter 7. Here, we will stay with the larger idea of collective security and how the United Nations can authorize a full-scale war. Chapter VII of the Charter provides the mechanism by which a UN collective security resolution would be approved and implemented. First, the Security Council approves a resolution, stating that an act of aggression has occurred and names the aggressor(s)/state(s). All the permanent members need to agree on this determination (or at least not veto this), as would a majority of the Council as a whole. The aggressor is then ordered to stop its hostile actions and return to the pre-aggression status quo. If the aggressor fails to comply with this order, the Council can impose economic and diplomatic sanctions to compel compliance. If these fail, or if there is insufficient time for these sanctions to work, the Council can order member states to use all means necessary, which would include armed force, to restore international peace and security.

Analysts disagree about which later cases might be labeled "collective security," but all agree that the first instance in which UN collective security was invoked involved the North Korean invasion of South Korea. In June 1950, the Communist forces of North Korea launched an invasion across the thirty-eighth parallel which formed the internationally recognized border between the divided Korean nation. The Security Council met on June 25, 1950, and declared that the invasion was a breach of international peace. In Resolution 82 (June 25, 1950), the Council ordered an immediate cessation of hostilities and called for the withdrawal of North Korean forces. Two days later, the Council declared "that the authorities in North Korea have neither ceased hostilities nor withdrawn their armed forces to the 38th parallel, and that urgent military measures are required to restore international peace and security" (Resolution 83, June 27, 1950). Toward that end, the Council recommended that members "furnish such assistance to the Republic of Korea [South Korea] as may be necessary to repel the armed attack and to restore international peace and security in the area." The Korean War, thereby, was authorized by the UN Security Council.

The vote in the Council was seven in favor and one opposed (Yugoslavia). At that time, the Council numbered eleven states, the P5 and six rotating members. Nonpermanent members Egypt and India did not participate in the vote, and the Soviet Union was absent when it was taken. The Soviet Union had been boycotting Council sessions to signal its political opposition to the seating of the Republic of China (Taiwan) rather than the Communist People's Republic of China in the China permanent seat. When Resolutions 82 and 83 were adopted, the Soviet ambassador was not there to cast votes. The practice of the Council is that absences do not count in the affirmative or the negative. Had the Soviet ambassador been present, it is most likely that he would have vetoed Resolution 82 rather than name a fellow Communist country as an aggressor. With the Soviet veto, the resolution would have died, and the United Nations might well have had no official stand on the war raging on the Korean Peninsula.

Instead, the war was authorized and the Council authorized the United States to command the UN forces in Korea. The Soviet Union returned to Council sessions and used its veto power to stop further substantive discussions of the war. In response, the United States used its strong majority support in the General Assembly to pass the Uniting for Peace Resolution that would give the United States a continuous UN stamp of approval for its war efforts in Korea. From this point on, great power agreement on naming an aggressor would be impossible to obtain until the 1991 Gulf War.

Discussions of the Korean War were moved to the General Assembly by the Uniting for Peace Resolution (General Assembly Resolution 377 [V], November 3, 1950). According to the UN Charter, the Security Council is the proper authority for discussing matters of international peace and security, and the General Assembly cannot discuss any matter under consideration in the Council. The Uniting for Peace Resolution declares that a "failure of the Security Council to discharge its responsibilities on behalf of all the Member States . . . does not relieve Member States of their obligations or the United Nations of its responsibility under the Charter to maintain international peace and security." Thus, the General Assembly resolved that whenever a "lack of unanimity of the permanent members" causes the Council to fail to exercise its Charter duties, an emergency session of the General Assembly can be called to consider the matter that has caused Council deadlock. This session can be requested by *any* seven Council members or by a majority of the General Assembly members. The veto does not apply.

The Uniting for Peace Resolution has been invoked twelve times, the last time was in 1997. In 2002–2003, a group of states and nongovernmental organizations opposed to the imminent American-British invasion of Iraq floated plans to enact the Uniting for Peace Resolution before the invasion. By the draft proposal, this resolution would have declared "that military action against Iraq without a Security Council resolution authorizing such action is contrary to the UN Charter and customary international law."[18] What would have been the value in invoking the Uniting for Peace Resolution against the United States and Britain? On the one hand, the General Assembly has no enforcement authority; thus, this resolution would amount only to a recommendation. On the other hand, such a resolution would carry moral and public opinion weight. The United States understood the importance of this kind of resolution in 1950 and used the General Assembly to promote its interests in the Korean conflict. Such a statement coming from the General Assembly in late 2002 or early 2003 might have been a strong counter to the Bush administration plans for Iraq.

Forty years after the start of the Korean War, the Security Council authorized another full-scale Chapter VII operation. The instance that revived UN collective enforcement action was the 1990 Iraqi invasion of Kuwait. The context that allowed UN collective enforcement action was the end of the Cold War and the preoccupation of Soviet authorities with holding their country together. In the years between the 1950 Korean War authorization and the November 1990 Gulf War authorization, the Security Council authorized peacekeeping operations that intentionally and expressly were not like collective security actions (see chapter 7). The end of the Cold War shifted expectations about what the United Nations might accomplish, and member states, including the P5, seemed to have developed some political willingness to act cooperatively at times on matters of peace and security.

On August 2, 1990, Iraq invaded Kuwait. The countries had been engaged in open dispute regarding sovereignty over oil reserves and the terms of the repayment of loans made by Kuwait to Iraq during the Iraq-Iran War of the previous decade. On the day of the invasion, the Security Council met and voted fourteen to none (Yemen abstaining) to condemn the invasion, demand "that Iraq withdraw immediately and unconditionally all its forces to the positions in which they were located on 1 August 1990," and call on both Iraq and Kuwait "to begin immediately intensive negotiations for the resolution of their differences" (Resolution 660, August 2, 1990).

Four days later, the Council voted thirteen to none (Yemen and Cuba abstaining), acting under Chapter VII authority, to impose economic and diplomatic sanctions on Iraq for failure to comply with its earlier resolution (Resolution 661, August 6, 1990). In Resolution 661, the Council noted that Kuwaiti government officials had signaled their readiness to comply with the earlier Council call to negotiate but that Iraq had not. In response to Resolution 661, Iraq announced it would annex Kuwait, leading the Council to denounce the annexation and to call on all states and international organizations not to recognize it (Resolution 662, August 9, 1990).

Resolution 678 (November 29, 1990) noted the continued Iraqi refusal to comply with the multiple Council resolutions regarding its invasion and occupation of Kuwait. Acting under Chapter VII, the Council authorized "Member States co-operating with the Government of Kuwait, unless Iraq on or before 15 January 1991 fully implements . . . the above-mentioned resolutions, to use all necessary means to uphold and implement resolution 660 (1990) and all subsequent relevant resolutions and to restore international peace and security in the area." The phrase "use all necessary means" is the authorization to use force. Resolution 678 passed with twelve yes votes, two no votes (Cuba and Yemen), and China abstaining.

Resolution 678 was an agreement among the great powers on how to manage the world order. The United States wanted Council approval to use force and wanted to use that force on its own terms. The US administration essentially said to the other veto-wielding members of the Security Council something like this: "We intend to go to war; tell us what would make this okay with you." Ever since it replaced the Republic of China in the United Nations in 1971, the People's Republic of China had opposed UN peacekeeping as unlawful intervention in the domestic affairs of sovereign states. UN peacekeeping does not compare to Resolution 678 in terms of the implications for Iraqi sovereignty, yet China apparently never threatened to block 678. Instead, when the vote was taken, China abstained, registering neither approval nor disapproval of the resolution. Was there a quid pro quo or some accommodation made between the United States and China resulting in China's accordance with US interests? After the Tiananmen Square pro-democracy protests in China in June 1989, there had been restricted diplomatic exchanges between the United States and China. On the same day that Resolution 688 was passed, China received its first loan from the Asian Development Bank since June 1989,[19] and two days after the resolution was passed, the Chinese foreign minister was welcomed back to the White House explicitly because the United States and China had found "common ground" in standing up to Iraq's aggression.[20]

Were accommodations made between the Soviets and Americans? The Bush administration and the Gorbachev government seemed to have reached accord about the use of force against Iraq despite news reports that Soviet military advisers were actively working in Iraq months after the Kuwaiti invasion.[21] The US administration persuaded "Saudi Arabia to give \$1 billion in aid to help the Soviets through the winter" in order to foster Soviet support for Resolution 678.[22] Then, in the last days before the January 15, 1991, deadline for Iraq to withdraw from Kuwait or face war, Soviet troops launched an attack on a Lithuanian broadcasting center, killing thirteen and wounding more than 160.[23] This attack culminated a year of Soviet repression of a nonviolent Lithuanian independence movement. The Bush administration had been lukewarm in opposing this crackdown. The Soviet use of force in January 1991 received only a statement of concern from the Bush administration, signaling to the pro-independence members of the Lithuanian parliament that they were on their own.[24] Possibly in return for this, the Soviet Union did not block the Gulf War through any last-minute diplomatic efforts or deals with Iraq.

Even as the two most likely opponents to the Gulf War were accommodated by the United States, the European Community states (particularly Britain and France) were receiving assurances that the Bush administration would use force only to liberate Kuwait, not attack Iraq itself.[25] Taken together, the road to war was paved through a series of great power agreements that coalesced in Security Council Resolution 678 and the subsequent UN-authorized Gulf War. These great power agreements resulted from accord over how to manage the international order in the face of the Iraqi invasion of Kuwait and kept great power management duties (in this case, war) within the UN framework. Moreover, none of the great powers felt their own interests threatened by the Gulf War resolution, or, if they did, the tangible payoff for cooperation was greater than the potential payoff for blocking the war resolution.

The Gulf War episode demonstrated what Claude had hoped for the United Nations some forty years before. Claude had hoped the United Nations might "be able to continue the development of its capability to serve the interests of the great powers—and of the rest of the world—by helping them to contain their conflicts, to limit their competition, and to stabilize their relationships."[26] Claude continued,

> The greatest potential contribution of the United Nations in our time to the management of international power relationships lies not in implementing collective security or instituting world government, but in helping to improve and stabilize the working of the balance of power system, which is, for better or for worse, the operative mechanism of contemporary international politics. The immediate task, in short, is to make the world safe for the balance of power system, and the balance system safe for the world.[27]

Between the Korean War and the November 1990 Gulf War resolution, the Security Council failed to pass a single collective enforcement resolution. Great power disagreement over Korea deadlocked the Council. In 1956, a crisis in the Sinai Peninsula put into question the ability of the UN great power system to manage the balance in a way that was safe for great powers, for the world, and for the new global organization. Working within the UN framework, some visionaries found a way to protect the balance and protect the United Nations. This is the story of UN peacekeeping, a topic taken up in chapter 7.

Recap

In this chapter, we explored why and how states create multilateral systems to protect states from war. We discussed how the United Nations collective security system is organized and how it works, and how the system allows the P5 special privileges. The two most potent tools of the UN Security Council are the ability to impose economic sanctions and the authorization of the use of force. We examined the sanctions regimes on Iraq, North Korea, and Iran, and the UN-authorized Korean War and the 1991 Gulf War.

Discussion Questions

1. Discuss this quote, "No state, no matter how powerful, can by its own efforts make itself invulnerable to today's threats."
2. What is a collective security system, and how is it dependent on overwhelming military power?
3. Discuss how the P5 are effectively exempted from the UN Charter prohibition on the use of force.
4. Discuss how Chapter VII, Articles 41 and 42 of the UN Charter work together.
5. Why is there no standing United Nations army?
6. Discuss how economic sanctions are an effort to compel compliance.
7. Compare the relative success of the sanctions regimes imposed on Iraq, North Korea, and Iran.
8. Describe the political events that created the circumstances in which the UN Security Council authorized war in Korea.
9. Describe the political events that created the circumstances in which the UN Security Council authorized the 1991 Iraq War.

7

United Nations Peacekeeping and Peace Enforcement

In This Chapter

Introduction
Traditional Peacekeeping
Precedents for a New Era
Peace Enforcement
Multidimensional Peace Operations
Improving Peace Support Operations
Hybrid Peace Operations
Recap
Discussion Questions

Introduction

The war in Syria that began in 2011 was a serious threat to international peace and security. The war crimes committed by the government and its supporters as well as by ISIL and other combatants, the millions of people endangered and displaced, the spillover violence, the massive refugee flows, the terrorist plots hatched there and executed elsewhere, and the presence of foreign fighters and terrorists from around the world who might take what they had learned back to incite other conflicts—all of these matters merited action by the United Nations Security Council. But, Russia was bombing the opposition on Assad's behalf, propping up the regime, and some of the antigovernment forces were supported by the air support (that is, bombing) provided by the United States, United Kingdom, and France. Many other state players were involved in the war as discussed in chapter 5, but the presence of four out of five veto-wielding permanent Council members on opposite sides of the war made Security Council consideration and action impossible.

In the history of the United Nations, there have been other times when major powers were involved in conflicts, or had political stakes in conflicts and so creative work-arounds had to be found. Indeed, creativity is at the foundation of UN peace operations. These work-arounds developed historically in response to events, and so to understand UN peace operations we must take an historical view.

Not all stories start in the Middle East, but the story of what the United Nations can do to protect international peace and security in the face of permanent five disagreement has its roots in the Middle East. The first Arab-Israeli war began on May 15, 1948, the day after Israel declared its independence in defiance of United Nations plans for the partition of Palestine into separate Jewish and Arab states. The Security Council called for a cease-fire and in June 1948 sent a small group of military observers to supervise, investigate, and report on issues surrounding the cease-fire. The group of observers was called the UN Truce Supervision Organization (UNTSO). The UNTSO precedent led to the deployment of another small military observer group, the UN Military Observation Group in India and Pakistan (UNMOGIP), to supervise a cease-fire in Jammu and Kashmir between India and Pakistan in 1949. These military observer missions might be understood as the eyes and ears of the Security Council—but eyes and ears with military expertise useful for detecting any military action that might disrupt the cease-fire and require stronger Council intervention. Both UNTSO and UNMOGIP are still operational at the start of 2017, nearly seventy years after they started—which means there has been no movement toward a political settlement in either case.

In October 1956, two major events put the Security Council great power balance into question. The first involved efforts by a liberal government in Hungary to establish its political independence from the Soviet Union and to sever its military ties with the newly created Warsaw Pact. This revolution was crushed by Soviet tanks. The Soviet military kept a heavy hand in Hungarian politics thereafter to ensure Hungary's continued membership in and contribution to the Soviet bloc. The second major event was on October 29 when Israel launched an attack on Egypt with the help of the United Kingdom and France. Both events created deadlock in the Council, and both became the subject of emergency General Assembly sessions. The crisis in Hungary resulted in the further consolidation of the Soviet sphere of influence, and the crisis in the Middle East resulted in the creation of the first UN peacekeeping force. The two events no doubt were linked in the minds of top decision makers with the politics of each impacting to some degree the resolution of the other.[1]

A complex set of events preceded the Israeli-British-French attack on Egypt. The precipitating event was Egypt's nationalization of the Suez Canal. The British and French wanted their colonial possession back, and Israel had its own security issues with Egypt, and so the three colluded. As per their plan, Israeli forces crossed into Egyptian territory, to which Egypt responded in self-defense. Then, the British and French ordered Israel and Egypt to stand down and withdraw their forces from the canal area. Israel agreed (again, as planned) and Egypt did not, and so the British and French "launched an air attack against targets in Egypt, which was followed shortly by a landing of their troops near Port Said at the northern end of the Canal."[2]

In an odd twist in the early Cold War, the Americans and Soviets joined to condemn the British, French, and Israeli actions. The Soviets, recall, were massively involved in stopping the Hungarian revolution in this very same month. In the Security Council, the British and French vetoed US and Soviet resolutions demanding a cease-fire and return to pre-invasion positions. Then, in Resolution 119 (October 31, 1956), the Council noted that a "lack of unanimity of its permanent members . . . has prevented it from exercising its primary responsibility for the maintenance of international peace and security." The Security Council then approved a Uniting for Peace Resolution, sending the matter to the General Assembly for discussion. A similar resolution enacting an emergency General Assembly session on the matter of the Soviet occupation of Hungary noted quite boldly that the Soviet forces were to blame; the corresponding resolution on the Suez crisis simply noted that "a grave situation has been created by an action undertaken against Egypt," but no perpetrators of that action were named.

Not naming the perpetrators became key to defusing the Suez crisis. The Security Council permanent members were split but not in the pattern that developed during the Korean War. This split over the canal crisis had the Americans and Soviets (with the ROC always on the side of the United States) on one side versus the British and French. While the United States tacitly acknowledged the Soviet Union's right to police its own sphere of influence in Hungary, it agreed with the Soviet Union that the British and French had no such claim or right in the Middle East. Yet, the diplomats involved in the crisis did not want the British and French to be humiliated or named as aggressors in this situation. Instead, some politically neutral egress point would be created to restore the pre-invasion balance.

UN secretary-general Dag Hammarskjöld and Canadian foreign minister Lester Pearson are credited with imagining a way out of this great power impasse. Their idea was to establish a neutral UN peacekeeping force in the area. In General Assembly Resolution 998 (ES-1, November 4, 1956), the secretary-general was asked to submit "a plan for the setting up, with the consent of the nations concerned, of an emergency international United Nations Force to secure and supervise the cessation of hostilities." Several elements of future United Nations peacekeeping were included in this resolution and in subsequent General Assembly resolutions. We will turn to those elements shortly. For now, it is important to note two critical elements of the proposed peacekeeping force: First, it was intended to monitor a cease-fire and should not do anything else to "influence the military balance in the current conflict, and thereby the political balance affecting efforts to settle the conflict."[3] Second,

> The Force obviously should have no rights other than those necessary for the execution of its functions, in cooperation with local authorities. It would be more than an observer corps, but in no way a military force temporarily controlling the territory in which it was stationed; nor should the Force have functions exceeding those necessary to secure peaceful conditions, on the assumption that the parties to the conflict would take all necessary steps for compliance with the recommendations of the General Assembly.[4]

The force would carry weapons only for self-defense since it was not an intervention nor occupation force and was present with the good-will and compliance of all the disputants.

The UN Emergency Force (UNEF I) was so constituted and deployed as the first official UN peacekeeping operation. Peacekeeping fulfilled the mission of the United Nations to restore international peace and security in situations in which combatants had agreed already to seek a peaceful resolution of their disagreements. At times, combatants might need to be persuaded by the Security Council to come to the negotiating table, but the payoff for combatants would be far better than the political and military costs of being named as an aggressor by the world body.

In the Suez crisis, it would have been politically impossible for the Security Council to name the British and French as aggressors. The Council was designed to maintain these states' great power privileges and, as discussed previously, to exempt them from the same threat of collective punishment to which other states were subject. The problem at hand, however, was that the faith of *all* UN members in the basic legitimacy of the UN system had to be maintained, and this meant that practical measures were needed to overlook the great powers' aggression (without seeming too obvious) and to ease their way back into the great power consultations over managing the crisis. The peace-keeping solution presented the United Nations with a mechanism through which the British and French (and Israelis) could bow out of the confrontation without incurring any costs for starting it. Peace could be restored, and the UN system would remain intact, thereby ensuring international stability.

Traditional Peacekeeping

The essential practice of peacekeeping was established with UNEF I. Because peacekeeping was a creative response to great power stalemate over Suez, there was no specific UN Charter foundation for it. Instead, peacekeeping sometimes is said to fall under Chapter VI, Pacific Settlement of Disputes, and sometimes under Chapter VII, Action with Respect to Threats to the Peace, Breaches of the Peace, and Acts of Aggression. Because of this, analysts sometime refer to the fictional "Chapter VI and a half" that authorizes peacekeeping.

Traditional peacekeeping dominated the Cold War era. Some peacekeeping operations in the twenty-first century still follow the traditional form or have some traditional elements. Following the first operation, traditional peacekeeping was understood in principle to include the following elements: First, each operation is approved by the Security Council and tasked to the secretary-general for implementation. Second, each operation is under the command and control of a force commander appointed by the secretary-general and answerable to the United Nations. Third, prior to the deployment of the peacekeeping force, a cease-fire or truce must be agreed to by the disputants. Fourth, the consent of local authorities is also secured prior to the deployment in order to respect the sovereignty of member states. Consent also signifies that the locals will act in compliance with the peacekeepers. Fifth, the mission would consist of supervising a cease-fire and reporting violations thereof to local and UN officials. In more complex peacekeeping, peacekeepers are tasked with facilitating peace talks, voluntary disarmament, supervising arms embargoes, assisting in the provision of humanitarian relief, securing environments for elections, and many other tasks. Sixth, the peacekeeping force is neutral regarding all the combatants, naming no party as an "aggressor" and taking no military action against particular parties. Seventh, the peacekeeping force is neutral regarding the contributors, avoiding the use of officers and troops from the permanent five and other interested countries (e.g., former colonial powers). And finally, because of all the previously mentioned points, peacekeepers carry sidearms only for self-defense purposes. In more complex operations, peacekeepers might employ heavier weapons but also only for defensive purposes.

For each of these aspects of traditional peacekeeping, there are many examples when the practice did not match the theory. Many times deviations from peacekeeping principles resulted from ambiguities in local conditions, inadequate mandates, and/or inadequate resources given to peacekeepers. Other deviations resulted from the lack of genuine will on the part of disputants to comply with cease-fire and other political agreements. Many exceptions to the principles, too, resulted from contributing states' reluctance to allow the UN force commander any real control over their troops.

UN peace operations of any type happen in this way: First, the UN Security Council establishes the mandate for the operation. The resolution mandate explains the type of operation, its tasks, the size of the forces to be deployed, and also may discuss related activities such as sanctions and activities under way by regional and other relevant actors. In the mandate, the secretary-general is given the job of setting up the operation. The secretary-general then dispatches a technical assessment team to determine the exact needs of the operation, and appoints a special representative of the secretary-general (called an SRSG) as the political head of the mission and a force commander as the military head of mission. Then, the secretary-general and the force commander go begging member states for troops, police, vehicles, supplies, logistical and communications support, and whatever else is needed to deploy the operation. All of this is voluntary, since no member state is obligated in any way to assist in a peacekeeping (or peace enforcement) operation. When sufficient personnel and material support are assembled, the operation deploys. It is important to note here that many operations deploy much later than anticipated and at much lower capacity than mandated because of the failure of member states to supply the personnel and materials needed. Once the mission is deployed, the secretary-general must make regular reports to the Security Council regarding the progress—or the problems—of the operation. With these reports in mind, the Security Council makes adjustments to the mandate or ends the operation on a predetermined schedule or if events on the ground require quicker action.

For most of the Cold War period (1945–1989), peacekeeping operations were limited in number and usually in size and mandate (with the exception of the UN Operation in the Congo, 1960–1964). During the Cold War, only eighteen peacekeeping operations were approved and deployed. Five of these operations—three in the Middle East, one in Kashmir, and one in Cyprus—remained active at the start of 2017.

At the close of the Cold War, UN member states had some real enthusiasm and optimism about making the United Nations a bold and effective tool for conflict management and resolution. Growing great power accord in this period allowed for the first UN-sanctioned war since Korea—the 1991 Gulf War as discussed in the previous chapter. Great power accord also opened the door to many more and more ambitious UN peacekeeping efforts and to UN-sanctioned peace enforcement operations.

Precedents for a New Era

The Gulf War of 1991 and two other contemporaneous operations established precedents that still shape UN peace operations—in all forms—today. Operation Provide Comfort (OPC) started an era of humanitarian intervention and peace enforcement. The UN Transitional Authority in Cambodia (UNTAC), from 1992 to 1993, set the standard for complex or multidimensional peacekeeping.

At the conclusion of the Gulf War of 1991, Iraqi Kurds and Shi'a attempted to rise up against the Iraqi government. The regime responded with force resulting in tens of thousands of deaths, and then Kurds and Shi'a attempted to flee the violence. Shi'a who made it across the border into Iran were welcomed and given safe haven, although international aid and attention were scarce. Kurds who fled north to Turkey were stopped at the border by the Turkish army. Death by starvation, winter conditions, and human rights abuses by Turkish border guards resulted in more mass casualties.[5]

Because this crisis came on the heels of the 1991 Gulf War, there were still hundreds of thousands of foreign troops in the area. The national leaders of key members of the Gulf War coalition were willing to use their troops in what would soon be called a humanitarian intervention. The goal would be to stop the immediate suffering of Kurds on the Turkish border and to create conditions that would provide future security for Kurds in Iraq.

On April 5, 1991, the Security Council passed Resolution 688, in which the Council first honored the provisions of Article 2, paragraph 7, of the Charter, that

> Nothing contained in the present Charter shall authorize the United Nations to intervene in matters which are essentially within the domestic jurisdiction of any state or shall require the Members to submit such matters to settlement under the present Charter; but this principle shall not prejudice the application of enforcement measures under Chapter VII.

How a government chooses to govern its own territory was and is a matter of domestic jurisdiction. The United Nations is dedicated to protecting the sovereign rights of its member states. Article 2 both reaffirms these ideas and suggests that there are limitations on them—limitations created by spillover problems for other states.

In Resolution 688, the Council condemned the repression of the Iraqi people, declared that this had created problems for international peace and security in the region, called on the Iraqi government to stop the repression and to allow humanitarian organizations immediate access to all parts of Iraq, and appealed to member states to contribute to the humanitarian relief efforts. This brief description of Resolution 688 highlights all of its key elements. The resolution did not authorize what happened next.

US military planners and humanitarian relief organizations determined that the best way to help the Kurds stranded on the Turkish border was to move them off the mountains and back to their hometowns and villages. To do this safely, Iraqi forces would need to be denied the ability to threaten the Kurds both on the way home and once resettled there. Iraqi forces were terrorizing the Kurds by the air, so a no-fly zone was established. Later another no-fly zone was established in the south to protect the Shi'a. A multinational coalition of the United States, Austria, Belgium, Canada, France, Germany, Italy, Luxembourg, the Netherlands, Portugal, Spain, and the United Kingdom responded massively to the Kurdish humanitarian crisis and in so doing they also ensured longer-term Kurdish security and effective autonomy from the Iraqi government. This operation and the 1991 Gulf War itself established precedents for peace enforcement operations approved by the Council but commanded by a lead state and executed by a coalition of the willing.

In Cambodia—the other precedent-setting case from this period— the United Nations launched a complex peacekeeping operation that combined some traditional peacekeeping with peace building. A four-party Cambodian civil war was brought to an end in October 1991 with the signing of peace accords in Paris. The four parties to the accords—the State of Cambodia, the United National Front for an Independent, Neutral, Peaceful and Cooperative Cambodia, the Khmer People's National Liberation Front, and the Khmer Rouge— agreed to a plan that would involve a massive peace support operation called the United Nations Transitional Authority in Cambodia (UNTAC). This operation was tasked to maintain the cease-fire, demobilize combatants, establish a political administration and law and order in the country, establish security forces that would honor and support human rights, and oversee elections.

Despite a mandate that went well beyond a traditional peacekeeping mandate, UNTAC was still a traditional peacekeeping mission. UNTAC's success depended on the willing compliance of local parties. In Security Council Resolution 745 (February 28, 1992), the Council strongly urged

> the Cambodian parties to agree to the complete demobilization of their military forces prior to the end of the process of registration for the elections as well as to the destruction of the weapons and ammunition deposited into the Authority's custody in excess of those, if any, which may be deemed necessary by the Authority for the maintenance of civil order and national defense, or which may be required by the new Cambodian Government.

UNTAC was also traditional in that it was required to maintain neutrality regarding all Cambodian parties. This meant that the peacekeepers would treat the Khmer Rouge the same as all the Cambodian parties. The Khmer Rouge was responsible for killing between one and two million Cambodians when it controlled Cambodia from 1975 to 1978. Despite this, UNTAC had to treat it like every other party to the peace accords.

The United Nations calls UNTAC a successful peacekeeping operation. A national election was freely and fairly conducted with nearly 90 percent of eligible voters participating. A coalition government was formed and managed to steer Cambodia toward greater political stability. Yet for all its success in holding elections, UNTAC failed to disarm and demobilize the combatants. The Khmer Rouge refused to disarm, and the other combatants followed suit. Despite this, UNTAC managed to hold the mandated elections and then departed Cambodia in 1993 with a coalition government in place. But when the peacekeepers departed a smaller civil war erupted. This war between the coalition government and the Khmer Rouge lasted four more years until 1997 when the Cambodians settled it without international intervention.

OPC in Iraq and UNTAC offered models of what the international community might do about intrastate conflicts. A new ethic of humanitarian intervention designed to protect populations in distress was endorsed, departing from the earlier tradition of strict nonintervention in the sovereign affairs of UN member states. The success of UNTAC gave the United Nations the confidence to deploy large, complex, and multidimensional peacekeeping operations. The success of OPC in northern Iraq demonstrated how rapid, massive, short-term military intervention could stop a humanitarian crisis when UN members shared the political will to act.

Peace Enforcement

A pattern took hold during the optimistic and somewhat-reckless early to mid-1990s in which the Security Council would authorize a complex peacekeeping operation even though there might be at best a tentative cease-fire and peace on the ground. The peacekeepers would be tasked with complicated mandates but with traditional rules of engagement and never enough personnel or equipment. The operation would soon fail or even fail to deploy, as the peace on the ground would prove illusive. Eventually, a powerful country with a particular interest in the conflict would offer to lead a UN-approved peace enforcement mission that would be unencumbered by the traditions and expectations of peacekeeping. This force would create better conditions on the ground for a short time into which a follow-on peacekeeping operation would be launched. With some variation, this pattern was apparent in Somalia, Haiti, Rwanda, Bosnia, Liberia, Sierra Leone, Kosovo, and East Timor, and in the twenty-first century in the Democratic Republic of the Congo, Côte d'Ivoire, and Mali.

Peace enforcement appeared to be the remedy to the problems inherent to peacekeeping. Both types of operations were given UN Security Council authorization; thus, neither was a violation of international law or the UN Charter. Peacekeeping required the consent and cooperation of parties to the dispute; peace enforcement created its own consent through overwhelming numbers and firepower. Technically, peacekeepers operated under a unified UN command, but in practice they followed separate, often conflicting directives from their national capitals. Peace enforcement troops, conversely, operated under the unified command of the dominant contributing state. Peacekeepers typically could use their weapons only in self-defense; peace enforcement troops had liberal rules of engagement to use all means necessary, including force, to achieve their objectives.

Somalia was the first testing ground for the combination pack of complex peacekeeping and peace enforcement. The central government of Somalia collapsed in 1991, leaving multiple combatants contesting to define and control the state. This state failure did not draw the attention of the Security Council. Instead, a humanitarian disaster of enormous proportions did: State failure and civil war led to the displacement of 29 percent of the entire population at the same time that three waves of famine struck the people of Somalia.

On April 24, 1992, the Security Council passed Resolution 751, in which it noted that the "magnitude of the human suffering caused by the conflict" in Somalia constituted a threat to international peace

and security. The parties to the civil conflict had signed multiple let-
ters of agreement on a cease-fire to allow a peacekeeping operation to
deploy. The UN Operation in Somalia (UNOSOM) was authorized to
facilitate an end to all hostilities, maintain a cease-fire, promote political reconciliation, and help provide "urgent humanitarian assistance."
A small group of military observers were to be dispatched to monitor
the cease-fire in Mogadishu, while the secretary-general worked to
achieve agreement among the Somali combatants about the details of
deploying UNOSOM.

It took from April through September before UNOSOM could
deploy because the Somalis would not agree on the details of its
operation. Agreement from each of the dominant armed factions was
considered the equivalent of local consent and thus was necessary
for the deployment of peacekeepers. Ultimately, different factions
had different expectations about the peacekeeping operation. The
situation in Somalia soon reverted to open violence and the regular
armed robbery of famine relief supplies. Peacekeepers and humanitarian workers alike came under fire. The peacekeepers had only a
mandate to protect themselves, but even self-protection was difficult
given their size and capabilities. By early December, it was clear that
the operation would need to be reconsidered. In Resolution 794 on
December 3, 1992, the Council approved giving Chapter VII authority
to an unnamed member state and others to "use all necessary means
to establish as soon as possible a secure environment for humanitarian
relief operations in Somalia." This UN-approved enforcement action
would be known as the United Task Force (UNITAF), and it would be
commanded by the United States.

If the enforcement operation in northern Iraq set the precedent,
UNITAF established the operating manual for future missions. UNI-
TAF deployed up to 38,000 troops (26,000 Americans) for an intentionally short mission. The Council did not require the secretary-general
to get the consent of the different factions on the ground—UNITAF
and other enforcement operations would create their own consent
through massive military might and flexible rules of engagement.
UNITAF approached all Somalis the same—anyone who cooperated
with it would not be harmed, and anyone who impeded the mission
would be dealt with using force if necessary. The Somali factions

learned how to comply with UNITAF and wait until the time when the enforcement mission ended and a weaker peacekeeping force replaced it.

The secretary-general understood what the Somali factions understood, and he urged UNITAF to do more than just tolerate warehoused weapons. The secretary-general wanted UNITAF to use its superior firepower, discipline, unified command and control, and liberal mandate to forcibly disarm the Somali factions and destroy their weapons. This was seen as essential to preparing a more secure environment for the follow-on peacekeeping mission that would be able to turn its attention to facilitating humanitarian relief and long-term political reconciliation. But the peace enforcement mission was not under UN command. In Somalia, the George H.W. Bush and the Bill Clinton administrations decided that UNITAF should facilitate humanitarian aid but not do anything more, especially anything that might entail some risk-taking for US troops. The secretary-general urged disarmament to no avail.

Because the United States won the argument about disarmament in Somalia, the follow-on UN peacekeeping mission, UNOSOM II, deployed into an environment in which there was no peace to keep. Recognizing this, the Security Council gave UNOSOM II authorization to employ liberal rules of engagement to achieve its mission. Despite this, national contingents deployed to UNOSOM II decided to read the rules of engagement in their own way, leading to wide variations in activities by the participants. This individual interpretation of mandates continues in all operations, a natural result of the nonbinding nature of Security Council resolutions. In Somalia and elsewhere, confusion over the mandate and rules of engagement created chaos for the peacekeepers. The Somali factions saw this chaos and took advantage of it.

In early June, a confrontation between the Somali National Alliance (SNA) led by Mohammed Farah Aideed and Pakistani UNOSOM II troops resulted in the killing of twenty-four Pakistanis and the wounding of scores of others. The Security Council then issued Resolution 837 (June 6, 1993) condemning the deaths and reaffirming that the secretary-general could order UNOSOM II to take "all necessary measures against all those responsible for the armed attacks." To US policymakers and military commanders, this was a green light for US troops to take measures to apprehend Aideed and key leaders of the SNA. From June to early October, the US troops assigned to UNOSOM II made it their business to protect other countries' peacekeepers by going on the offensive against Somalis who had targeted peacekeepers. The infamous "Black Hawk Down" incident on October 3, 1993, in which eighteen US servicemen were killed, resulted from this split mandate. Thereafter, the entire UNOSOM II operation became a self-protection mission until it disbanded the following March.

What happened in Somalia probably influenced the poor treatment of peacekeepers in other ongoing and future operations. The UN Protection Force (UNPROFOR) in the former Yugoslavia, deployed from 1992 through 1995, was routinely attacked and impeded by Bosnian Serb and Bosnian Croat forces, as well as by the forces of the government of Croatia. The UNPROFOR force commander declared that the peacekeeping operation would maintain its neutrality even in the face of this provocation because he did not want to cross the "Mogadishu line" and get the peacekeepers embroiled in the civil war with disastrous consequences.[6] Ultimately, the Security Council authorized NATO to protect the UN peacekeepers, so mistreated were they by the combatants. Even in the face of NATO threats, in the spring of 1994 Bosnian Serb forces took peacekeepers hostage, killed a British peacekeeper, and shot down a British Harrier. The knowledge that NATO was committed to the protection of UNPROFOR only made UNPROFOR troops pawns to be played with by the Bosnian Serb forces. Over the next year, a pattern developed "in which the Western alliance threatened but did not straightforwardly respond to Serbian aggression, because they feared all-out war between the 100,000-strong Serbian forces and the significantly outnumbered UN forces."[7] And, the presence of peacekeepers and the air strikes of NATO did nothing to stop the mass murder of Bosnian Muslim men and boys committed by Serbian forces, particularly in the horrible summer of 1995.

Lessons from Somalia were no doubt learned by combatants in Rwanda as well. The Rwandan *génocidaires* learned that peacekeepers would have neither the means nor the mandate to respond forcefully even in self-defense and that Western countries would pull out of an operation rather than suffer Black Hawk Down–like fatalities among their troops. The UN Security Council ordered the peacekeeping forces to be withdrawn at the start of the Rwandan genocide that killed 800,000 people in three months. Some courageous peacekeepers stayed to witness and help in whatever way they could.

In the 1990s alone, the Security Council authorized thirty-four peacekeeping operations (involving both forces and military observer missions), compared to the eighteen operations launched from 1948 to 1988. Many of these blended UN peacekeeping and UN-authorized peace enforcement operations with increasingly complex tasks for the peacekeepers.

Multidimensional Peace Operations

The United Nations says this about present-day peacekeeping:

> Today's multidimensional peacekeeping operations are called upon not only to maintain peace and security, but also to facilitate political processes, protect civilians, assist in the disarmament, demobilization and reintegration of former combatants; support constitutional processes and the organization of elections, protect and promote human rights and assist in restoring the rule of law and extending legitimate state authority.[8]

These operations deploy to places where violence may still be occurring; local authorities may not be able to provide security; large numbers of people may have been displaced; society may be divided along ethnic, regional, or religious lines; large numbers of people may be armed including children; and grave human rights violations may have occurred or still be occurring. Increasingly peacekeepers have been given broader authority to respond in these situations, but not always with the means to respond. Often, other actors must intervene militarily to provide the muscle when the peacekeepers cannot.

Another example from the end of the last century and into the twenty-first century illustrates the types of tasks—and limitations— facing peace operations today. The United Nations Mission in Sierra Leone (UNAMSIL), according to the United Nations,

may serve as a model for successful peacekeeping, as well as a proto-
type for the UN's new emphasis on peacebuilding. Over the course
of its mandate, the Mission disarmed tens of thousands of ex-fighters,
assisted in holding national elections, helped to rebuild the country's
police force, and contributed towards rehabilitating the infrastructure and bringing government services to local communities.[9]

UNAMSIL was the first peacekeeping operation to be given Chapter VII
authorization to protect civilians, an authorization that did not protect UNAMSIL from having hundreds of its own troops from being
taken hostage. UNAMSIL is thus a lesson but not just because of its
success.

War came to Sierra Leone in 1991 when a small antigovernment
group calling itself the Revolutionary United Front (RUF) took up
arms against the government. The RUF was supported in part by
Charles Taylor's militia in neighboring Liberia. The Liberian civil war
had brought the Economic Community of West African States military observer group known as ECOMOG to Sierra Leone. When the
RUF started the war in Sierra Leone, ECOMOG was preoccupied with
ending the war in Liberia and remained out of the fighting in Sierra
Leone. After a year of fighting the RUF, the Sierra Leone army overthrew the government. The war with the RUF continued. This phase
of the war came to an end with the muscular intervention of a mercenary group from South Africa called Executive Outcomes that was
employed to protect the diamond mining area. Another mercenary
group, Sandline, participated in the civil war as a weapons supplier,
and it was also funded by diamond mines. The Sierra Leone war was
the diamond conflict.

In February 1996, an election was held, and a civilian government
was brought to power. The RUF, however, did not participate in
the elections and continued its fight. The weak civilian government
had not yet stood up an effective security force when it ordered
Executive Outcomes to leave the country at the start of 1997. Within
a few months, an alliance of the RUF and the army overthrew the
government. In Resolution 1132 in October, the UN Security Council
imposed an oil and arms embargo on the rebel alliance/junta and
authorized ECOMOG to implement the embargo. This authorization
became the basis for ECOMOG's military intervention in the civil

war. Initially, just the threat of ECOMOG intervention brought the junta and the exiled civilian government together to agree to a cease-fire. All sides agreed to work toward normalized politics and allow ECOMOG, the United Nations, and various UN agencies to enter and assist Sierra Leone. This agreement was never implemented, and the fighting continued.

The war took on a new dimension in February 1998 when ECOMOG was attacked by the rebel alliance and so launched a massive coun-terattack. Within weeks, ECOMOG had expelled the junta from the capital, Freetown, and within a month the civilian government was restored. The Security Council then ended the oil and arms embargo and, in June, established a small military observer mission, the UN Observer Mission in Sierra Leone (UNOMSIL). UNOMSIL was tasked with monitoring and advising the government on matters related to the disarming of combatants and the restructuring of security forces. UNOMSIL's work was to be under the protection of ECOMOG. The fight with the rebel alliance continued, however, culminating in a fierce rebel attack on Freetown in December–January in which some 6,000 persons may have been killed. UNOMSIL was evacuated in early January on the order of the Security Council. By the end of the month, ECOMOG had fought its way back into Freetown, expelling the rebels and again reinstalling the civilian government.

Within a few months, talks had concluded with an agreement to form a unity government, in which the head of the RUF would serve as vice president. In October 1999, UNOMSIL was officially dis-banded, and a 6,000-person strong United Nations Mission in Sierra Leone (UNAMSIL) was started. UNAMSIL was given Chapter VII authority to protect civilians in its areas of control and within its abil-ity. This was the first time a peacekeeping operation would be given a civilian protection mandate. By early 2000, the Security Council noted that the RUF violence continued with widespread human rights violations. Further, because of the RUF, little progress had been made on the disarmament, demilitarization, and reintegration program for former combatants, and no progress had been made on abductees and child soldiers. In February 2000, in Resolution 1289, UNAMSIL was increased to 11,000 uniformed personnel with an expanded mandate that included the provision of law enforcement and security at key sites, roads, buildings and the airport, and the guarding and destruction of weapons and munitions collected from combatants. To complete its expanded mandate, the Security Council affirmed that UNAMSIL "may take the necessary action to ensure the security and freedom of movement of its personnel and, within its capabilities and areas of deployment, to afford protection to civilians under imminent threat of physical violence, taking into account the responsibilities of the Government of Sierra Leone." The key problem here is suggested in the phrase "within its capabilities" since its capabilities were on paper and not in reality. Fortunately for UNAMSIL, ECOMOG was still present with as many as 8,000 battle-tested troops.

Then, in April 2000, the remaining ECOMOG troops departed, creating a security vacuum. The next month, 500 UNAMSIL peace-keepers were taken hostage by the RUF. The RUF took control of the peacekeepers' armored troop transports, uniforms, and weapons, and started advancing on Freetown. At this point, another external actor intervened. The United Kingdom had up to 500 diplomatic and military personnel in its former colony. When the RUF started marching on Freetown in May 2000, the UK ordered the evacuation of its personnel. To facilitate this, and to liberate the peacekeepers, the British government ordered 1,200 ground forces and five warships to Sierra Leone. By the middle of May, the British forces began engaging the RUF in battle. The British government and military command made it clear that British forces were not in Sierra Leone to serve under the UN command. While the British military intervention was under way, the Security Council authorized the expansion of UNAMSIL to 13,000 uniformed personnel.

By the end of May 2000—an action-packed month—British forces had altered their mission away from engaging the RUF to training and equipping the Sierra Leone army. Because the army—like the rebels—was packed with child soldiers, this meant that British forces were training and arming children. UNAMSIL took over the training of police forces. To stop the financing of RUF weapons purchases, the Security Council imposed an embargo on diamonds from Sierra Leone in July.

The war in Sierra Leone was one in which loyalties shifted continuously and groups took whatever advantage they had. One rebel group called the West Side Boys had joined forces with the army when the British forces arrived. In August 2000, the West Side Boys took their British-supplied weapons and turned them on their British military partners, taking them hostage. The British freed their personnel in a military action in September. Then, the British returned to train and assist, staying two more years until the war ended. While the British troops were present, UNAMSIL disarmed "tens of thousands of ex-fighters, assisted in holding national elections [in May 2002], helped to rebuild the country's police force, and contributed towards rehabilitating the infrastructure and bringing government services to local communities."[10] The May 2002 elections brought to office the same person elected in 1996 (and deposed many times). The British withdrew in July 2002, although 200 personnel remained behind to advise and protect the government. Finally, three years later, UNAMSIL was disbanded. Another United Nations political operation was begun to assist Sierra Leone to consolidate its achievements and move forward.

UNAMSIL had significant achievements once the situation was secure enough for it to work. Securing the environment required more force than UNAMSIL was able or willing to use, despite its size and a civilian protection mandate. The combatants needed to be forcibly stopped and not allowed to simply lay low and redeploy when the situation allowed. Two different limited military interventions—by ECOMOG and the British—were effective when their forces were on the offense, but less effective when they went into a defensive, train, and assist mode.

The United Nations Development Programme summarized the conflict in Sierra Leone in a way that captures the essence of the conflicts faced by peacekeepers today:

> The war was characterized by widespread atrocities, including the abduction of children and systematic rape. The conditions that led to the war included a repressive predatory state, dependence on mineral rents, the impact of structural adjustment, a large excluded youth population, the availability of small arms after the end of the Cold War, and interference from regional neighbours.[11]

Peacekeeping and peace enforcement within the United Nations system were creative interpretations of what the Charter and the interests of member states would allow. Clearly, traditional peacekeeping can work only in limited situations, and peace enforcement is limited by the interests of the lead states. In Sierra Leone, the British government did not permit its forces to engage in offensive actions that might have eliminated the threat posed by the RUF years before war finally ended. In Somalia, a decade before, the UN secretary-general begged the US enforcement forces of UNITAF to disarm combatants, but the US government wanted the engagement to be limited in scope and time frame. The combatants waited out UNITAF and then turned on the UN peacekeepers when the mission changed. The combatants in Sierra Leone did the same thing when ECOMOG withdrew.

Improving Peace Support Operations

In August 2000, the secretary-general published a report on how to improve the effectiveness of UN peacekeeping operations. That report is known as the Brahimi Report for its chair, Lakhdar Brahimi. The report offered this summary of the challenges facing peacekeeping in 2000, challenges which persist still:

> Without renewed commitment on the part of Member States, significant institutional change and increased financial support, the United Nations will not be capable of executing the critical peacekeeping and peace-building tasks that the Member States assign to it in coming months and years. There are many tasks which United Nations peacekeeping forces should not be asked to undertake and many places they should not go. But when the United Nations does send its forces to uphold the peace, they must be prepared to confront the lingering forces of war and violence, with the ability and determination to defeat them.[12]

The report made fifty-seven recommendations for improving peacekeeping that were incorporated into a *Handbook on United Nations Multidimensional Peacekeeping Operations* in 2003. First and foremost, as the *Handbook* notes, "there must be a peace to keep. The parties to a conflict must be willing to cease fighting and pursue their objectives through political and other non-violent means." Peacekeeping must be an appropriate option, and it "must be part of a more comprehensive strategy to help resolve a conflict." And, "the comprehensive strategy must take into account the regional dimension to ensure that gains made in addressing the problems that contributed to a conflict are not undermined by problems in neighboring countries."[13] And, of course, mandates must be achievable, with an appropriate number of trained and equipped troops authorized and provided by members. Above all, member states must be committed to the long-term effort necessary to ensure lasting peace.

A decade later after some reorganization, the heads of the departments of peacekeeping operations and field support issued a "nonpaper" (i.e., not official policy but a statement to facilitate more discussion) on peacekeeping. The "nonpaper" suggested that the same problems with peace support operations continued, as

> the scale and complexity of peacekeeping today are mismatched with existing capabilities. The demands of the past decade have exposed the limitations of past reforms and the basic systems, structures and tools of an organization not designed for the size, tempo and tasks of today's missions. Political strains are also showing. Divisions within the international community impact the ability of some missions to act effectively on the ground, and Member States' attention is at times spread thin among competing peace and security priorities. Each new operation is built voluntarily and from scratch on the assumption that adequate resources can be found and is run on individual budget, support and administrative lines. Peacekeeping in its current form requires more predictable, professional and adaptable capabilities. It needs a global system to match the global enterprise it has become.
>
> Peacekeeping is a core function of the United Nations. Continuous improvement is essential but a piecemeal approach is not an option.[14]

The "nonpaper" went on to call for a "new agenda for partnership" between its member states, the United Nations system, and regional organizations.

In this same period, the Security Council made a point of recognizing that peacekeeping mandates needed to consider special circumstances. In Resolution 1261 in 1999, the Council noted that all actors to a conflict should refrain from using children as combatants and that the United Nations system should facilitate the disarmament, demobilization, rehabilitation, and reintegration of child soldiers. In Resolution 1612 in 2005, the Council reminded actors of their obligations to protect children and called for the inclusion of child-protection language in all peacekeeping mandates. In this same resolution, the Council reminded peacekeepers to refrain from engaging in the sexual exploitation of children—a practice of some peacekeepers in far too many operations. Through 2016, the special needs of children in war have been noted in at least ten Council resolutions.

The Security Council also noted the special circumstances of women in peace and security in a series of resolutions starting with Resolution 1325 in 2000. The Council noted the special toll conflict takes on women and children because of rape, other sexual abuse, and exploitation, and noted the obligation of peacekeeping operations to consider the postconflict needs of women and children. Peacekeeping operations were ordered to adopt a "gendered understanding" of the situation at hand, which would require greater inclusion of women in all roles in peacekeeping. According to a report called "Gender Equality in UN Peacekeeping Operations," UN operations should be inclusive of men and women in the areas deployed, nondiscriminatory in the execution of the mandate including protecting women and girls from "sexual and gender based violence and harmful traditional practices," balanced in terms of the staffing in all posts and levels, and efficient in promoting peace activities to women and men, girls and boys.[15]

The results of this call for gender awareness and inclusion in the fielding of operations have been uneven at best.[16] For example, one of the largest current operations, the United Nations Mission in Republic of South Sudan (UNMISS), had 10,000 troops in mid-2016, but only 400 or so of these were women. The inclusion of women in UNMISS is critical since South Sudan has been the site of massive and pervasive rape and sexual violence against women and girls.[17] Women leaders are rare in peacekeeping as well. The United Nations Peacekeeping Force in Cyprus (UNFICYP) is the only operation with women in the leadership roles of political head and force commander. UNFICYP has a few more than 1,000 personnel and has been a feature of the Cypriot political/military landscape since it deployed in 1964.

Hybrid Peace Operations

One of the key suggested improvements for peacekeeping was to make greater use of regional forces to provide "regional solutions to regional problems."[18] Countries in a region are assumed to have more immediate interests in local peace and security, and so they should be expected to devote more time and energy to build lasting peace. Thus, the United Nations would partner with regional organizations to create hybrid peace operations. This idea was facilitated by a negative phenomenon as well—Western peacekeepers had retreated from participation in United Nations peacekeeping in the 2000s as they turned inward for financial reasons or turned elsewhere in the global war on terror.

Regional solutions for regional problems have been only directed at problems in Africa. The first hybrid mission was in Darfur in Sudan. In July 2007, in Resolution 1769, the Security Council authorized the African Union/United Nations Hybrid operation in Darfur (UNAMID). This operation is an integrated effort of the two organizations under the single command of the designated AU force commander. The mission is funded through the United Nations. UNAMID has Chapter VII authority to "take the necessary action, in the areas of deployment of its forces and as it deems within its capabilities" to protect itself, humanitarian workers, and civilians, as it assists with the implementation of the Darfur Peace Agreement. UNAMID has a multidimensional peacekeeping mandate, yet it remains dependent on the consent and goodwill of the local and national authorities of Sudan.

Earlier that same year—2007—the Security Council authorized the African Union to deploy a peace enforcement operation in Somalia (Resolution 1744). Although not called a hybrid operation, the African Union Mission in Somalia (AMISOM) operated as one. AMISOM was authorized by the UN Security Council, assisted by a UN political mission, commanded by the African Union using troops from

AU member states, and funded by the European Union through the United Nations Trust Fund for Somalia. AMISOM was the product of the integrated actions of three organizations—the United Nations, the African Union, and the European Union. And, AMISOM benefitted from the air power and special operations forces of the United States. AMISOM was given a Chapter VII authorization to use all necessary means to support the long-term stabilization of Somalia.

Earlier in this chapter, we discussed the UN peace operations in Somalia from 1992 to 1995. After UNOSOM II was withdrawn in March 1995, Somalia and its people were abandoned to civil war. Transitional governments were attempted in fits and starts, but warfare continued in parts of the country. In 2006, the Islamic Courts Union (ICU) managed to exert control over the southern part of Somalia and the capital Mogadishu. The ICU established Sharia law in its areas of control. Claiming to be under threat by the ICU and on the invitation of the (deposed) Somali transitional government, Ethiopia launched a military intervention into Somalia with US air support in July 2006. By the end of the following year, the Ethiopian force had expelled the ICU from Mogadishu, causing the ICU to splinter. One of its splinters was al Shabaab, a group loyal to al Qaeda. The war continued even as the Security Council began some preparations to field a peacekeeping operation to support the transitional government.

Fearing what would happen in the interim between an Ethiopian withdrawal and the creation of a peacekeeping operation, the African Union proposed sending an enforcement operation to Somalia. The Security Council, in Resolution 1744 (February 2007), authorized AMISOM to support the "long-term stabilization and post-conflict restoration of Somalia" in conjunction with the transitional government. AMISOM was authorized to use all necessary measures in support of the government for six months. In the meantime, the secretary-general would send out a technical assessment team to assess what kind of peacekeeping operation would be necessary. Ethiopia continued its combat operations with US air support for another year or so, waiting on AMISOM to deploy.

Al Shabaab proved a difficult group to eject particularly in AMISOM's early years when its troops tended to stay within more secure areas.

By 2014, AMISOM—with the help of US air strikes, drone attacks, and raids—had become more effective against al Shabaab, hurting it so much that Shabaab started resorting to asymmetrical actions as it lost control of areas and lost fighters. Recall that AMISOM was authorized in 2007 to help stabilize Somalia and seven years later it finally managed to strike decisive blows against al Shabaab. Al Shabaab retained considerable local support in places where the Somali national forces and AMISOM were viewed with suspicion. And, AMISOM commanders made their own troops vulnerable by using regular full-troop replacements. According to a January 2016 report by the BBC, Shabaab would plan its attacks around these full-troop replacements, attacking new troops who had not yet familiarized themselves with their new area of deployment.[19]

AMISOM's drawn-out war with Shabaab had consequences for its contributors. Kenya suffered from al Shabaab terrorist attacks in its own territory, notably the Westgate Mall attacks in 2013 and an attack on a university that left nearly 150 Kenyans dead. The price of terrorist attacks and maintaining the world's largest refugee camp were issues of contention in Kenyan domestic politics. And, multiple media reported that AMISOM personnel went unpaid for months, causing more domestic controversy in the troop-contributing countries.

In mid-2016, AMISOM remained a war-fighting force, as clearly demonstrated in Resolution 2297 in July 2016 in which AMISOM was authorized to "continue to conduct offensive operations against al Shabaab and other armed opposition groups" for the period until May 2017 when the Council would revisit the situation. In this same resolution, the Security Council noted that the situation in Somalia still remained too insecure for a peacekeeping operation. And, the Council made several appeals for more states to contribute to the UN Fund for Somalia. The length of this joint operation had taken its toll on the funders: In January 2016, the European Union cut its funding to the operation by 20 percent. In the same month, al Shabaab launched an attack on a camp of Kenyan troops, killing perhaps 200 Kenyans.

UNAMID is the face of hybrid peacekeeping, and AMISOM is the face of hybrid peace enforcement. Both suffer from the same problems that have beset peace operations in the past although they face bigger, more complicated scenarios. The needs remain intense, even as the contributing countries grow more depleted and frustrated. Unfortunately for all, the United Nations has few alternatives at its disposal.

In August 2016, Security Council Resolution 2304 authorized the expansion of UNMISS. This mission was started in July 2011 to help the newest UN member state after it achieved independence from Sudan. In 2014, South Sudan plunged into civil war. In the summer of 2016, the fighting came home to the UN mission with attacks against "civilians, United Nations personnel, premises and property." In Resolution 2304, the Council authorized UNMISS to use all necessary means to carry out its mandate. To facilitate that in the face of civil war, UNMISS would be increased to 17,000 troops, including a 4,000-strong Regional Protection Force. The details of this will be difficult to negotiate and implement—such as who will send the additional forces to either UNMISS or the Regional Protection Force—given the exhaustion of the African Union. Regional solutions for regional problems meant that the African Union's members were already engaged in UNMISS, in UNAMID in Darfur, in the African Union Mission in Sudan (AMIS), as well as in AMISOM in Somalia, and other operations on the continent. And, of course, a new trust fund will need to be established with a new set of benefactors.

In the next chapter, we finally introduce the concept of human security. The civilian protection mandates given now to peacekeepers and the enforcement operations designed to confront humanitarian disasters are, of course, about protecting human beings. But in the next chapter, we learn when and how human security finally gets a place on the international agenda.

Recap

In this chapter, we discussed how the UN Charter has been creatively interpreted to allow the United Nations to field peace support operations first for interstate and then for intrastate conflicts. We examined the development of traditional peacekeeping, peace enforcement and multidimensional peacekeeping, and the evolving idea of civilian protection. More recently, the United Nations has approved hybrid peacekeeping operations and hybrid peace enforcement operations.

Discussion Questions

1. Discuss the events that led to the creation of neutral peacekeeping.
2. What are the UN Charter foundations for peacekeeping?
3. Discuss the elements of UN peacekeeping operations.
4. Discuss the elements of UN-approved peace enforcement operations.
5. Describe the environment into which multidimensional peace operations are deployed.
6. What types of tasks are required of multidimensional peace operations?
7. Discuss what a civilian protection mandate is and how it developed in UNAMSIL.
8. Describe the continuing difficulties facing UN peace operations.
9. What special circumstances beyond civilian protection must be included in peacekeeping mandates?
10. Discuss how UNAMID is a hybrid peacekeeping operation.
11. Discuss how AMISOM is a hybrid peace enforcement operation.

8

Human Security

In This Chapter

Introduction
Defining Human Security
The Geneva Conventions
The Post–Cold War Human Security Agenda
Protecting People from Large-Scale Violence
Civilian Protection Becomes Humanitarian War
The Future of Human Security
Recap
Discussion Questions

Introduction

The world can sometimes seem to be full of scared people—those displaced, those running for their lives, those looking for something better, and those who do not want foreigners among them. According to the United Nations, in the world today there are sixty-five million forcibly displaced people, twenty-one million of them are refugees, and forty million are internally displaced. At the same time, the domestic politics of so many countries is infused with anti-immigrant, antiforeigner, anti-refugee sentiments. The campaign in favor of Brexit in 2016 was waged using pictures of scores of walking Syrian refugees with the suggestion that they were breaching Britain's shores. In the United States a major party's presidential candidate engaged in the same fear-filled rhetoric aimed at keeping unwanted others out.

At the United Nations in early September 2016, member states argued over a nonbinding draft agreement on refugees and migrants. Western Europe and Russia objected to making any pledge to resettle refugees; African and Latin American countries wanted language about migrants, not refugees; and "the United States suggested a phrase asserting that detention is 'seldom' good for children" because it detains unaccompanied, undocumented children coming into it from Mexico and Central America.[1] Someone must have wanted the draft document to say that detention is never good for children, prompting the US suggestion. The discussions were in advance of a special world summit on refugees in September 2016.

The United States got what it wanted in the draft document called the New York Declaration for Refugees and Migrants (A/71/L.1, September 13, 2016):

> Recognizing that detention for the purposes of determining migration status is seldom, if ever, in the best interests of the child, we will use it only as a measure of last resort, in the least restrictive setting, for the shortest possible period of time, under conditions that respect their human rights and in a manner that takes into account, as a primary consideration, the best interest of the child, and we will work towards the ending of this practice.

Those who opposed detaining children got the "if ever" put in the statement, one might imagine. And, African and Latin American countries got what they wanted as the declaration put upfront that "though their treatment is governed by *separate legal frameworks*, refugees and migrants have the same universal human rights and fundamental freedoms" (emphasis mine). And, the only mention of pledges to take in refugees was to those already made and not to those that should be made.

Still, a fundamental point in the draft New York Declaration evokes the sentiments of *A More Secure World* in 2004 (discussed in chapter 6) which stated: "No State, no matter how powerful, can by its own efforts alone make itself invulnerable to today's threats." The declaration makes this call to common purpose:

> Large movements of refugees and migrants have political, economic, social, developmental, humanitarian and human rights ramifications, which cross all borders. These are global phenomena that call for global approaches and global solutions. *No one State can manage such movements on its own* [emphasis mine].

Meanwhile, the International Organization for Migration reported that 3,198 migrants had perished attempting to cross the Mediterranean in 2016.[2]

By now, readers of this book will know that the reason states can put such obstacles in the way of human safety is because states come first. And, of course, the state has an absolute right to defend itself against threats, and no one but the state may sit in judgment of how threats are defined and protected against. This is the case even though there would be no need for countries if there were no people! People form the basis of countries—and this point comes to shape the evolving idea of human security that we finally discuss in this penultimate chapter.

Defining Human Security

Like so many essential terms we have discussed, the term "human security" does not have a standard definition. But, there are commonly accepted elements or characteristics of human security. In 2005, the UN General Assembly approved a nonbinding document (A/RES/60/1 2005) that contained a paragraph on human security that set out some of the accepted elements:

> We stress the right of people to live in freedom and dignity, free from poverty and despair. We recognize that all individuals, in particular vulnerable people, are entitled to freedom from fear and freedom

from want, with an equal opportunity to enjoy all their rights and fully develop their human potential. To this end, we commit ourselves to discussing and defining the notion of human security in the General Assembly.

Human security is conceptualized as the freedom from fear of violence, the freedom from want, and the freedom to live in human dignity. The Human Security Unit of the UN secretariat's Office for the Coordination of Humanitarian Affairs makes a useful distinction between these freedoms. The freedom from fear involves a more immediate-term matter of *protection* through national and international norms, practices, and institutions. This freedom "implies a 'top-down' approach," with states having the primary responsibility for its protection.[3] This freedom from fear is the basis of the discussion in this chapter. The freedom from want and the freedom to live in dignity constitute longer-term freedoms that come with the *empowerment* of individuals from the "bottom-up," in that economic development, education, and full participation in decision-making processes allow "people to develop their resilience to difficult conditions" while upholding human dignity.[4]

All of these freedoms are modern conceptualizations. It took a long time historically to reach a point where discussions of human security achieve some international prominence. But, "human security" is still "based on national ownership" according to a 2012 General Assembly statement (A/RES/66/290 2012). We'll return to this at the end of the chapter. For now, let's consider the development of the idea of human security in terms of the freedom from the fear of violence.

The Geneva Conventions

Despite the grasp of Westphalian ideas on the state system since 1648, there have been arguments all along that an emphasis on states-first missed the more primary and ethical goal of securing human beings. But because of Westphalia, we know that the state system understands human security primarily as derivative of and instrumental for state security.

There are modern international agreements whose purpose is to protect humans from the excesses of states pursuing their security through violence. Perhaps the most important of these agreements are the Geneva Conventions and their Additional Protocols. The Geneva Conventions were started by the humanitarian work of a single person who wanted to alleviate human suffering caused by war. States agreed to the Geneva Conventions over time because these conventions were for the most part about protecting soldiers—a key state asset.

The idea for an agreement between states regarding the treatment of soldiers began in a single bloody battle over Italian unification in June 1859. The Battle of Solferino involved 300,000 French and Austrian troops. Over the course of one day, 6,000 troops were killed and 40,000 wounded. Caring for the wounded was a French medic named Henry Dunant, who took from the ordeal some ideas about alleviating the suffering of soldiers on the battlefield.[5] Dunant and a handful of other men formed the Geneva Public Welfare Society to put his ideas into practice. At the bidding of this society—later to be called the International Committee of the Red Cross—the Swiss government hosted a conference of governments, organizations, and individuals. The First Geneva Convention was adopted in 1864 as a result of this conference.

Four Geneva Conventions and two Additional Protocols describe the proper treatment of combatants and civilians in war. A third Additional Protocol concerning the emblems of the Red Cross and Red Crescent societies came into force in 2005. The third Additional Protocol is not important for this discussion. The titles of the relevant agreements inform us of their content:

- First Geneva Convention (adopted in 1864 and last revised in 1949): Convention (I) for the Amelioration of the Condition of the Wounded and Sick in Armed Forces in the Field
- Second Geneva Convention (adopted in 1949 as a successor to a 1907 treaty): Convention (II) for the Amelioration of the Condition of the Wounded, Sick and Shipwrecked Members of Armed Forces of Sea

- Third Geneva Convention (adopted in 1929 and last revised in 1949): Convention (III) relative to the Treatment of Prisoners of War
- Fourth Geneva Convention (adopted in 1949): Convention (IV) relative to the Protection of Civilian Persons in Time of War
- Protocol I (adopted 1977): Protocol Additional to the Geneva Conventions of 12 August 1949, and relating to the Protection of Victims of International Armed Conflicts
- Protocol II (adopted 1977): Protocol Additional to the Geneva Conventions of 12 August 1949, and relating to the Protection of Victims of Non-International Armed Conflicts

The Fourth Geneva Convention and first and second Additional Protocols concern the protection of civilians in armed conflicts. During wartime, individuals are either civilians or combatants. These designations are important since each has certain rights and protections. A combatant is a member of the armed forces of a party to a conflict, whether the forces are under the command of a recognized government or not. Combatants have "the right to participate directly in hostilities," according to Protocol I, Article 43, Section 2. The category of "special quasi-combatants"—which might include military subcontractors and perhaps even international terrorists—was rejected in the negotiations of Protocol I.[6] Civilians who take "a direct or active role in hostilities" can be subject to attack. This would apply to civilians accompanying or supporting parties to a conflict, such as military subcontractors.[7]

"A civilian is any person who does not belong to any of the following categories: members of the armed forces, militias or volunteer corps, organized resistance movements, and residents of an occupied territory who spontaneously take up arms."[8] Protocol I, Article 50, Section 1, states, "In case of doubt whether a person is a civilian, that person shall be considered to be a civilian." Further, "the presence within the civilian population of individuals who do not come within the definition of civilians does not deprive the population of its civilian character" (Protocol I, Article 50, Section 3). Thus, subjecting a civilian neighborhood to siege or attack because of the alleged or actual presence of combatants is illegal since the neighborhood and its people retain the protections afforded to civilians.

Civilians, civilian objects, and civilian livelihoods cannot be subject to attack by parties to a conflict; only combatants and military property can be subject to attack. Civilians cannot be used as hostages or human shields or receive differential treatment based on race, religion, nationality, or political allegiance. Civilians cannot be subject to torture, rape, or enslavement; "outrages upon personal dignity"; collective punishment and reprisals; or deportation; and cannot be attacked with biological or chemical weapons.[9]

Despite the Geneva Convention definition of a civilian, the concept seems difficult for combatants to grasp in practical terms. Hanadi Jaradat, the Palestinian suicide bomber discussed in chapter 1, lost protected civilian status when she obtained and put on her explosive belt. In response to Jaradat's suicide bombing, Israeli authorities destroyed her family's home. Unless all the members of her family were combatants and their home was a military installation, the Israeli authorities violated the Geneva Conventions by this act of reprisal. But Israeli authorities might respond that Jaradat's family and all the families of terrorists serve as a support network for terrorism against Israel. To eradicate terrorist threats to the state and people of Israel, Israeli authorities must treat all Palestinians as enemies. Israeli authorities have not hesitated to act preemptively in the name of national security, at times rounding up all young Palestinian men who meet the "terrorist" profile, although this, too, would violate the Geneva Conventions. Yet this example and the broader Israeli-Palestinian situation are marked by ambiguity and complexity; as Hugo Slim notes, many people find the idea of protected civilians to be meaningless in militarized societies.[10]

In the Syrian conflict, the Assad regime and its Russian ally used "scorched-earth tactics of siege and bombardment" to clear opposition-held cities and neighborhoods. *New York Times* reporters Anne Barnard and Somini Sengupta explain the Syrian and Russian policy: "Make life intolerable and death likely. Open an escape route, or offer a deal to those who leave and surrender. Let people trickle out. Kill whoever stays. Repeat until a deserted cityscape is yours."[11]

This "starve-or-submit" policy violated the Geneva Conventions. Syria and Russia took their violations further in September 2016 when they launched three hours of air strikes on a United Nations and Red Crescent aid convoy—which they had previously agreed could go into opposition-held neighborhoods in Aleppo. The strikes did more than attack the convoy, they also targeted the headquarters of local aid workers, and their vehicles, and the aid workers themselves in order to kill the first-responders. All of these acts are violations of the Geneva Conventions. In the Security Council, the United States and United Kingdom called Russia's actions "barbarism" and "war crimes."[12] The civilians throughout Syria but particularly those targeted in the aid convoy attack were distinguishable from combatants. There could be no legitimate claims of the fog of war.

In such cases where civilians and combatants *are* distinguishable from one another, claims of "military necessity" are not legitimate. So, in such cases, what happens? Would there have been any way to stop the harm to civilians or prevent it in the first place? Is there any way to hold the responsible parties accountable? These questions will be considered later in this chapter in the discussions of the International Criminal Court and *The Responsibility to Protect*, important parts of the post–Cold War human security agenda.

The Post–Cold War Human Security Agenda

The *Human Development Report 1994* (*HDR 1994*) of the UN Development Programme (UNDP) is credited with creating the momentum for post–Cold War discussions designed to link national security to human security. The *HDR 1994* begins with a simple, evocative statement: "The world can never be at peace unless people have security in their daily lives."[13] The UNDP's mission is to promote sustainable human development, and in 1994 the UNDP boldly linked development with human security. Human development, the UNDP said, is about the "process of widening the range of people's choices," and human security concerns whether "people can exercise these choices safely and freely" with relative confidence in the future. Thus, these are presented as complementary goals.[14] Human development involves what the founders of the United Nations called the "freedom from want," while human security involves the "freedom from fear."

The political context in which the UNDP engaged the issue of human security in the 1990s has been discussed at length throughout this book. A few events might be recalled here to understand why the UNDP linked human development with security in 1994. The Cold War had ended five years before the report, and this initiated a period of optimism regarding international cooperation. The 1991 Gulf War and the follow-on humanitarian intervention in northern Iraq demonstrated how force could be used in common purpose and how broad agreement on the management of international conflict could be achieved. Then the United Nations conducted a largely unsuccessful and in some ways disastrous humanitarian intervention in Somalia and dispatched peacekeepers to Bosnia, facilitating the disintegration of Yugoslavia and a larger war. As the *HDR 1994* went to press with its assertion that human development must be linked to human security, the international community had decided to abandon Somalia, was doing little to stop ethnic cleansing in the former Yugoslav republics, and was about to pass on doing anything about genocide in Rwanda. Human insecurity seemed to be everywhere.

The *HDR 1994* argued that the concept of security needed to be broadened from its previous anchor in state-state conflict. Post–Cold War threats affected rich and poor states differently in the immediate term, but because of global interdependence and interconnections, threats anywhere ultimately were threats everywhere. The UNDP identified seven broad categories of threats to human security: economic, food, health, environmental, personal, community, and political. The UNDP sought to establish clear sets of human security indicators that might serve as an early warning system for the international community to know when to intervene to help prevent crises. Prevention was critical because, in the UNDP's words, "it is less costly and more humane to meet these threats upstream rather than downstream, early rather than late."[15] Moreover, alarms were going off all over the globe.

The UNDP set forth a comprehensive framework for security but one that was "awkward as a policy framework"[16] in the words of a key human security proponent. Lloyd Axworthy served as Canada's minister of foreign affairs from 1996 to 2000. He was instrumental in establishing Canada's human security foreign policy. His view was that the UNDP's broad framework "tended to distract from the central realization that underdevelopment cannot be addressed in the presence of war and its attendant insecurity."[17] Thus, Axworthy proposed that the human security agenda should be focused on personal security from violence as the first and necessary step to achieving broader, longer-term goals.

The first and noteworthy accomplishment of human security advocates was the Ottawa Treaty, formally known as the Convention on the Prohibition of the Use, Stockpiling, Production and Transfer of Anti-Personnel Mines and on Their Destruction. The treaty signatories agreed never to use, develop, produce, stockpile, retain, or transfer antipersonnel mines; to destroy all mines held; and to clear all mine areas within their territories within ten years of signing the treaty.

The landmine ban was initially encouraged by the International Committee of the Red Cross in the 1970s. Later, the issue was taken up by the Vietnam Veterans of America and US senator Patrick Leahy. Ultimately, an organized, coherent International Campaign to Ban Landmines (ICBL) resulted from the efforts of nongovernmental organizations, some governments, and what Axworthy called "citizen-diplomats."[18] Axworthy used his office as Canadian foreign minister to fast-track the campaign, and the treaty was signed in December 1997 and entered into force fifteen months later. There are 161 states parties to the treaty.

"The [landmine] ban was possible because its proponents were able to superimpose a human security framework over what had traditionally been treated as an arms control and dis-armament issue," conclude Mark Gwozdecky and Jill Sinclair.[19] This was facilitated by widespread publicity about the devastating human toll of landmines. Even Superman, Wonder Woman, and Batman appeared in graphic novels published in many languages depicting the dangers of landmines and warning children about them. The campaign to ban landmines found an issue that had resonance for citizens and governments alike.

Not all states are members of the Ottawa Treaty, of course. Some of the countries that did join—states with no landmine problems on their own territory—were initially opposed to it. The United Kingdom and France were shamed into joining the treaty by domestic constituents. British participation in the treaty came at cross-purposes with some British companies that were major manufacturers of antipersonnel mines. But critical civil society groups—who were joined in their mission by Diana, princess of Wales—were more motivated than the status quo business interests to influence official British policy, and the British government finally agreed to join the treaty process.

The Bill Clinton administration pledged to stop all use of landmines by 2006, although it did not sign the Ottawa Treaty. In March 2004, the George W. Bush administration revoked this pledge, reserving the right to use "smart" landmines where it deemed necessary. China and Russia and thirty-three other countries also refused to sign the treaty. Despite not signing the treaty, the United States became "one of the main financial contributors to the global campaign"[20] leading the way in researching better de-mining technologies.

Most of the other nonsignatories were countries with immediate security issues. Chechnya in Russia, according to the ICBL, was one of the most heavily mined places on earth. Nuclear rivals and old foes Pakistan and India did not sign the treaty, nor did North and South Korea. Both sets of countries have deployed mines along their disputed borders. And, finally, the Middle East is a region in which the ban was rejected by all but one country (Jordan).

The same three Security Council permanent members that refused to join the landmine ban treaty also refused to participate in another important human security accomplishment—the International Criminal Court (ICC). The ICC is not the same as the International Court of Justice (ICJ). The ICJ is one of the six main organs of the United Nations. The ICC came into being in July 2002 with the ratification of the Rome Statute by sixty countries. As of mid-2016, there were 124 state parties to the ICC.

The ICC has jurisdiction over crimes of genocide, crimes against humanity, and war crimes (as enumerated in the Geneva Conventions). The Rome Statute also included the "crime of aggression" in

ICC jurisdiction, but there still is no agreement on the definition of "aggression." The primary purpose of the ICC is to hold heads of state accountable for the planning, instigating, ordering, or otherwise aiding and abetting of the execution of the covered crimes.[21] Previously, "violence carried out in the name of the state was shielded from accountability by the fiction of corporate responsibility."[22] That is, national leaders could commit acts of mass violence with impunity because they claimed to be acting not as private people but as representatives of sovereign states.

There are some important limitations on the ICC, limitations that remind us that this is still a states-first system dominated by the fifteen-member Security Council. First, although the ICC is said to be complementary to national criminal courts, in practical terms national prosecution bars ICC action. Second, the court has jurisdiction only over states who are party to the Rome Statute or over states that choose to allow ICC jurisdiction in particular cases. Third, the Security Council retains control over the ICC because it can block ICC investigations and prosecutions on an annual, renewable basis. Finally, Article 98 of the Rome Statute forbids the court to request the surrender of a foreign national for prosecution when the requested state has a treaty obligation with the government of the foreign national that bars surrender of its citizens and personnel.

The power of the Security Council permanent members over the ICC was demonstrated as it came into existence in the summer of 2002. The United States was an early supporter of a standing international criminal court, but by the time the Rome Statute was signed US support had been withdrawn. The Bill Clinton administration signed the Rome Statute without intending to ask the US Senate for its ratification; the George W. Bush administration went further and "unsigned" the Rome Statute. The US position was that the ICC will be used for frivolous and politically motivated prosecutions of US officials. As the court was coming into existence on July 1, 2002, the Bush administration linked it to a veto threat regarding the unrelated matter of renewing the mandate for UN peacekeeping in Bosnia. The United States insisted that the Security Council bar the ICC from investigating and prosecuting any "current or former officials or personnel from a con-tributing State not a Party to the Rome Statute over acts or omissions relating to a United Nations established or authorized operation." The Security Council approved such a limitation for a year, and indicated its intention to renew the suspension each July for another twelve months. The suspension was renewed the following year. But by 2004, the matter did not come before the Security Council. The US-led war in Iraq was under way, and few Americans were involved in UN-led or UN-endorsed peacekeeping operations anywhere. Further, the Bush administration took a different route to avoid the ICC because of a 2002 US law that required countries receiving US military assistance to sign Article 98 agreements with the United States. Like the United States, Russia signed the Rome Statute but did not ratify it. China never signed the statute in the first place.

The ICC could be politically useful to states, and this fact ultimately helped the ICC gain greater authority. In 2005, acknowledging the wishes of some important domestic constituents calling for inter-vention to stop genocide in Darfur, Sudan, the Bush administration abstained on a Security Council referral of the situation in Darfur to the ICC (S/RES/1593, 2005). An abstention does not stop an action; a "no" vote would. The United States did get the Council to insert some qualifications into the referral, including that ICC expenses on the referral would be "borne by the parties to the Rome Statute and those States that wish to contribute voluntarily." After the abstention (which was matched by China, Algeria, and Brazil), the US representative said that the United States remained opposed to the ICC but would not veto the resolution because "of the need for the international com-munity to work together in order to end the climate of impunity in the Sudan" (UNSC Press Release SC/8351, March 31, 2005).

For an administration so opposed to multilateralism of most sorts and the ICC particularly, this was a considerable concession. The next natural step for the ICC was to indict Sudanese president Omar al-Bashir for crimes committed in Darfur (ICC-02/05–01/09). Thus, the self-interested choice of the Bush administration—responding to domestic constituents—opened the door for the ICC to indict a sitting head of state, a remarkable achievement. In 2011, when the Council authorized military action for the purposes of civilian protection in Libya (S/RES/1973), the Council simultaneously made an ICC referral. The Barrack Obama administration strongly supported the resolution and registered no caveats regarding the ICC.

One should not conclude that the Obama administration had no objections to the ICC because it was more multilateral-minded than the Bush administration. The Obama administration did not "re-sign" the Rome Statute or even float the idea of having the Senate consider it. The administration seemed just as inclined to invoke the states-first and America-first claim as its predecessor. Consider the 2008 Convention on Cluster Munitions.

The Convention on Cluster Munitions begins with a clear statement that the banning of cluster munitions is motivated by the singular human security concern "that civilian populations and individual civilians continue to bear the brunt of armed conflict" and that states parties are determined "to put an end for all time to the suffering and casualties caused by cluster munitions at the time of their use, when they fail to function as intended or when they are abandoned." The cluster munitions convention bans the use, development, production, stockpiling, retaining, and transferring of cluster munitions. It came into force in 2010 and currently has 100 states parties.

The United States is not a party to the cluster munitions treaty, nor are Russia, China, Israel, India, and Pakistan. In 2011, these states and more than one hundred others—with the United States taking the lead—tried to write an alternative treaty and urged states to abandon the 2008 treaty. The United States wanted to legitimize the use of *some* cluster munitions (newer and more reliable) and so would not support a ban on the use of any and all cluster munitions. The US proposal was defeated and so the 2008 total ban remained a human security commitment. The United States continued to sell cluster munitions to India, Saudi Arabia, South Korea, Taiwan, and the United Arab Emirates, according to the Arms Control Association.[23] Saudi Arabia used US cluster munitions in 2015 in Yemen, despite an end user agreement that put conditions on the use of the weapons.

Protecting People from Large-Scale Violence

To the extent that any agreement emerged on the issue of international security after the turbulent 1990s, the agreement was that the international community was ill prepared to deal effectively with mass killings. In so many cases in the 1990s, states seemed unable or unwilling to stop violence being done to their own people, and often states were the perpetrators of the abuse. And the community of states seemed unwilling at some times and unable at others to mount effective international humanitarian interventions.

Continuing its human security focus, the government of Canada—again under the leadership of Lloyd Axworthy—sponsored yet another ambitious international effort "to find tactics and strategies of military intervention that [could] fill the current gulf between outdated concepts of peacekeeping and full-scale military operations that may have deleterious impacts on civilians."[24] The effort became the independent International Commission on Intervention and State Sovereignty (ICISS). The "policy challenge" before the ICISS was summed up in this way:

> External military intervention for human protection purposes has been controversial both when it has happened—as in Somalia, Bosnia and Kosovo—and when it has failed to happen, as in Rwanda. For some the new activism has been a long overdue internationalization of the human conscience; for others it has been an alarming breach of an international state order dependent on the sovereignty of states and the inviolability of their territory. For some, again, the only real issue is ensuring that coercive interventions are effective; for others, questions about legality, process and the possible misuse of precedent loom much larger.[25]

Before the commission finished its report, the 9/11 terrorist attacks on the United States occurred. Responding to this event, the commission noted that "human security is indeed indivisible"—both in the sense that human insecurity anywhere was a threat to human security everywhere *and* in the sense that human insecurity in a faraway country could facilitate a successful attack on the world's most powerful state. The events of 9/11 demonstrated that "in an interdependent world, in which security depends on a framework of stable sovereign entities, the existence of fragile states, failing states, states who through weakness or ill-will harbour those dangerous to others, or states that can only maintain internal order by means of gross human rights violations, can constitute a risk to people everywhere."[26]

The ICISS proposed that sovereignty as it developed and has been understood over time entails more than absolute rights; it also entails responsibilities. The responsibilities have two levels: "The primary responsibility for the protection of its people lies with the state itself." But "where a population is suffering serious harm, as a result of internal war, insurgency, repression or state failure, and the state in question is unwilling or unable to halt or avert it, the principle of non-intervention yields to the international responsibility to protect."[27]

How did the ICISS arrive at this responsibility to protect? Sovereignty, as understood since the Treaty of Westphalia, is located in the state rather than in any extraregional authority. In democratic systems, sovereignty resides in the people—popular sovereignty—and the state is granted only that authority necessary to protect the interests of the people—that is, the sovereigns. When a state fails to protect the sovereigns, the state loses its legitimacy. Because the international system is organized to protect the interests of sovereign states, the system also must protect the *source* of the legitimacy of those states—the people. When large-scale loss of life or ethnic cleansing occurs or is likely to occur in the immediate term, someone must protect the sovereigns. If the state cannot or will not, the community must step up to the task.

This may sound like a monumental shift of authority or a monumental interruption or suspension of state authority, but the ICISS made great efforts to indicate that state sovereignty was still critical and that the first line of defense for human protection remained the state. The ICISS also made it clear that the responsibility to protect required more than military intervention. The responsibility was envisioned in three parts: a responsibility to prevent crises, a responsibility to react in "situations of compelling human need with appropriate measures," and a responsibility to rebuild.[28]

Military intervention, if it occurred, should be guided by "just war" principles. First, the intervention must be for the right purpose—to prevent large-scale loss of life and/or genocide—which would be ensured by its multilateral nature. The appropriate authority for determining right purpose was the Security Council, then the General Assembly, then regional organizations, and then, only if all else fails, individual states. The Security Council would authorize such an intervention as a Chapter VII civilian protection mandate. Interventions aimed at stopping systematic political repression, racial discrimination, and similar human rights abuses, thwarting a military coup (even a coup against a democratic government), regime change, or "in response to a terrorist attack on a state's territory and citizens," were *not* envisioned under this proposal.[29] The UN Charter already provided methods for dealing with these problems.

Further, military intervention would be an act of last resort unless impending large-scale loss of life or genocide required immediate reaction. When it occurred, military intervention would employ proportional force rather than engage in tactics that amount to traditional war fighting (i.e., the objective is to save lives, not defeat or destroy an enemy).[30] The intervention force would be given appropriate rules of engagement and plentiful resources to complete the task at hand. Additionally, the mission must have a reasonable prospect for military success and not create greater human insecurity than it seeks to stop. In the words of the ICISS, "It will be the case that some human beings simply cannot be rescued except at unacceptable cost—perhaps of a larger regional conflagration involving major military powers. In such cases, however painful the reality, coercive military action is no longer justified."[31] Because of this, military intervention against any of the permanent members of the Security Council or the other major powers was not envisioned on utilitarian grounds; the prospects for success against a major power would be small to none, and the chances of a greater war would be far too large. Despite the appearance of double standards, political reality and feasibility should govern the responsibility to protect in order to avoid promising more than can or will be delivered to a population in distress. Finally, the inability to mount an intervention in one case should not preclude intervention in any other case.[32]

The Responsibility to Protect was designed to offer a practical and effective method for determining when and how the United Nations should intervene to protect human beings. The effort made by the ICISS to respect the political realities of the international system—that is, to accommodate states and their interests—while still promoting human security was admirable. In this respect, the effort approximated the campaign to ban landmines. Unfortunately, the idea that there is a *responsibility* to prevent, react, and rebuild still fails today in the face of many states' unwillingness to accept international responsibilities.

The invasion of Iraq by a US-led coalition in March 2003 created discord within the UN Security Council and among UN member states. The Bush administration argued after the invasion that the intervention was required to stop massive human rights abuses. The administration claimed that it acted to uphold the principles of the United Nations when other states were not inclined to do so. These assertions—if not examined too closely—might fit into a responsibility to protect argument. But the implications of the Bush administration contention caused alarm in Global South states that the responsibility to protect would be a new excuse for regime change.

Kofi Annan, the then-secretary-general of the United Nations, opposed the US-led war in Iraq as an illegal war and kept pressing forward on developing a strong responsibility to protect ethic. Later, in 2011, Annan's successor Ban Ki-moon would be one of the loudest voices calling for a civilian protection mandate for Libya and Côte d'Ivoire. Annan assembled a High-level Panel on Threats, Challenges and Change to consider war, terrorism, other security and general reform issues confronting the United Nations. The panel's report, *A More Secure World: Our Shared Responsibility*, was issued in December 2004. It embraced the responsibility to protect and attempted to refocus collective security on issues of human security and on the borderless security threats challenging all states. It also repudiated Bush administration justifications for the war in Iraq. But the Iraq War had a shaping impact on the responsibility to protect idea, as demonstrated in the Outcome Document of the 2005 World Summit.

In March 2005, the UN secretary-general issued a report titled *In Larger Freedom: Towards Development, Security and Human Rights for All.*

This report was devoted primarily to suggesting measures that the UN member states should take to reduce extreme poverty or the freedom from want. But attention was paid as well to the freedom from fear of violence. This report formed the agenda for discussions at the World Summit held in the days before the opening of the Sixtieth UN General Assembly session. The 2005 Outcome Document of the World Summit was a reality check for those who advocated a strengthened human security ethic embodied in an international responsibility to protect. The words "responsibility to protect" were included in the Outcome Document but not in association with an expectation about state responsibility that is backed by an international responsibility to prevent, react, and rebuild. The document instead declared that "each individual State has the responsibility to protect its populations from genocide, war crimes, ethnic cleansing and crimes against humanity," and the international community had a limited role to play in this, encouraging and helping states "as appropriate" using "appropriate diplomatic, humanitarian and other peaceful means" in accordance with the UN Charter. Collective action through Chapter VII should be taken in a "timely and decisive manner" on a case-by-case basis (A/60/L.1 para. 138, 139).

As for human security, the Outcome Document had a single paragraph on the subject that came after two paragraphs on children's rights. The paragraph embraced a wide and amorphous definition of human security:

> We stress the right of people to live in freedom and dignity, free from poverty and despair. We recognize that all individuals, in particular vulnerable people, are entitled to freedom from fear and freedom from want, with an equal opportunity to enjoy all their rights and fully develop their human potential. To this end, we commit ourselves to discussing and defining the notion of human security in the General Assembly. (A/RES/60/1, para. 143)

We will return shortly to the General Assembly's views on human security.

Alex Bellamy has offered a history of the 2005 Outcome Document, a history that shows that the "2005 consensus was produced not by the power of humanitarian argument but by bargaining away key tenets of the ICISS's recommendations."[33] The Bush administration's desire not to be bound by any international obligation was promoted successfully by the (acting) US ambassador to the United Nations. The Outcome Document emphasized that the responsibility to protect fell greater on the host state than on the international community and that the Security Council should decide each case on its own merits rather than apply a uniform standard with set criteria that would trigger action.[34]

The poor treatment of the responsibility to protect in the Outcome Document led some to conclude that a window of opportunity to further the human security agenda had been opened and shut too fast.[35] Bellamy concluded in 2006 that "powerful states are no more likely [after the Outcome Document] to feel obliged to act to save distant strangers, and there is no more likelihood of agreement about what to do in particular cases."[36] Yet, the *discourse had changed* as seen in Security Council Resolution 1674 in 2006 in which the Council affirmed that there is a responsibility to provide civilian protection. The wording in 1674 is, though, vague as to who bears this responsibility and is silent on how to operationalize the responsibility.

By the late 2000s, the responsibility had entered the international discourse enough to generate debate about which cases were and were not appropriate for UN intervention based on human protection. For example, in May 2008, Myanmar was hit by Cyclone Nargis. The storm's destruction and subsequent flooding resulted in 138,000 or more deaths initially, yet the military government refused to allow humanitarian groups into the worst-hit areas. The government confiscated UN relief supplies amid growing international fears that 100,000 more people faced certain death for lack of food, water, shelter, and medical care. The French foreign minister proposed that the Security Council invoke the responsibility to protect to force the Myanmar government to accept relief aid. This interpretation of the responsibility to protect fits the ICISS's just cause threshold, particularly the idea that there should be military intervention to stop "large scale loss of life, actual or apprehended, with genocidal intent or *not*, which is the product of either deliberate state action, or *state neglect or inability to act*, or a failed state situation" where the large scale loss of life results or may result from an "internal war, insurgency, repression or *state failure*."[37]

The French foreign minister's invocation of the responsibility to protect was proclaimed to be a serious *misreading* of the responsibility, especially as it was "embraced by the World Summit." Gareth Evans, one of the primary architects of the responsibility ethic, proposed that the responsibility was "not about human security generally, or protecting people from the impact of natural disasters, or the ravages of HIV-Aids or anything of the kind" but instead was about "mass atrocity crimes." If "the sharp military end" of the responsibility to protect were to be used in anything "other than a context of mass atrocity crimes, then such consensus as there is in favor of the new norm will simply evaporate in the global south."[38]

At the start of 2009, the Sri Lankan government conducted a surge in its decades-long war against the Liberation Tigers of Tamil Eelam (LTTE or Tamil Tigers). The surge resulted in the physical elimination of the Tamil Tigers. The government's surge also killed an incredible number of Tamil civilians. Some of the civilian deaths resulted from direct government shelling of Tamil-displaced persons camps, and some from the horrific conditions within those camps in the aftermath of the bombardment. Tamil-displaced persons camps were critical sites of conflict in the last years of the war. Government bombardment may have resulted in 40,000 deaths in the last months of the war. Urgent calls came from humanitarian organizations for the Security Council to stop the Sri Lankan government from attacking the camps and to force the government to allow humanitarian aid to be given to the Tamil civilians. However, the Security Council never formally discussed the situation in Sri Lanka that year.

Civilian Protection Becomes Humanitarian War

Civilian protection took on the mantle of the responsibility to protect in March 2011. Recall from the previous chapter how peace operations have been asked to provide civilian protection in their areas and within their capabilities. In March 2011, civilian protection became synonymous with forced regime change.

When the Arab Spring came to Libya, Qaddafi mobilized his mercenaries and threatened to make the streets run with the blood of the protestors. The Security Council adopted Resolution 1674 (2006) which authorized a civilian protection mandate to stop the impending mass loss of lives at the hand of the Qaddafi regime (S/RES/1973). Alex Bellamy and Paul Williams declared that this marked "a shift in the terms of [Council] debates from questions about *whether* to act to protect civilians to questions about *how* to engage."[39] This conclusion may have been premature.

Resolution 1973 reaffirmed that the armed parties to a conflict have the primary responsibility to protect civilians and reaffirmed the Security Council's "strong commitment to the sovereignty, independence, territorial integrity and national unity" of Libya. Then, acting under Chapter VII, the Council authorized states "acting nationally or through regional organizations or arrangements . . . to take all necessary measures," short of deploying troops on Libyan soil, to protect civilians and civilian-populated areas. To achieve the protection of civilians, the Council imposed a no-fly zone over Libyan airspace, imposed an arms embargo, banned flights by Libyans intended to obtain more mercenary armies, and froze the foreign assets of key government officials. The League of Arab States and the Organization of the Islamic Conference had called for muscular intervention by the United Nations, and NATO stepped up to be the muscle. Resolution 1973 was passed with ten votes in favor, no votes against and five abstentions (Russia, China, Brazil, Germany, and India).

On March 19, 2011, the US military began an air campaign against Libyan government forces and facilities to degrade their capacity for harming civilians. Ten days later, the operation was handed off to other NATO members. The air campaign provided support for anti-regime forces on the ground, but it also targeted government facilities in an effort to topple the regime. Finally, in October, Qaddafi was captured and killed by opposition forces, and the operation declared a success. For states participating in the campaign, the regime needed to be removed to ensure mass killing would not happen. Many other states, particularly in the Global South, were alarmed by the Western interpretation of "civilian protection" to mean regime change. The countries that had abstained on the vote were some of the loudest critics of the regime change interpretation.

In the same month—March 2011—the situation in Côte d'Ivoire had taken a turn for the worse. The United Nations had had a peacekeeping operation (UNOCI) in place there since the 2004 conclusion of a civil war. In late 2010, an election was held with the incumbent losing. The incumbent, Laurent Gbagbo, refused to relinquish office and the civil war reignited. UNOCI had a civilian protection mandate, but it had no way to compel actors to comply with the elections and end the fighting. The French also had troops in Côte d'Ivoire. After the muscular civilian protection mandate was approved for Libya, the Council authorized UNOCI and the French troops to use all necessary means to protect civilians (S/RES/1975). The intervention in Côte d'Ivoire then became an enforcement operation premised on the grounds of civilian protection. Although it was still in name a peacekeeping operation, UNOCI set aside impartiality and assisted in the military removal of Gbagbo and his forces and supporters. At the end of May, Gbagbo and his supporters were arrested, and Lassane Dramane Ouattara was sworn in as president. UNOCI resumed its previous role and remains in Côte d'Ivoire as of the beginning of 2017.

The intervention in Côte d'Ivoire did not raise as many objections as that in Libya. Perhaps this is because what happened in Côte d'Ivoire resembled precedents. There have been many enforcement operations authorized to create a short-term fix to facilitate peacekeeping. And, peacekeepers had been authorized to use force in other cases. But Libya was different. Williams and Bellamy and other scholars contended that the intervention in Libya was the result of years of patient promotion and acceptance of the norms of the responsibility to protect.[40] Others, like Charles Ziegler, contend that the responsibility to protect cannot withstand the weight of state sovereignty and state claims.[41] And, the Global South had deep misgivings that the "responsibility" was a repackaging of Western or Northern imperialism.

When the General Assembly met in September 2001, before Qaddafi had been captured and amid international worries about whether the conflict in Libya would have an end point, the Brazilian president Dilma Rousseff argued for "responsibility while protecting." The real responsibility, she argued, was for the United Nations to respect the sovereignty of its member states. And, the United Nations had a responsibility to not cause more harm than good; regime change could destabilize countries and regions. Instead, she argued that the international community should pay more attention to prevention.[42] *The Responsibility to Protect* document called for these things in 2001, but the full idea of the *Responsibility*—to prevent, protect, and rebuild with all its cautionary notes—was not endorsed by the Security Council, as we have seen. Once the *Responsibility* got identified with Western-induced regime change and once Libya descended into chaos after the regime fell, UN-approved humanitarian intervention in other places—such as Syria—became difficult to imagine.[43]

The Future of Human Security

Human security advocates have established an array of nongovernmental and intergovernmental organizations to promote and make practical the human security agenda. The United Nations secretariat has created the office of the Special Adviser on the Responsibility to Protect which works with the Special Adviser on the Prevention of Genocide. The United Nations also has a Trust Fund for Human Security to which countries can contribute. The Trust Fund is based on two pillars: protection and empowerment. Similarly, the United Nations Office for the Coordination of Humanitarian Affairs establishes a framework for responses to humanitarian disasters. These offices work with various nongovernmental organizations to advocate for people in situations of extreme insecurity.

But, the states-first ethic remains firmly in place—perhaps because of Libya. In 2012, the General Assembly revisited the idea of human security and endorsed a vision of human security that is limited and conservative. In A/RES/66/290, the General Assembly noted that "human security is an approach to assist Member States in identifying and addressing widespread and cross-cutting challenges to the survival, livelihood and dignity of their people." The Assembly embraced the wider view of human security, which it noted includes:

"The right of people to live in freedom and dignity, free from poverty and despair. All individuals, in particular vulnerable people, are entitled to freedom from fear and freedom from want, with an equal opportunity to enjoy all their rights and fully develop their human potential." And then the General Assembly—the most democratic part of the United Nations—reasserted the states-first nature of the United Nations and gutted the human security agenda. The words of the resolution are pointed and not open to much interpretation:

- The notion of human security is distinct from the responsibility to protect and its implementation;
- Human security does not entail the threat or the use of force or coercive measures. Human security does not replace State security;
- Human security is based on national ownership. Since the political, economic, social and cultural conditions for human security vary significantly across and within countries, and at different points in time, human security strengthens national solutions which are compatible with local realities;
- Governments retain the primary role and responsibility for ensuring the survival, livelihood and dignity of their citizens. . .
- Human security must be implemented with full respect for the purposes and principles enshrined in the Charter of the United Nations, including full respect for the sovereignty of States, territorial integrity and non-interference in matters that are essentially within the domestic jurisdiction of States. Human security does not entail additional legal obligations on the part of States. (A/RES/66/290 2012)

Recap

This is the final recap. In this chapter, we examined how human security gets inserted into the states-first world by appealing to the needs of states. We explored the rising prominence of human security from the Geneva Conventions to the civilian protection mandates in Libya and Côte d'Ivoire in 2011. The lack of any multilateral interest in promoting human security in Syria has been apparent throughout this book.

Human security supporters have been able to make some headway against the states-first system. These gains should not be dismissed as trivial. But, the pursuit of security for human beings remains debilitated by the insecurities of states. States fear any infringement on their sovereign rights—and this is obvious in how the UN General Assembly endorsed a restricted and diminished notion of human security: "Human security is based on national ownership," and, "human security does not entail additional legal obligations on the part of States."

The formidable opposition to civilian protection and any notion of a responsibility to protect after Libya, the naked pursuit of narrow interests in the destruction of Syria and its people, and the hostility and barriers being built against refugees and migrants—including that little girl on the cover—are signposts that point to this continuing feature of life on earth: The bedrock principle of the international system is that states come first.

Discussion Questions

1. Discuss the three freedoms in the idea of human security.
2. What was the original purpose of the Geneva Conventions?
3. Discuss how the Geneva Conventions define "civilian" and "combatant" and why these definitions matter.
4. Describe the ways in which the parties to the Syrian conflict have violated the Geneva Conventions.
5. Discuss the context in which the UNDP asserted the importance of human security to human development.
6. Describe the treaties that banned the use of landmines and cluster munitions and the opposition to each.
7. What crimes are under the jurisdiction of the International Criminal Court?
8. Discuss the states-first limitations put on the International Criminal Court.
9. Discuss what motivated the writers of *The Responsibility to Protect*.

10. Discuss how the World Summit, Security Council, and General Assembly embraced limited and truncated versions of a responsibility to protect and human security.

11. Describe the civilian protection mandate approved by the Security Council for Libya, how the mandate was interpreted, and the controversy that erupted over that interpretation.

9

Conclusion

Resilience and Imagination

This book has examined national, international, and human security in the contemporary international system using the states-first framework imposed on the system centuries ago. The purpose was to educate the reader about the security-seeking policies and practices of states, and how these policies and practices contribute to security and insecurity at many levels. In this chapter, the road forward is outlined. It is a road that is more secure for states, the international community, and humans alike. And, it is a road that is already being cut through the tangles of insecurities present today. But, first, a reminder of the road we have been on in this states-first world.

As we have discussed, state security has been the primary focus of security discussions and policies for centuries. Yet, the pursuit of security—which comes at increasingly higher costs—only brings more or less tolerable (and intolerable) degrees of insecurity. This situation in which states continually pursue (in)security comes to absurdity in the twentieth-century creation and deployment of nuclear weapons. "Stable" or "mature" nuclear deterrence is achieved between two rivals when both acknowledge that *they cannot protect their people* from the nuclear threat levied by the other. Some might see this as a desirable end point. Extended globally, a world of nuclear armed states would be "stable" and "mature" because every state can play the role of the grim reaper for itself and every other state, and with this knowledge each state holds back. But this reasoning is difficult to accept; why would states go to great lengths to achieve such weapons and then never use them? Why even start down that road?

Further, the state-first logic tells us that states *will not be content* with any particular weapons capability. Consider this: Keir Lieber and Daryl Press conclude that by 2006 the US nuclear arsenal had become so enhanced by an accuracy revolution and the next-nearest competitor's arsenal so degraded that the era of mutual assured destruction likely was over.[1] Lieber and Press ran a computer model "of a hypothetical U.S. attack on Russia's nuclear arsenal using the standard unclassified formulas that defense analysts have used for decades." Their model showed that "a simplified surprise attack would have a good chance of destroying every Russian bomber base, submarine, and ICBM."[2] US nuclear primacy will, of course, threaten others, causing them to attempt to bandage their hemorrhaging national security positions.

Russian military aggression in Georgia, Ukraine, and Syria, and its crippling cyberattack on Estonia in 2007 and Western Ukraine in 2016 can be seen as efforts to respond to this security dilemma. Russian cyberattacks on Estonia took down the computer systems of every institution of government, major political parties, news organizations, banks, and communications companies. Russian cyberattacks in Western Ukraine (where Russian troops are not present) turned off the power grid for several hours. Russian hacking of the websites of US political institutions and the Democratic Party threatened to undermine public confidence in the 2016 elections and the legitimacy of elected officeholders. At the same time, Russia threatened US air forces in Syria should they attack the forces of the Assad regime.

These aggressive moves by Russia—locked in the realists' security dilemma—have required increasingly militarized responses by the United States and NATO. Indeed, few would question the logic of these militarized responses; it is necessary to respond to real threats of violence. But the *implications* of these strategies are terrible. And, given the lessons in this book, the endgame is just more violence and less security. Jonathan Schell reminds us that,

> The terrible violence of the twentieth century . . . holds a lesson for the twenty-first. It is that in a steadily and irreversibly widening sphere, violence, always a mark of human failure and a bringer of sorrow, has now also become dysfunctional as a political instrument. Increasingly it destroys the ends for which it is employed, killing the user as well as his victim. It has become the path to hell on earth and the end of the earth. This is the lesson of the Somme and Verdun, of Auschwitz and Bergen-Belsen, of Vorkuta and Kolyma; and it is the lesson, beyond a shadow of a doubt, of Hiroshima and Nagasaki.[3]

The world in the middle of the second decade of the twenty-first century is raging with insecurities. A 2015 report of the United Nations secretary-general (A/70/357-S/2015/682, September 2, 2015) starts with this frightful summary:

> Since 2008 the number of major violent conflicts has almost tripled. Long-simmering disputes have escalated or relapsed into wars, while new conflicts have emerged in countries and regions once considered stable. Labels assigned to conflict, such as "internal," "inter-State," "regional," "ethnic," or "sectarian," have become increasingly irrelevant as transnational forces of violent extremism and organized crime build on and abet local rivalries. Environmental degradation and resource deprivation are not contained by borders. Exclusion at home is driving tension abroad.

This report called for states to recommit to United Nations peace operations with the primary goal of pursuing lasting political settlements. These settlements should be aimed at building longer-term stability because "societies with effective, inclusive and accountable institutions are more likely to withstand crises and peacefully manage disputes. Communities that recognize the dignity of each individual stand less chance of fueling resentments that can manifest in extremism."

Such communities are also able to move beyond a preoccupation with the fear of violence toward securing for their people the freedom from want and the freedom to live in human dignity. Recall that these three together are the broader goals of human security; the latter two goals get deprioritized because of the ubiquitous fear of violence. There are many reasons for states and people to live in fear, as the secretary-general's report sets out. And clear and present security threats must be managed, of course, but this should not condemn states and people to unending violent conflict in all its many forms. There is nothing inevitable about violent conflict within and between states.

This situation is not working. The pursuit of national security brings no national security; the pursuit of international security based on a state-centric ethic also brings no security. Human security, as we have seen, is the afterthought in all of this even though most people would agree that human beings should be the natural starting point in any security discussion. To achieve real security and to put the focus on human beings, we must reimagine politics. This reimagining is not just a project for the future—and it is not an exercise in wishful thinking—but instead has been with us for at least as long as the Westphalian war system has had us in its grasp.

Practically speaking, we cannot "destate" the world; we must work with what is and be more clear-eyed about how the present reality provides little security to states and people. History offers alternatives to the state system—empires, caliphates, and other supranational authorities have operated previously. These historical alternatives would not be able to address the problems, threats, and challenges contained in the present globalized era. Indeed, the state was preferable to the empires of the past in terms of its ability to respond to local interests, needs, and desires. The birth of the modern state in the mid-seventeenth century was part of a process of human advancement despite its brutal circumstances. A hundred years or so later, further and substantial human advancement occurred with the birth of democracy and the recognition that sovereignty resides in citizens.

Democratic states were an improvement on the absolutist national security states that arose in the mid-seventeenth century. Are the present-day democratic states better than present-day nondemocratic states in terms of respecting broad human rights? Absolutely they are. Can present-day democratic states themselves be improved on? It is undeniable that there is room for improvement in both the domestic and foreign policies of democratic states. But democracy itself maintains the public space for imagining and implementing such improvements. Democratic states are by design institutions that can constantly evolve.

There is also empirical evidence that democratic states are more internally secure and better international neighbors than other types of states. Moreover, there is evidence that human security—defined by the freedom from the fear of violence, the freedom from want, and the freedom to live in human dignity—is enhanced in democracies.

What is the evidence for this? Social scientists have been trying to understand violent conflict and peace for a long time. Philosophers, theologians, and military strategists have been trying to do this for even longer. Some compelling evidence regarding the practical elements of peace comes from the Institute for Economics and Peace (IEP), a not-for-profit think tank that partners with a range of actors from international organizations to cause groups, including the United Nations Development Programme, the Economist Intelligence Unit, the Stockholm Institute for Peace Research, the Organization for Economic Cooperation and Development, the International Crisis Group (founded by one of the architects of *The Responsibility to Protect*), Rotary International, and Religions for Peace.[4]

Since 2008, the IEP has produced the Global Peace Index (GPI) which measures "the level of safety and security in society, the extent of domestic or international conflict, and the degree of militarization."[5] Much of the GPI concerns what we have examined in this book under the idea of the freedom from fear of violence, or what is called "negative peace." The IEP also produces a Positive Peace Report, which uses twenty-four indicators of "positive peace" to examine peace inside countries and overall in the world.[6] In chapter 4, we discussed a "positive peace" idea called "defensive defense." The IEP is interested in positive peace from a data-analytics perspective. Thus, the IEP studies the relationship between indicators from 163 states and territories that demonstrate the "presence of the attitudes, institutions and structures that create and sustain peaceful societies."[7]

Eight factors are associated with positive peace, factors that the IEP calls the "pillars of peace." These factors are important in their own right but also in how they interact with and reinforce each other. The pillars of peace are: "a well-functioning government; a sound business environment; an equitable distribution of resources; an acceptance of the rights of others; good relations with neighbors; free flow of information; a high level of human capital; and low levels of corruption."[8] A consistent IEP finding over the years is that "peace creates resilience, thereby allowing societies to absorb shocks and disturbances more easily. . . resilience is seen as the capacity of social systems to absorb stress and repair themselves, as well as a capacity for renewal and adaptation."[9] And, the countries that are most resilient and that have the strongest positive peace are democracies.[10]

A resilient country responds to natural disasters as well as terrorist attacks in ways that do not undermine the structure of legitimate government. The citizens and government of a resilient country react to natural and human-made disasters in ways that show a deep and enduring commitment to human rights and the acceptance of ethnic, religious, racial, and socioeconomic differences. A resilient country is also a country in which gender equality and workers' rights are protected, free and independent media exist, and where education is prioritized.[11]

There are significant anti-immigrant and anti-other nationalistic movements present today in some of the most established democracies; these movements wish to close down open societies and make them less inclusive. The IEP's conclusion—found over many years of data analysis—should offer optimism in the face of these backlash movements. Democratic states and societies are resilient, and they will resist antidemocratic social movements, even as they continue to improve and extend human security to all of their citizens.

That there are places in the world in which humans thrive means that it is possible to create more places in which humans can thrive. This is why the 2015 report by the secretary-general (quoted earlier in this chapter) says that states must recommit to UN peace operations, and that UN peace operations must be aimed at building lasting political settlements and not just providing stopgap, temporary measures. Lasting settlements are necessary because "societies with effective, inclusive and accountable institutions are more likely to withstand crises and peacefully manage disputes." It is in the interests of all states to help other states embody the elements of positive peace and human security.

The mid-seventeenth century seems a long time ago. The self-defeating security practices arising at that moment in history *are* entrenched but not inevitable; they are not indelible reality. The development of democracy was a step away from the states-first ethic. The democracies of today are not perfect entities, but they have in them the institutions and attitudes that make them evolve and adapt. We just need to keep taking steps down that path. Indeed, for the sake of human beings everywhere, we need to pick up the pace and confront our mutual challenges with urgency.

Rejecting the states-first ethic and the antidemocratic backlash requires seeing with eyes wide open what has been and what is, and then imagining a better way of being in the world. Here, the ideas of Susan Griffin are useful:

> Imagination is as necessary to a social order as any legal agreement. That in America we imagine ourselves to be a democracy is crucial, even when democracy is failing . . . .
>
> Such a moment does not require less but rather more imagination. For to imagine is not simply to see what does not yet exist or what one wants to exist. It is also a profound act of creativity to see what is.[12]

This has been one goal of the present book—to show the reader what is and to suggest why and how at many different points the states-first security ethic does not secure states, the community of states, or human beings. Another less tangible but equally important goal has been to facilitate change in how the readers see this world and the security problématique. As Griffin writes, "The act of seeing changes those who see." And,

> Perception is not simply a reflection of reality but a powerful element of reality. Anyone who meditates has had this experience: Observing the activities of the mind changes the mind until, bit by bit, observation creates great changes in the soul. And the effect is the same when the act of perception is collective. A change in public perception will change the public. This is why acts of imagination are so important.[13]

In chapter 1 of this book, I wrote that in these pages the defini-tion of security would remain a persistent problem. I stated that the definitional problem drives an operational problem: Without a clear understanding of what we are securing and what we are securing against, how do we know when we have found the right policy, doctrine, weapon, or alliance that will in fact secure us? Definitional and operational problems ultimately are political problems. Political problems turn on value judgments, and the ultimate value judgment is determining what must be secured at what expense. In this world, we proceed as if some of the ultimate value judgments were cast in stone centuries ago and cannot be recast. But people have been recasting, remaking, and reshaping their political institutions before and after the start of the Westphalian system. We can insist that our institutions protect what we most value—human beings in faraway places, ourselves, our parents, our children, and the young girl on the cover of this book.

"What we seek to protect reflects what we value."[14] States can be required to put human beings first in security matters at home and abroad through democratic accountability. Dire human needs and seemingly pervasive insecurities on the one hand and spreading democracy and the irreversible growth of international society on the other will combine to compel states to reassess their old (in)security methods. In one sense, we have no choice—the old methods create greater insecurity. In another sense, we have many choices—we can look at the turn of human events and say that it *went* this way, not that it *was* this way.

Notes

Chapter 1: The Elusive Nature of Security

1. "Migrant Crisis: Migration to Europe Explained in Seven Charts," BBC, March 4, 2016, accessed May 24, 2016, http://www.bbc.com/news/world-europe-34131911.
2. Institute for Economics and Peace, *Global Terrorism Index 2015*, 3, accessed May 23, 2016, http://economicsandpeace.org/wp-content/uploads/2015/11/Global-Terrorism-Index-2015.pdf.
3. Council of the European Union, "EU-Turkey Statement, 18 March 2016," accessed May 24, 2016, http://www.consilium.europa.eu/en/press/press-releases/2016/03/18-eu-turkey-statement/.
4. International Commission on Intervention and State Sovereignty (ICISS), *The Responsibility to Protect* (Ottawa: International Development Research Centre, 2001), 5.
5. Graham Evans and Jeffrey Newnham, *Penguin Dictionary of International Relations* (New York: Penguin, 1998), 490.
6. High-level Panel on Threats, Challenges and Change, *A More Secure World: Our Shared Responsibility* (New York: United Nations, 2004), 17, accessed November 14, 2005, http://www.un.org/secureworld/.
7. Laura Barnett, "Global Governance and the Evolution of the International Refugee Regime," Working Paper No. 54, UN High Commissioner for Refugees, February 2002, 8–9.
8. Barnett, "Global Governance," 7.

9. Barnett, "Global Governance," 2.
10. "Migrant Crisis: Migration to Europe Explained in Seven Charts."
11. Edward Newman, "Refugees, International Security, and Human Vulnerability: Introduction and Survey," in *Refugees and Forced Displacement*, ed. Edward Newman and Janne van Selm (New York/Paris: United Nations University Press, 2003), 3.
12. Newman, "Refugees, International Security," 3.
13. Newman, "Refugees, International Security," 7.
14. "Migrant Crisis: Merkel Warns of EU 'Failure,'" BBC, August 31, 2015, accessed June 14, 2016, http://www.bbc.com/news/world-europe-34108224.
15. "Merkel's Refugee Policy Divides Europe," *SpeigelOnline*, September 21, 2015, accessed May 24, 2016, http://www.spiegel.de/international/germany/refugee-policy-of-chancellor-merkel-divides-europe-a-1053603.html.
16. Sara Miller Llana, "Hollande, Merkel Call for 'More Europe' to Fight Crises Afflicting EU," *Christian Science Monitor*, October 7, 2015, accessed September 30, 2016, http://www.csmonitor.com/World/Europe/2015/1007/Hollande-Merkel-call-for-more-Europe-to-fight-crises-afflicting-EU.
17. Llana, "Hollande, Merkel Call for 'More Europe.'"
18. Justin Huggler, "Germany to Deport Syrian Refugees as Minister Reverses Merkel's Policy," *Daily Telegraph*, November 12, 2015, 15.

Chapter 2: National Security

1. Friedrich Meinecke, "*Raison d'État*," in *Basic Texts in International Relations*, ed. Evan Luard (New York: St. Martin's Press, 1992), 170.
2. Arnold Wolfers, *Discord and Collaboration* (Baltimore: The Johns Hopkins University Press, 1962), 150.
3. Wolfers, *Discord and Collaboration*, 149.
4. R. B. J. Walker, "Security, Sovereignty, and the Challenge of World Politics," *Alternatives* 15 (1990): 5–6.
5. Brazil, "National Strategy of Defense," December 18, 2008, accessed September 30, 2016, http://www.defesa.gov.br/projetosweb/estrategia/arquivos/estrategia_defesa_nacional_ingles.pdf.
6. South Africa, "South African Defence Review 2014," accessed September 30, 2016, http://www.gov.za/sites/www.gov.za/files/dfencereview_2014.pdf.
7. Barry Buzan, *People, States & Fear*, 2nd ed. (Colchester: ECPR Press, 2007), 219.

8. Buzan, *People, States & Fear*, 219.

9. Charles W. Kegley Jr. and Gregory A. Raymond, *Exorcising the Ghost of Westphalia* (Upper Saddle River, NJ: Prentice Hall, 2002), 190.

10. Kegley and Raymond, *Exorcising the Ghost of Westphalia*, 190.

11. Kegley and Raymond, *Exorcising the Ghost of Westphalia*, 190.

12. Evans and Newnham, *Penguin Dictionary of International Relations*, 504.

13. Walker, "Security, Sovereignty, and the Challenge of World Politics," 9.

14. Kegley and Raymond, *Exorcising the Ghost of Westphalia*, 90.

15. Kegley and Raymond, *Exorcising the Ghost of Westphalia*, 93.

16. Kegley and Raymond, *Exorcising the Ghost of Westphalia*, 93.

17. Kegley and Raymond, *Exorcising the Ghost of Westphalia*, 94.

18. Kegley and Raymond, *Exorcising the Ghost of Westphalia*, 97.

19. Kegley and Raymond, *Exorcising the Ghost of Westphalia*, 4.

20. Karen Mingst, *Essentials of International Relations*, 2nd ed. (New York: Norton, 2003), 218.

21. Charles Tilly, "War Making and State Making as Organized Crime," in *Bringing the State Back In*, ed. Peter B. Evans, Dietrich Rueschemeyer, and Theda Skocpol (New York: Cambridge University Press, 1985).

22. For more on this argument, see Ian S. Lustick, "The Absence of Middle Eastern Great Powers: Political 'Backwardness' in Historical Perspective," *International Organization* 51, no. 4 (1997): 653–83.

23. For more on this argument, see Robert H. Jackson, "Juridical Statehood in Sub-Saharan Africa," *Journal of International Affairs* 46, no. 1 (1992): 1–16.

24. Mohammed Ayoob, *The Third World Security Predicament* (Boulder, CO: Lynne Rienner, 1995), 32–33.

Chapter 3: Internal Security

1. Buzan, *People, States & Fear*, 78.

2. Ilaria Parogni, "By Misunderstanding Crimea, the West Is Pushing Russia Further Away," *HuffPost*, April 15, 2015, accessed September 30, 2016, http://www.huffingtonpost.com/ilaria-parogni-/misunderstanding-crimea-west-russia_b_7073322.html; "Crimean Tatars Kicked Out of Their Office," *The Moscow Times*, September 24, 2014, accessed September 30, 2016, https://themoscowtimes.com/news/crimean-tatars-kicked-out-of-their-office-39739.

3. Michael Birnbaum, "Eight Months after Russia Annexed Crimea from Ukraine, a Complicated Transition," *Washington Post*, November 27, 2014, accessed September 30, 2016, https://www.washingtonpost.com/

world/europe/eight-months-after-russia-annexed-crimea-from-ukraine-a-complicated-transition/2014/11/27/d42bcf82–69b3–11e4-bafd-6598192a448d_story.html; Parogni, "By Misunderstanding Crimea."

4. Buzan, *People, States & Fear*, 71.
5. Zachary Laub and Jonathan Masters, "The Islamic State," Council on Foreign Relations, CFR Backgrounders, March 22, 2016.
6. Buzan, *People, States & Fear*, 71.
7. International Crisis Group, "Justice at the Barrel of a Gun: Vigilante Militias in Mexico," Latin America Briefing No. 29, May 28, 2013, 2, accessed September 30, 2016, https://www.crisisgroup.org/latin-america-caribbean/mexico/justice-barrel-gun-vigilante-militias-mexico.
8. International Crisis Group, "Justice at the Barrel of a Gun," 7.
9. International Crisis Group, "Justice at the Barrel of a Gun," 7.
10. Vanda Felbab-Brown, "Changing the Game or Dropping the Ball? Mexico's Security and Anti-Crime Strategy under President Enrique Peña Nieto," Latin America Initiative, Brookings, November 2014, 32, accessed September 30, 2016, https://www.brookings.edu/research/changing-the-game-or-dropping-the-ball-mexicos-security-and-anti-crime-strategy-under-president-enrique-pena-nieto/.
11. Felbab-Brown, "Changing the Game," 17, 15.
12. Azam Ahmed and Eric Schmitt, "Mexican Military Runs Up Body Count in Drug War," *New York Times*, May 26, 2016, accessed September 30, 2016, http://www.nytimes.com/2016/05/27/world/americas/mexican-militarys-high-kill-rate-raises-human-rights-fears.html?_r=0.
13. Ahmed and Schmitt, "Mexican Military."
14. Kirk Semple, "Missing Mexican Students Suffered a Night of 'Terror,' Investigators Say," *New York Times*, April 24, 2016, accessed September 30, 2016, http://www.nytimes.com/2016/04/25/world/americas/missing-mexican-students-suffered-a-night-of-terror-investigators-say.html.
15. Buzan, *People, States & Fear*, 74.
16. Buzan, *People, States & Fear*, 49.
17. Buzan, *People, States & Fear*, 52.
18. Lizette Alvarez, "British Court Says Detentions Violate Rights," *New York Times*, December 17, 2004, 1.
19. Donohue, "Fear Itself," 283.
20. Donohue, "Fear Itself," 276.
21. Donohue, "Fear Itself," 275.
22. Donohue, "Fear Itself," 277, 278.

23. William McCants, *The ISIS Apocalypse* (New York: St. Martin's Press, 2015), 98.
24. Guy Faulconbridge and Jonathan Saul, "Islamic State Oil Is Going to Assad, Some to Turkey, U.S. Official Says." *Reuters*, December 20, 2015, accessed September 25, 2016, http://www.reuters.com/article/us-mideast-crisis-syria-usa-oil-idUSKBN0TT2O120151210.
25. McCants, *The ISIS Apocalypse*, 85, 98, 99.
26. McCants, *The ISIS Apocalypse*, 98.
27. Buzan, *People, States & Fear*, 85.
28. McCants, *The ISIS Apocalypse*, 86.
29. McCants, *The ISIS Apocalypse*, 85.
30. Buzan, *People, States & Fear*, 53.
31. UNHCR, "Figures at a Glance," accessed July 18, 2016, http://www.unhcr.org/en-us/figures-at-a-glance.html.
32. UNHCR, "UNHCR Mid-Year Trends 2015," accessed September 30, 2016, http://www.unhcr.org/en-us/statistics/unhcrstats/56701b969/mid-year-trends-june-2015.html.
33. Fund For Peace, "Fragile States Index for 2015," accessed September 30, 2016, http://fsi.fundforpeace.org/rankings-2015.
34. Institute for Economics and Peace, *Global Terrorism Index 2015*, 2.
35. Institute for Economics and Peace, *Global Terrorism Index 2015*, 5.

Chapter 4: Unilateral Pursuit of External Security

1. Kegley and Raymond, *Exorcising the Ghost of Westphalia*, 109.
2. Kegley and Raymond, *Exorcising the Ghost of Westphalia*, 104.
3. Kegley and Raymond, *Exorcising the Ghost of Westphalia*, 106.
4. James E. Dougherty and Robert L. Pfaltzgraff Jr., *Contending Theories of International Relations*, 5th ed. (New York: Longman, 2001), 286.
5. John J. Mearsheimer, *The Tragedy of Great Power Politics* (New York: Norton, 2001), 21.
6. Nicholas J. Spykman, *American Strategy and World Politics* (New York: Harcourt Brace, 1942), 21–22, as quoted in Dougherty and Pfaltzgraff, *Contending Theories of International Relations*, 43.
7. Glenn H. Snyder, "The Security Dilemma in Alliance Politics," *World Politics* 36, no. 4 (July 1984): 461.
8. Klaus Knorr, "Threat Perception," in *Historical Dimensions of National Security Problems*, ed. Klaus Knorr (Lawrence: University Press of Kansas, 1976), 79.
9. Buzan, *People, States & Fear*, 277.
10. Buzan, *People, States & Fear*, 277.

11. Michael E. O'Hanlon, "The Future of Land Warfare," Brookings, August 31, 2015, accessed September 30, 2016, https://www.brookings.edu/blog/order-from-chaos/2015/08/31/the-future-of-land-warfare/.

12. Kyle Mizokami, "If India and Pakistan Went to War: 5 Weapons Pakistan Should Fear," *The National Interest*, August 16, 2014, accessed September 30, 2016, http://nationalinterest.org/feature/if-india-pakistan-went-war-5-weapons-pakistan-should-fear-11089.

13. Bruno Tertrais, "Nuclear Policy, France Stands Alone," *Bulletin of the Atomic Scientists* (July/August 2004): 52.

14. Thomas C. Schelling, "The Diplomacy of Violence," in *Essential Readings in World Politics*, ed. Karen A. Mingst and Jack L. Snyder (New York: Norton, 2004), 302.

15. Upendra Choudhury, "Too Close for Comfort," *Bulletin of the Atomic Scientists* (March/April 2003): 24.

16. Jennifer Taw, "Preventive Force: The Logic of Costs and Benefits," in *Preventive Force: Drones, Targeted Killing, and the Transformation of Contemporary Warfare*, ed. Kerstin Fish and Jennifer M. Ramos (New York: New York University Press, 2016), 36.

17. Geoffrey Wiseman, *Concepts of Non-Provocative Defense* (New York: Palgrave, 2002), 4.

18. Evert Jordaan and Abel Esterhuyse, "South African Defence since 1994: The Influence of Non-Offensive Defence," *African Security Review* 13, no. 1 (2004): 59.

19. Johan Galtung, "Transarmament: From Offensive to Defensive Defense," *Journal of Peace Research* 21, no. 2, Special Issue on Alternative Defense (June 1984): 128.

20. Wiseman, *Concepts of Non-Provocative Defense*, 5.

21. *Wiseman, Concepts of Non-Provocative Defense*, 5.

22. See, for example, Bjørn Møller, *Resolving the Security Dilemma in Europe: The German Debate on Non-Offensive Defence* (London: Brassey's, 1991).

23. See Radmila Nakarada and Jan Oberg, eds., *Surviving Together: The Olof Palme Lectures on Common Security 1988* (Brookfield, VT: Dartmouth Publishing, 1989).

24. Wiseman, *Concepts of Non-Provocative Defense*, 26.

25. Galtung, "Transarmament," 128, especially figure II.

26. Wiseman, *Concepts of Non-Provocative Defense*, 5; Jordaan and Esterhuyse, "South African Defence since 1994," 61.

27. Wiseman, *Concepts of Non-Provocative Defense*, 57–58, emphasis added.

28. Galtung, "Transarmament," 136.

29. Galtung, "Transarmament," 135.

30. Galtung, "Transarmament," 135.
31. Avery Plaw and João Franco Reis, "The Contemporary Practice of Self-Defense: Evolving toward the Use of Preemptive or Preventive Force?" in *Preventive Force*, ed. Fish and Ramos, 231.
32. Plaw and Reis, "The Contemporary Practice of Self-Defense," 231.
33. Richard K. Betts, "Striking First: A History of Thankfully Lost Opportunities," *Ethics and International Law* 17, no. 1 (2003): 18.
34. Neta C. Crawford, "The Slippery Slope to Preventive War," *Ethics & International Affairs* 17, no. 1 (2003): 31.
35. Chris Brown, "Self-Defense in an Imperfect World," *Ethics & International Affairs* 17, no. 1 (2003): 2.
36. Michael J. Glennon, "The Fog of Law: Self-Defense, Inherence, and Incoherence in Article 51 of the United Nations Charter," *Harvard Journal of Law and Public Policy* 25, no. 2 (2002): 541–42.
37. Betts, "Striking First," 19.
38. Laura Neack, *The New Foreign Policy: Complex Interactions, Competing Interests*, 3rd ed. (Lanham, MD: Rowman & Littlefield, 2014), 35.
39. Randall L. Schweller, "Domestic Structure and Preventive War: Are Democracies More Pacific?" *World Politics* 44 (January 1992): 236.
40. Betts, "Striking First," 18.
41. For example, see John J. Mearsheimer, "Why the Ukraine Crisis Is the West's Fault," *Foreign Affairs* 93, no. 5 (2014): 77–89; Michael Mcc-Gwire, "NATO Expansion: 'A Policy Error of Historic Importance,'" *Review of International Studies* 24, no. 1 (1998): 23–42.
42. Taw, "Preventive Force," 33.
43. Taw, "Preventive Force," 38.
44. Taw, "Preventive Force," 43, table 2.1.
45. Robert Farley, "The Five Most Deadly Drone Powers in the World," *The National Interest*, February 16, 2015, accessed September 30, 2016, http://nationalinterest.org/feature/the-five-most-deadly-drone-powers-the-world-12255.
46. New America Foundation, "World of Drones: Military," accessed July 20, 2016, http://securitydata.newamerica.net/world-drones.html.
47. Cora Currier, "Everything We Know So Far about Drone Strikes," *ProPublica*, February 5, 2013, accessed July 20, 2016, https://www.propublica.org/article/everything-we-know-so-far-about-drone-strikes; Tom Junod, "The Lethal Presidency of Barack Obama," *Esquire*, August 2012, accessed February 13, 2014, http://www.esquire.com/news-politics/a14627/obama-lethal-presidency-0812/.
48. Plaw and Reis, "The Contemporary Practice of Self-Defense," 246.

Chapter 5: Multilateral and Bilateral Responses to External Security Threats

1. Kathleen J. McInnis, "Coalition Contributions to Countering the Islamic State," Congressional Research Service, 7–5700, August 24, 2016, www.crs.gov.
2. Glenn H. Snyder, "Alliance Theory: A Neorealist First Cut," *Journal of International Affairs* 44, no. 1 (1990): 104.
3. Snyder, "Alliance Theory," 105.
4. Stephen M. Walt, *The Origins of Alliances* (Ithaca, NY: Cornell University Press, 1987), 12.
5. Walt, *The Origins of Alliances*, 12.
6. James Stavridis, "It's Time for a Formal U.S. Alliance with Israel," *Foreign Policy*, September 25, 2015, accessed September 12, 2016, http://foreignpolicy.com/2015/09/25/its-time-for-a-formal-u-s-alliance-with-israel-collective-defense-treaty/.
7. Miles Kahler, "Multilateralism with Small and Large Numbers," *International Organization* 46, no. 3 (1992): 681.
8. John Gerard Ruggie, "Multilateralism: The Anatomy of an Institution," in *Multilateralism Matters: The Theory and Praxis of an Institutional Form*, ed. John Gerard Ruggie (New York: Columbia University Press, 1993), 11.
9. Walt, *The Origins of Alliances*, 5.
10. Christopher Hemmer and Peter J. Katzenstein, "Why Is There No NATO in Asia? Collective Identity, Regionalism, and the Origins of Multilateralism," *International Organization* 56, no. 3 (2002): 575–76.
11. Hemmer and Katzenstein, "Why Is There No NATO in Asia?" 575.
12. Michael Beckley, "The Myth of Entangling Alliances: Reassessing the Security Risks of U.S. Defense Pacts," *International Security* 39, no. 4 (2015): 7.
13. Steve Weber, "Shaping the Postwar Balance of Power: Multilateralism in NATO," *International Organization* 46, no. 3 (1992): 635–36.
14. North Atlantic Treaty Organization, "Enlargement," December 3, 2015, accessed September 12, 2016, http://www.nato.int/cps/en/natohq/topics_49212.htm.
15. Schweller, "Domestic Structure and Preventive War," 74.
16. Schweller, "Domestic Structure and Preventive War," 93.
17. Neil MacFarlane, "Realism and Russian Strategy after the Collapse of the USSR," in *Unipolar Politics: Realism and State Strategies after the Cold War*, ed. Ethan B. Kapstein and Michael Mastanduno (New York: Columbia University Press, 1999), 236.

18. Michael Emerson, "Post-Mortem on Europe's First War of the 21st Century," CEPS Policy Brief, No. 167, Centre for European Policy Studies, August 2008, 2.

19. Emerson, "Post-Mortem on Europe's First War," 1.

20. Jonathan Masters, "The Russian Military," CFR Backgrounder, Council on Foreign Relations, September 28, 2015, accessed September 11, 2016, http://www.cfr.org/russian-federation/russian-military/p33758.

21. Emerson, "Post-Mortem on Europe's First War," 4.

22. Liz Fuller, "Georgia's Hopes of NATO Membership Recede," *Radio-FreeEurope/RadioLiberty*, April 26, 2016, accessed September 16, 2016, http://www.rferl.org/a/georgia-hopes-of-nato-membership-recede/27699636.html.

23. Nick Bisley, "An Ally for All the Years to Come: Why Australia Is Not a Conflicted US Ally," *Australian Journal of International Affairs* 67, no. 4 (2013): 405.

24. Beckley, "The Myth of Entangling Alliances," 9–10.

25. Beckley, "The Myth of Entangling Alliances," 7.

26. Beckley, "The Myth of Entangling Alliances," 10.

27. Beckley, "The Myth of Entangling Alliances," 11.

28. James Kilner, "Uzbekistan Withdraws from Russia-Lead Military Alliance," *Telegraph* (London), July 2, 2012, accessed September 11, 2016, http://www.telegraph.co.uk/news/worldnews/asia/uzbekistan/9369392/Uzbekistan-withdraws-from-Russia-lead-military-alliance.html.

29. GobalSecurity.org, "Collective Security Treaty Organization (CSTO)," accessed September 11, 2016, http://www.globalsecurity.org/military/world/int/csto.htm.

30. GobalSecurity.org, "Collective Security Treaty Organization."

31. McInnis, "Coalition Contributions," 1.

32. McInnis, "Coalition Contributions," 2.

33. McInnis, "Coalition Contributions," 6.

34. Fazel Hawramy, Shalaw Mohammad, and David Smith, "Kurdish Fighters Say US Special Forces Have Been Fighting ISIS for Months," *Guardian*, November 30, 2015, accessed July 29, 2016, https://www.theguardian.com/us-news/2015/nov/30/kurdish-fighters-us-special-forces-isis-combat.

35. Michael D. Shear, Helene Cooper, and Eric Schmitt, "Obama Administration Ends Effort to Train Syrians to Combat ISIS," *New York Times*, October 9, 2015, accessed July 29, 2016, http://www.nytimes.

com/2015/10/10/world/middleeast/pentagon-program-islamic-state-syria.html?_r=0.

36. Thomas Gibbons-Neff, "This Is Where American Special Operations Forces Are Helping Advise U.S. Allies," *Washington Post*, April 17, 2016, accessed July 29, 2016, https://www.washingtonpost.com/news/checkpoint/wp/2016/04/17/this-is-where-american-special-operations-forces-are-helping-advise-u-s-allies/.

37. Paul D. Williams, "Enhancing U.S. Support for Peace Operations in Africa," Council Special Report No. 73, Council on Foreign Relations, May 2015, 11, accessed September 30, 2016, http://www.cfr.org/peacekeeping/enhancing-us-support-peace-operations-africa/p36530.

38. Williams, "Enhancing U.S. Support," 18.

39. Williams, "Enhancing U.S. Support," 11.

40. Security Assistance Monitor, "4 Charts on Spike in U.S. Military and Police Aid to Africa," June 3, 2015, accessed September 10, 2016, http://securityassistance.org/blog/4-charts-spike-us-military-and-police-aid-africa?language=en.

41. "AFRICOM Campaign Plan Targets Terror Groups," *CQ Federal Department and Agency Documents*, January 5, 2016.

Chapter 6: International Security: Multilateral Efforts to Achieve Security

1. High-level Panel on Threats, Challenges and Change, *A More Secure World: Our Shared Responsibility* (New York, December 2004), 16, accessed November 1, 2005, http://www.un.org/secureworld.

2. Karen Mingst, *Essentials of International Relations* (New York: Norton, 2005), glossary entry.

3. Inis L. Claude Jr., *Power and International Relations* (New York: Random House, 1964, 3rd printing), 126.

4. Claude, *Power and International Relations*, 113.

5. Claude, *Power and International Relations*, 123.

6. Claude, *Power and International Relations*, 272–74.

7. Claude, *Power and International Relations*, 283–84.

8. Soffer, "All for One or All for All," 62.

9. Soffer, "All for One or All for All," 61.

10. Soffer, "All for One or All for All," 61.

11. Soffer, "All for One or All for All," 66.

12. Jim Wurst, "UN Command of Gulf Action Unlikely," *Bulletin of the Atomic Scientists* (January/February 1991): 4.

13. Stephen D. Krasner, "Structural Causes and Regime Consequences: Regimes as Intervening Variables," *International Organization* 36, no. 2 (1982): 185.

14. Jess McHugh, "North Korea Missiles Fired from Yemen into Saudi Arabia, South Korean Official Says," *International Business Times*, July 30, 2015, accessed August 19, 2016, http://www.ibtimes.com/north-korea-missiles-fired-yemen-saudi-arabia-south-korean-official-says-2031548.

15. Jim Walsh and John Park, "To Stop the Missiles, Stop North Korea, Inc.," *New York Times*, March 10, 2016, accessed August 16, 2016, http://www.nytimes.com/2016/03/10/opinion/to-stop-the-missiles-stop-north-korea-inc.html.

16. Zachary Laub, "International Sanctions on Iran," CFR Backgrounder, Council on Foreign Relations, July 15, 2015, accessed July 29, 2016, http://www.cfr.org/iran/international-sanctions-iran/p20258.

17. Kelsey Davenport and Daryl G. Kimball, "An Effective, Verifiable Nuclear Deal with Iran," Iran Nuclear Policy Brief, Arms Control Association, July 23, 2015, accessed July 29, 2016, https://www.armscontrol.org/files/ACA_Iran%20Brief_July28_D.pdf.

18. For a longer discussion of this movement, see the Center for Constitutional Rights, "There Is a Way to Stop the War," accessed November 14, 2005, http://www.ccr-ny.org/v2/reports/ report.asp?ObjID=0hZHHegENn&Content=186.

19. Peter Ellingsen, "UN Gulf Vote Returns China to World Stage," *Financial Times*, November 30, 1990, 4.

20. Robert Pear, "Mideast Tensions; Bush, Meeting Foreign Minister, Lauds Beijing Stand Against Iraq," *New York Times*, December 1, 1990, accessed September 30, 2016, http://www.nytimes.com/1990/12/01/world/mideast-tensions-bush-meeting-foreign-minister-lauds-beijing-stand-against-iraq.html.

21. Graham E. Fuller, "Moscow and the Gulf War," *Foreign Affairs* 70, no. 3 (1991): 60.

22. Thomas L. Friedman, "How the US Won Support to Use Mideast Forces," *New York Times*, December 2, 1990, 1.

23. Paul Quinn-Judge, "Lithuania Leaders Urge Calm, Soviet Assault Leaves 13 Dead," *Boston Globe*, January 14, 1991, 1; Annika Savill, "The Soviet Crackdown: Iraq Crisis Stifles US Action on Baltic," *Independent* (London), January 14, 1991, 1.

24. Quinn-Judge, "Lithuania Leaders Urge Calm."

25. Marc Fischer, "Some Europeans States More Open to Negotiated Settlement in Gulf," *Washington Post*, January 4, 1991, A19.

26. Claude, *Power and International Relations*, 283–84.

27. Claude, *Power and International Relations*, 284.

Chapter 7: United Nations Peacekeeping and Peace Enforcement

1. For more on potential linkages, see Gustáv Kecskés, "The Suez Crisis and the 1956 Hungarian Revolution," *East European Quarterly* 35, no. 1 (2001): 47–57, and William R. Keylor, *The Twentieth Century World: An International History*, 3rd ed. (New York: Oxford University Press, 1996), 294–95.
2. UNDPO, First United Nations Emergency Force (UNEF I), "Background," accessed November 14, 2005, http://www.un.org/Depts/dpko/dpko/co_mission/unef1backgr2.html.
3. UNDPO, First United Nations Emergency Force (UNEF I), "Background."
4. UNDPO, First United Nations Emergency Force (UNEF I), "Background."
5. Thomas G. Weiss, *Military-Civilian Interactions: Humanitarian Crises and the Responsibility to Protect*, 2nd ed. (Lanham, MD: Rowman & Littlefield, 2005), 44.
6. Walter Clarke and Jeffrey Herbst, "Somalia and the Future of Humanitarian Intervention," *Foreign Affairs* 75, no. 2 (1996): 70.
7. Weiss, *Military-Civilian Interactions*, 85.
8. United Nations, "Maintain International Peace and Security," accessed August 26, 2016, http://www.un.org/en/sections/what-we-do/maintain-international-peace-and-security/index.html.
9. United Nations Mission in Sierra Leone (UNAMSIL), "Background," accessed August 26, 2016, http://www.un.org/en/peacekeeping/missions/past/unamsil/background.html.
10. UNAMSIL, "Background."
11. United Nations Development Program (UNDP), "Case Study Sierra Leone," 4, accessed August 26, 2016, http://web.undp.org/evaluation/documents/thematic/conflict/SierraLeone.pdf.
12. Report of the Panel on United Nations Peace Operations, A/55/305, S/2000/809, August 21, 2000, Executive Summary, viii, accessed November 14, 2005, http://www.un.org/peace/ reports/peace_operations/.
13. United Nations Department of Peacekeeping Operations, *Handbook on United Nations Multidimensional Peacekeeping Operations*, December 2003, 6, accessed September 30, 2016, http://www.un.org/en/peacekeeping/documents/Peacekeeping-Handbook_UN_Dec2003.pdf.
14. United Nations Department of Peacekeeping Operations and Department of Field Support, *A New Partnership Agenda: Charting a New Horizon for UN Peacekeeping*, July 2009, iii, accessed September 30, 2016, http://www.un.org/en/peacekeeping/documents/newhorizon.pdf.

15. United Nations Department of Peacekeeping Operations, Department of Field Support, *Gender Equality in UN Peacekeeping Operations*, July 28, 2010, 3, accessed September 30, 2016, http://www.un.org/en/peacekeeping/documents/gender_directive_2010.pdf.
16. For example, see Nicole George and Laura J. Shepherd, "Women, Peace and Security: Exploring the Implementation and Integration of UNSCR 1325," *International Political Science Review* 37, no 3 (2016): 297–306; Sheri Lynn Gibbings, "No Angry Women at the United Nations: Political Dreams and the Cultural Politics of United Nations Security Council Resolution 1325," *International Feminist Journal of Politics* 14, no. 4 (2011): 522–38.
17. CARE, "'The Girl Has No Rights': Gender-Based Violence in South Sudan," May 2014, accessed August 27, 2016, http://insights.careinternational.org.uk/media/k2/attachments/CARE_The_Girl_Has_No_Rights_GBV_in_South_Sudan.pdf.
18. For example, see Comfort Ero, "The Problems with 'African Solutions,'" International Crisis Group, December 2, 2013, accessed September 30, 2016, http://blog.crisisgroup.org/africa/2013/12/02/the-problems-with-african-solutions/.
19. "Kenyan Report Details Blunders by AU Mission in Somalia," BBC Worldwide Monitoring, January 24, 2016.

Chapter 8: Human Security

1. Somini Sengupta, "U.N. Deadlocked Over Draft Agreement on Refugees and Migrants," *New York Times*, August 1, 2016, accessed August 1, 2016, http://www.nytimes.com/2016/08/02/world/americas/un-united-nations-refugees-migrants.html.
2. International Organization for Migration, "Missing Migrants Project," accessed September 9, 2016, http://missingmigrants.iom.int/.
3. United Nations Trust Fund for Human Security, "Human Security in Theory and Practice," 2009, 7, accessed October 1, 2016, http://www.un.org/humansecurity/sites/www.un.org.humansecurity/files/human_security_in_theory_and_practice_english.pdf.
4. United Nations Trust Fund for Human Security, "Human Security in Theory and Practice," 7.
5. International Committee of the Red Cross (ICRC), "The Battle of Solferino," accessed December 14, 2005, http://www.icrc.org/Web/Eng/siteeng0.nsf/html/57JNVR.
6. Lt. Col. Mark David "Max" Maxwell, "The Law of War and Civilians on the Battlefield: Are We Undermining Civilian Protections?" *Military Review* (September–October 2004): 19.

7. Maxwell, "The Law of War and Civilians on the Battlefield," 18–19.

8. Society of Professional Journalists, "Reference Guide to the Geneva Conventions," accessed November 21, 2005, http://www.genevacon ventions.org/.

9. Society of Professional Journalists, "Reference Guide to the Geneva Conventions."

10. Hugo Slim, "Why Protect Civilians? Innocence, Immunity and Enmity in War," *International Affairs* 79, no. 3 (2003): 481.

11. Anne Barnard and Somini Sengupta, "Syria and Russia Appear Ready to Scorch Aleppo," *New York Times*, September 25, 2016, accessed September 26, 2016, http://www.nytimes.com/2016/09/26/world/ middleeast/syria-un-security-council.html.

12. Barnard and Sengupta, "Syria and Russia"; Anne Barnard and Somini Sengupta, "'From Paradise to Hell': How an Aid Convoy in Syria Was Blown Apart," *New York Times*, September 24, 2016, accessed September 24, 2016, http://www.nytimes.com/2016/09/25/world/ middleeast/from-paradise-to-hell-how-an-aid-convoy-in-syria-was-blown-apart.html.

13. United Nations Development Programme (UNDP), *Human Development Report 1994* (New York: Oxford University Press, 1994), 1.

14. UNDP, *Human Development Report 1994*, 23.

15. UNDP, *Human Development Report 1994*, 3.

16. Lloyd Axworthy, "Introduction," in *Human Security and the New Diplomacy: Protecting People, Promoting Peace*, ed. Rob McRae and Don Hubert (Montreal: McGill-Queen's University Press, 2001), 4.

17. Axworthy, "Introduction," 4.

18. Axworthy, "Introduction," 5.

19. Mark Gwozdecky and Jill Sinclair, "Landmines and Human Security," in *Human Security and the New Diplomacy: Protecting People, Promoting Peace*, ed. Rob McRae and Don Hubert (Montreal: McGill-Queen's University Press, 2001), 28.

20. Fen Osler Hampson, *Madness in the Multitude: Human Security and World Disorder* (Don Mills, Ontario, Canada: Oxford University Press, 2002), 81.

21. Carla Del Ponte, "Holding Leaders Accountable," *Global Agenda* (January 2005): 74–75.

22. Michael Struett, "The Meaning of the International Criminal Court," *Peace Review* 16, no. 3 (2004): 318.

23. Arms Control Association, "Time to Ban Cluster Munitions Transfers, Rethink Approach to Treaty," *Issue Briefs* 8, no. 3 (July 13, 2016), accessed August 1, 2016, https://www.armscontrol.org.

24. International Commission on Intervention and State Sovereignty (ICISS), *The Responsibility to Protect* (Ottawa: International Development Research Centre, 2001), vii.
25. ICISS, *The Responsibility to Protect*, vii.
26. ICISS, *The Responsibility to Protect*, sec. 1, para. 21.
27. ICISS, *The Responsibility to Protect*, xi.
28. ICISS, *The Responsibility to Protect*, xi.
29. ICISS, *The Responsibility to Protect*, sec. 4, para. 25; para. 26; para. 33; para. 47.
30. ICISS, *The Responsibility to Protect*, sec. 7, para. 1.
31. ICISS, *The Responsibility to Protect*, sec. 4, para. 41.
32. ICISS, *The Responsibility to Protect*, sec. 4, para. 42.
33. Alex J. Bellamy, "Whither the Responsibility to Protect? Humanitarian Intervention and the 2005 World Summit," *Ethics & International Affairs* 20, no. 2 (2006): 167.
34. Bellamy, "Whither the Responsibility?" 164.
35. Laura Neack, "The Future of Human Security: Taking Advantage of a States-First World," in *State Responses to Human Security: At Home and Abroad*, ed. Courtney Hillebrecht, Tyler R. White, and Patrice C. McMahon (New York: Routledge, 2014), 217–18.
36. Bellamy, "Whither the Responsibility?" 169.
37. ICISS, *The Responsibility to Protect*, xi, xii, emphases added.
38. Gareth Evans, "Facing Up to Our Responsibilities," *Guardian*, May 12, 2008, accessed June 8, 2012, http://www.guardian.co.uk/commentisfree/2008/may/12/facinguptoourresponsbilities.
39. Alex J. Bellamy and Paul D. Williams, "The New Politics of Protection? Côte d'Ivoire, Libya and the Responsibility to Protect," *International Affairs* 87, no. 4 (2011): 825.
40. Bellamy and Williams, "The New Politics of Protection?"; Ramesh Thakur, "The Responsibility to Protect at 15," *International Affairs* 92, no. 2 (2016): 415–34.
41. Charles Ziegler, "Contesting the Responsibility to Protect," *International Studies Perspectives* 17, no. 1 (2016): 75–97; see also Saleh El Machnouk, "The Responsibility to Protect after Libya," *Harvard Kennedy School Review* XIV (January 2014): 88–93.
42. Jennifer Welsh, Patrick Quinton-Brown, and Victor MacDiarmid, "Brazil's 'Responsibility While Protecting' Proposal: A Canadian Perspective," Canadian Centre for the Responsibility to Protect, July 12, 2013, accessed September 10, 2016, http://www.responsibilitytoprotect.org/index.php/crises/178-other-rtop-concerns/4915-jennifer-welsh-patrick-quinton-brown-and-victor-macdiarmid-ccr2p-brazils-responsibility-

while-protecting-proposal-a-canadian-perspective; Kai Michael Kenkel and Cristina Stefan, "Brazil and the 'Responsibility While Protecting' Initiative: Norms and the Timing of Diplomatic Support," *Global Governance* 22, no. 1 (2016): 41–78.

43. See Richard Reeve, "Intervention in Libya: Why Here? Why Now? What Next?" ORG Briefing, February 29, 2016, accessed September 10, 2016, http://www.oxfordresearchgroup.org.uk/publications/briefing_ papers_and_reports/intervention_libya_why_here_why_now_ what_next.

Chapter 9: Conclusion: Resilience and Imagination

1. Keir A. Lieber and Daryl G. Press, "The Rise of U.S. Nuclear Primacy," *Foreign Affairs* 85, no. 2 (March/April 2006): 42–54.
2. Lieber and Press, "The Rise of U.S. Nuclear Primacy," 47, 48.
3. Jonathan Schell, *The Unconquerable World* (New York: Metropolitan Books, 2003), 6–7.
4. Institute for Economics and Peace (IEP), "Affiliations and Partners," accessed October 9, 2016, http://economicsandpeace.org/about/ affiliations-and-partners/.
5. Institute for Economics and Peace (IEP), *Positive Peace Report 2016*, 9, accessed October 9, 2016, http://economicsandpeace.org/wp-content/ uploads/2016/09/Positive-Peace-Report-2016.pdf.
6. IEP, *Positive Peace Report 2016*, 9.
7. IEP, *Positive Peace Report 2016*, 8.
8. IEP, *Pillars of Peace: Understanding the Key Attitudes and Institutions That Underpin Peaceful Societies*, 1–2, accessed October 9, 2016, http:// economicsandpeace.org/wp-content/uploads/2015/06/Pillars-of-Peace-Report-IEP2.pdf.
9. IEP, *Pillars of Peace*, 5.
10. IEP, *Positive Peace Report 2016*, 6.
11. IEP, *Positive Peace Report 2016*, 10.
12. Susan Griffin, "Can Imagination Save Us?" *Utne Reader*, July–August 1996, 45.
13. Griffin, "Can Imagination Save Us?" 45.
14. High-level Panel on Threats, Challenges and Change, *A More Secure World: Our Shared Responsibility* (New York: United Nations, 2004), 17, accessed November 14, 2005, http://www.un.org/secureworld/ (accessed November 14, 2005).

Index

Africa Command (AFRICOM), 99–101
Africa Contingency Operations Training and Assistance (ACOTA), 100
African Union Mission in Somalia (AMISOM), 154–56
al Qaeda, 44
American-Soviet nuclear relationship, 72
Annan, Kofi, 12, 176
Arab Spring, 51, 180
Arab-Israeli war, 79, 132
Article 41 of Chapter VII, 113–23
Article 42 of Chapter VII, 123–29
Assad regime, 22, 50, 55–58
Assad, Bashar al-, 29, 44, 49–51, 55–57
Assad, Hafez al-, 56–57
asylum seekers, 12–15
Australian government, 8–9, 11, 20
Axworthy, Lloyd, 173
Ayoob, Mohammed, 34–35

balance-of-power system, 63, 64
Bali bombings (2002), 11
Barnett, Laura, 10
Battle of Solferino, 163
Beckley, Michael, 90
Bellamy, Alex, 177
Betts, Richard, 78, 79
bin Laden, Osama, 57, 95
Brahimi Report, 151
Brexit, 25
Brown, Chris, 78
Bush, George H.W., 144
Bush, George W., 119
Buzan, Barry, 27, 42, 45, 48–50, 56

Calderón, Felipe, 46–47
China, 72
civilian protection, 179–82
Claude, Inis, 15, 108
Cold War, 11, 35, 138, 167
Collective Security Treaty Organization (CSTO) in 2002, 97

collective security, 104–9, 114, 123–29
Common European Asylum System (CEAS), 14
Commonwealth of Independent States (CIS), 92, 97
compellence, 114
Congressional Research Service (CRS) report, 97
Convention on the Status of Refugees (1951), 9–10
Côte d'Ivoire, 181
counterterrorism, 54–55
Crawford, Neta, 78
Criminal Justice (Terrorism and Conspiracy) Act, 53

defense, 66–68
defensive defense, 73–77
democracy, 50–53, 55, 58
deterrence, 68–73
Donohue, Laura, 53–54
drones, 81
drug trafficking organizations (DTOs), 45–46

Economic Community of West African States military observer group (ECOMOG), 147–50
Emerson, Michael, 93
entanglement theory, 96
ethnic conflict, 65
Eurozone Crisis (2009), 14
EU-Turkey agreement, 17
Evans, Gareth, 179
external security threats: military alliances, 86–88; multilateral and bilateral responses, 85–101; mutual defense arrangements, 88–97; train, advise, equip, and assist missions, 97–101
external security, 21; defense and, 66–68; defensive defense, 73–77; deterrence and, 68–73; dilemma, 62–66; preemptive self-defense, 77–82; preventive force, 77–82; unilateral pursuit of, 61–83
external sovereignty, 28

Farley, Robert, 81
Felbab-Brown, Vanda, 46–47
first-strike capability, 69
floating coalitions, 96
France, 70, 71
freedom of unilateralism, 96
French government, 21–22

Galtung, Johan, 74–77
Gender Equality in UN Peacekeeping Operations report, 153
Geneva Conventions, 162–66
Georgia, 92, 93
Global Peace Index (GPI), 191
Global Peace Operations Training (GPOI), 100
Global Terrorism Index, 13, 59
Griffin, Susan, 193
Grotius, Hugo, 31
Gulf War, 116, 138–40, 167

Haifa bombing, 5
Hama massacre (1982), 56
Hammarskjöld, Dag, 134
Hawaiian sovereignty movement, 38
Hemmer, Christopher, 89
Human Development Report 1994 (HDR 1994), 166, 167
human security, 3–4, 6, 8, 12, 18, 24, 31–32, 159–84; civilian protection and, 179–82; definition of, 161–62; future of, 182–83; Geneva Conventions, 162–66; large-scale violence, protecting people, 173–79;

post–Cold War human security agenda, 166–72
humanitarian war, 179–82
Hussein, Saddam, 41, 43
hybrid peace operations, 154–57

imagination, 187–94
Indo-Chinese border war, 72
Indonesia, 65
Indonesian ferry, 8
Institute for Economics and Peace (IEP), 191, 192
institutional expression, 42, 45, 48
internal security, 21, 37–60; effective government, 44–48; internal threats, state responses to, 50–59; legitimacy, 48–50; state components, 42–50; territory, 42–44
internal sovereignty, 28
internal threats, 50–59
International Atomic Energy Agency (IAEA), 118, 122
International Commission on Intervention and State Sovereignty (ICISS), 5, 173–75
International Committee of the Red Cross, 47
international community, 5
International Court of Justice (ICJ), 106, 169
International Criminal Court (ICC), 169–71
International Crisis Group, 46
International Organization for Migration, 13, 161
international security, 1, 3–6, 12, 25, 31–32; Article 41 of Chapter VII, 113–23; Article 42 of Chapter VII, 123–29; multilateral efforts for, 103–29; multilateral sanctions,

UN, 113–23; UN Charter, 109–13; and United Nations, 104–9
Iraq invasion to Kuwait (1990), 42–43
Islamic State of Iraq and the Levant (ISIL), 41, 44, 52, 55–58, 86

Jaradat, Hanadi, 5

Kalher, Miles, 88
Kargil War, 68, 72, 83
Katzenstein, Peter, 89
Kegley, Charles, 28–31
Khamenei, Ali, 122
Khmer Rouge, 141
Knorr, Klaus, 66
Kurds, 138, 139

large-scale violence, protecting people, 173–79
Laub, Zachary, 44
Lieber, Keir, 188
Locke, John, 50–51

Masters, Jonathan, 44
McCants, William, 55, 57
McVeigh, Timothy, 53
Mearsheimer, John, 64
Merkel, Angela, 14–15, 17
military alliances, 86–88
Mingst, Karen, 31
multidimensional peace operations, 146–51
multilateral UN sanctions, 113–23; on Iran, 121–23; against Iraq, 116–17; against North Korea, 118–21
multilateralism, 89, 90
multinationalism, 40–42
mutual assured destruction (MAD), 70

mutual defense arrangements,
    88–97; costs of joining, 94–97;
    states joining, 88–94

Nasser, Gamal Abdel, 79
nation, defined, 38
national security policies, 66
national security, 3–8, 12–13,
    16, 18, 19–36; internal *versus*
    external, 20–23; sovereign state,
    ways of, 28–35; sovereignty,
    28–35; state's core values, 23–27
nationalism, 38
New America Foundation, 81
New York Declaration for
    Refugees and Migrants, 160
New York Times (magazine), 47
Newman, Edward, 13
9/11 terrorist attacks, 8, 11, 20–21,
    52, 54, 70, 104
nongovernmental organizations
    (NGOs), 5, 11–12
nonoffensive defense, 74
Non-Proliferation Treaty (NPT),
    118, 120
nonprovocative defense, 74
North Atlantic Treaty
    Organization (NATO), 89,
    91, 145
nuclear deterrence, 70, 74, 187
nuclear power, 70
nuclear weapons, 69

Obama, Barack, 20, 90, 172
Operation Inherent Resolve, 98
Operation Provide Comfort
    (OPC), 138
Ottawa Treaty, 169

Pakistan, 82
paradox of "war for peace," 105
Paris terrorist attacks (2015), 1–2,
    15, 21

Park, John, 120
peace enforcement, 131–58
peace support operations,
    151–54
Pearson, Lester, 134
*Penguin Dictionary of International
    Relations* (Graham Evans and
    Jeffrey Newnham), 6
P5 veto power, 108
post–Cold War human security
    agenda, 166–72
potential threats, 66
Press, Daryl, 188
Prevention of Terrorism Act, 53

Raymond, Gregory, 28–31
resilience, 187–94
Revolutionary United Front
    (RUF), 149
Rio Treaty, 87, 89
Rouhani, Hassan, 122
Ruggie, John Gerard, 88
Russian military aggression, 188
Rwandan génocidaires, 145

Schell, Jonathan, 189
"starve-or-submit" policy, 166
Schelling, Thomas, 71
Schweller, Randall, 80, 91
security dilemma, 62–66
security, nature of, 1–18;
    definition, 3, 6–7; national
    security, 8–17; overview, 1–6, 18
shared community, 90
Shi'a, 138, 140
Sierra Leone war, 147
Six Days' War, 79
sleeper cells, 11, 21
Snyder, Glenn, 64
Somali National Alliance
    (SNA), 144
Soviet nuclear weapons
    program, 69

Spykman, Nicholas J., 64
state, defined, 38
state-building process, 33–34, 50
Strategic Arms Limitation Treaty
    (SALT I), 69
suicide bomber, 4–5
Suri, Abu Khalid al-, 57
Syrian conflict, 2, 12, 44,
    55–56, 165
Syrian Kurds, 99
Syrian refugee, 2–3, 15–17, 50
Syrian war, 17
systemic threats, 66

Taliban, 9, 12–13
Taw, Jennifer, 73, 80
terrorism, 1–3, 5–8, 11, 13, 15–17,
    20–23, 42, 52–54, 58–59
Thirty Years' War, 62
Tilly, Charles, 33
traditional peacekeeping, 136–38
Treaty of Westphalia (1648), 29,
    31, 33

UN Charter, 106–8, 175;
    international peace and security,
    109–13
UN Declaration, 92
UN Development Programme
    (UNDP), 166–68
UN Emergency Force (UNEF I),
    135, 136
UN High Commissioner for
    Refugees (UNHCR), 8, 10, 12, 58
UN Hybrid operation in
    Darfur, 154
UN Military Observation
    Group in India and Pakistan
    (UNMOGIP), 132
UN Mission in Republic of South
    Sudan (UNMISS), 153, 157
UN Mission in Sierra Leone
    (UNAMSIL), 146–50

UN Operation in Somalia
    (UNOSOM), 143, 144
UN Peacekeeping Force in Cyprus
    (UNFICYP), 153
UN peacekeeping operation
    (UNOCI), 181
UN peacekeeping, 131–58
UN Protection Force
    (UNPROFOR), 145
UN Security Council, 85
UN Transitional Authority in
    Cambodia (UNTAC), 138,
    140, 141
UN Truce Supervision
    Organization (UNTSO), 132
United Kingdom's Independence
    Party, 16
United States, 8, 11, 20, 22, 41,
    43, 47
United Task Force (UNITAF), 143,
    144, 151
unmanned aerial vehicles
    (UAVs), 81

violence, 4–5, 9–10,
    28–29, 32–35, 39,
    48, 56–57

wage preventive wars, 80
Walker, R.B.J., 24
Walsh, Jim, 120
Walt, Stephen, 86
Warsaw Pact, 90–91
Westphalian peace treaty, 63
Wiseman, Geoffrey, 73, 75
Wolfers, Arnold, 23–24
World War II, 10, 32, 51

Yanukovych, Viktor, 43–44

Zawahiri, Ayman al-, 57
Zer-Aviv, Bruriya, 5
Ziegler, Charles, 181

About the Author

Laura Neack is professor of political science at Miami University, Oxford, Ohio. She teaches courses in world politics, foreign policy analysis, and international security. Professor Neack is the author of three editions of *The New Foreign Policy* (2003, 2008, and 2014), and the author of the first edition of this book under the title *Elusive Security: States First, People Last*. She is the coeditor of two books, *Global Society in Transition* (2002) and *Foreign Policy Analysis: Continuity and Change in Its Second Generation* (1995). Professor Neack is the editor-in-chief of *International Studies Perspectives* (2015–2020). She received her doctorate in 1991 from the University of Kentucky and is a lifelong member of the BBN.